2005

Academic Library Trends and Statistics

for Carnegie Classification:
Associate's Colleges

compiled by
**Library Research Center
The Graduate School of Library and Information Science
University of Illinois at Urbana-Champaign**

Project Coordinator
**Hugh A. Thompson
Association of College and Research Libraries**

Association of College and Research Libra.
A division of the American Library Association
Chicago 2006

ISBN 0-8389-8403-7

Printed in the United States of America.

Association of College and Research Libraries
A division of the American Library Association
50 East Huron Street
Chicago, IL 60611

TABLE OF CONTENTS

INTRODUCTION

The publication of the *2005 Academic Library Trends and Statistics* marks the seventh year of ACRL's effort to provide timely data on academic library management on an annual basis. The ultimate goal is to represent libraries from all institutions of higher learning in the United States and Canada. With 1,104 institutions reporting out of a sample of 3,077, the total represents 36% of all institutions.

As was done previously, the survey collected data on a range of library operations, including collections, expenditures for operations, expenditures for computers and electronic resources, personnel and public services, and demographic information such as Ph.D.s granted and faculty and enrollment statistics. In addition, ratios such as support staff as a percent of total staff, serial expenditures as a percent of total library materials expenditures, and others, are provided. These data are intended to provide useful comparisons among peer groups as well as to facilitate benchmarking across various time frames. This year the survey also continued its examination of "trends": new activities or other developments of interest that might affect library operations and management.

The use of electronic resources by academic libraries has increased significantly during the last ten years. This trend has impacts ranging from expenditures to information delivery modes to use of space, among others. To quantify these impacts, the 2005 survey trends section adapted questions from the ARL supplementary form, as was done for the 2004 survey. These questions were originally part of the ARL E-metrics project. Principal areas of investigation in the trends section include electronic resources, network resources and services, and digitization activities.

ACRL feels that the data from the 2005 survey continues to meet a need among academic libraries for information on operations that can inform management decisions through comparison to other organizations, through benchmarking, and through awareness of current trends. We solicit your suggestions for ways this survey may be improved and for additional trends about which current data would be useful.

ACRL would like to acknowledge the contributions of Martha Kyrillidou from the Association of Research Libraries. The Association of Research Libraries publishes a separate publication entitled ARL Statistics. The ACRL publication on Academic Library Statistics would not have been possible without the generous support of the Association of Research Libraries (ARL) and its member libraries. ARL has supported the production of the ACRL/ALA publication on Academic Library Statistics by providing permission to utilize the ARL Statistics survey instruments and by providing full-access to the ARL Statistics data that are included in this compilation. For more information about the ARL Statistics and Measurement Program, please see: <http://www.arl.org/stats/>.

Hugh Thompson
Publications Manager
ACRL

The fiscal year 2005 Academic Library Trends and Statistics publication was prepared by the Association of College and Research Libraries (ACRL) and the Library Research Center (LRC) at the University of Illinois. Data was compiled from a web-based survey conducted January 6, 2006 through April 17, 2006.

Study Population

We defined the survey population as libraries at all accredited colleges and universities found in the United States (including Puerto Rico) and Canada. This population is defined in a similar manner to that of ACRL studies dating back to fiscal year 1999. The contact list originated as a commercially purchased list of college and university libraries. This list has been maintained and modified in previous years by the Center for Survey Research (CSR) at the University of Virginia. For the 2005 survey, the respondent population included 3,077 college and university libraries.

Questionnaire

As in previous years, ACRL has collaborated with the Association of Research Libraries (ARL) in this survey. The survey questionnaire and instructions were developed from the ARL Statistics survey. This was necessary to allow for the incorporation of data provided from ARL member libraries into the ACRL data set.

The 2005 ACRL survey gathered core information on collections, expenditures, personnel, instruction, public services, circulation, and interlibrary services. Additionally each year, ACRL selects a different area to gather information, referred to in the survey as the "trends" section. As in 2004, the survey collected data on E-metrics in the Trends section.

To simplify the data collection process, data was gathered through a web-based questionnaire. However, reporting libraries were given the option of completing and submitting a paper survey. The 2005 survey was administered by the LRC.

Survey Administration

The Library Research Center managed the development of the online form, the necessary web-hosting, data collection, analysis, and assisted in developing the final report. The web questionnaire was developed using commercial survey software. Each institution was assigned a unique respondent key, which served as both a unique identifier and a password for access to the web questionnaire.

All respondents were directed to an information website before entering the online survey. This website included the official invitation from ACRL Executive Director Mary Ellen Davis, survey instructions, instructions on the use of the online questionnaire, a frequently-asked-questions page, a link to the summary reports of previous surveys, and a link to begin the survey. The survey questionnaire itself was designed with a simple user interface to allow for navigation within the questionnaire and to save partial data. The questionnaire utilized "session" files so that respondents could save and resume the survey.

ARL member libraries were invited to the same questionnaire; if they had already provided most of the requested data in the ARL Statistics survey they were branched out of the main body of they survey and only asked to complete the Trends questions. In the survey form, ARL member libraries were asked if they would give permission for the use of their ARL Statistics data in the ACRL Academic Library Trends and Statistics survey. Their trends information was then incorporated with their data from the ARL Statistics survey. We thank ARL for its cooperation in sharing this data.

The contact e-mail list was checked using e-mail verifying software to isolate invalid e-mail addresses. Those institutions with valid e-mail addresses were sent e-mail invitations during the week of January 6, 2006. Institutions for which we had no valid e-mail address were sent a paper invitation via U.S. mail the following week. Multiple reminders were sent to both groups. Institutions for which we had valid e-mail addresses were sent reminder e-mails on February 27th, March 22nd and April 7th. Paper reminders were sent to those institutions for which we did not have valid e-mail invitations on February 27th, March 16th and April 3rd.

For the fiscal year 2005 survey, a total of 1,217 institutions responded. Of those 1,217 institutions, only 1,104 submitted surveys contained data. The following tables show the final disposition from the ACRL 2005 survey broken down by country as well as by invitation medium.

Table 1. Final Disposition – Overall			
	Population (N)	Completed Returns (N)	Response Rate (%)
United States	2,771	1,049	37.9
Canada	306	55	18.0
Combined	3,077	1,104	35.9

Table 2. Final Disposition – E-mail Invitations			
	Population (N)	Completed Returns (N)	Response Rate (%)
United States	2,229	1,014	45.5
Canada	136	50	36.7
Combined	2,365	1,064	45.0

Table 3. Final Disposition – U.S. Mail Invitations			
	Population (N)	Completed Returns (N)	Response Rate (%)
United States	73	35	47.9
Canada	54	5	9.3
Combined	127	40	31.5

Coding Procedure
In order to present a clean data set, the LRC made an effort to locate and correct errors in the data. However, given the abbreviated time frame of this year's survey, we were unable to contact all institutions that provided obvious data errors to determine the correct figure. In such cases, data was removed and replaced with the symbol "U/A" (data unavailable).

Institutions were assigned to one of four Carnegie Classifications based on the information provided by the Carnegie Foundation through a spreadsheet available on their website (cc2000-public.xls).

Canadian libraries were given the option of reporting expenditures in Canadian dollars. Expenditures indicated as reported in Canadian dollars were converted into U.S. dollars. The exchange rate used (0.8577, Canadian to U.S.) is the exchange rate as of 12/31/2005.

Institutions were given the option of providing a footnote for each question. Footnotes were published as is, with the exclusion of minor editorial changes and the removal of notes that did not provide information useful to the interpretation of an institution's data. Respondents also had the opportunity to communicate with ACRL and the LRC through the "notes to the editor." This field was reserved for general comments not pertaining to specific data and is not published.

Library Research Center Acknowledgments

Professor Leigh Estabrook, Director of the Library Research Center, and Edward Lakner, Assistant Director, gave valuable oversight throughout the project. Project Coordinators Megan Mustafoff and Lauren Teffeau gave additional assistance in the planning and execution of data collection and cleaning. Bridget Swift provided invaluable support in data cleaning and phone administration. Navadeep Khanal acted as the primary contact with ACRL and responding institutions, updated the online survey questionnaire and website, and oversaw data collection and cleaning. Megan Mustafoff worked on preparing the summaries and analyzing the variables. Charity Clevinger and Jennifer Roth helped as contact people for respondents with questions. Our greatest appreciation goes to the thousands of library personnel who took the time to respond to this project. Questions may be directed to the Library Research Center, Graduate School of Library and Information Science, University of Illinois at Urbana Champaign, 501 E. Daniel, Champaign, IL 61820. The LRC may be reached by telephone at (217) 333-1980, or on the World Wide Web at: http://lrc.lis.uiuc.edu.

(Blank page)

ACRL LIBRARY DATA TABLES 2005

SUMMARY DATA: COLLECTIONS

INSTITUTIONS GRANTING ASSOCIATE OF ARTS DEGREES (Carnegie Code A)

	Volumes in Library	Volumes Added (Gross)	Volumes Added (Net)	Mono-graphs Purchased	Current Serials Total	Current Serials Purchased	Current Serials Not Purchased	Microform Units
(Survey Question #)	1	1bi	1b	2	4	4a	4b	6
High	198,807	55,077	65,700	52,004	25,662	17,221	24,406	1,123,437
Mean	56,097	2,413	1,885	2,224	746	557	227	37,722
Median	46,296	1,427	926	1,142	249	224	10	6,827
Low	133	1	-9,947	0	29	1	0	0
Total	13,575,538	569,546	446,788	478,196	178,320	132,673	50,722	8,562,949
Libraries Reporting	242	236	237	215	239	238	223	227

ACRL LIBRARY DATA TABLES 2004

SUMMARY DATA: COLLECTIONS

INSTITUTIONS GRANTING ASSOCIATE OF ARTS DEGREES (Carnegie Code A)

Government Documents	Computer Files	Archives and Manus.	Carto-graphic Materials	Graphic Materials	Audio Materials	Film and Video	(Survey Question #)
7	8	9	10	11	12	13	
56,597	12,775	1,501	5,014	82,768	12,658	14,162	High
999	207	66	165	1,623	928	2,607	Mean
0	28	0	0	0	341	1,877	Median
0	0	0	0	0	0	0	Low
208,788	44,890	13,401	35,072	345,718	212,479	612,636	Total
209	217	204	212	213	229	235	Libraries Reporting

3

COLLECTIONS

INSTITUTIONS GRANTING ASSOCIATE OF ARTS DEGREES (Carnegie Code A)

Lib. No.	Survey Question # Institution	Volumes in Library 1	Volumes added (Gross) 1bi	Volumes added (Net) 1b	Monographs Purchased 2	Basis of Vol. Count 3	Total Serials Received 4	Serials Purchased 4a	Serials Received (not purchased) 4b	Gov Docs in Serial Count 5
1	A Baldwin Agrl C	73,116	872	872	853	P	269	264	5	N
2	Adirondack CC	62,358	1,909	207	2,000	P	434	434	0	N
3	Alpena CC	42,169	1,539	1,032	-1	B	-1	-1	-1	Y
4	Alvin CC	16,265	486	2,108	242	P	73	73	0	N
5	Am River C	82,393	4,844	3,079	4,644	P	254	254	0	N
6	Am Samoa CC	32,500	3,000	2,500	3,000	B	118	88	30	Y
7	Andover C	7,075	767	660	400 [1]	B	131	99	32	Y
8	Anne Arundel CC	137,453	2,972	1,904	0	P	350 [1]	350 [1]	0 [1]	Y
9	Anoka-Ramsey CC	39,365	1,118	1,109	-1	B	260	254	6	N
10	AR ST U Beebe	74,066	3,714	3,652	3,714	P	349	314	35	N
11	Athens Tech C	36,140	2,249	2,249	2,249 [1]	B	554	554	0	N
12	AZ Western C	92,254	11,916	8,930	1,955	B	360	335	25	Y
13	Bellingham Tech C	10,927	1,049	228	1,049	B	174	164	10	Y
14	Belmont Tech C	12,600	1,219	925	819	P	341	330	11	N
15	Bergen CC	123,203	6,041	899	5,207	B	20,196	15,737	4,463	N
16	Black Hawk C	64,798	2,232	1,167	2,173	P	302	298	4	Y
17	Blackhawk Tech C	21,822	1,244	1,007	557	B	296	286	10 [1]	N
18	Blue Mountain CC	41,711	925	165	635	P	367	345	22 [1]	Y
19	Blue Ridge CC	49,768	2,162	185	2,326	P	5,808	208	7,082	N
20	Brazosport C	91,356	3,524	1,598	3,392	B	350	345	5	N
21	Bunker Hill CC	66,494	1,270	541	769	P	321	316	5	N
22	Butler County CC	43,515	0	2,250	827	B	108	90	18	N
23	C Canyons	54,290	1,705	547	0	P	229	203	26	N
24	C Edouard Montpetit	105,977	2,246	-4,157	2,000	P	371	347	24	Y
25	C Lake Co	115,545	5,463	5,463	5,463	B	688	652	15	N
26	C Merici	34,764	1,381	1,197	0		156	111	45	N
27	C New Caledonia	157,299	8,664	7,664	4,000	P	450	350	100	Y
28	C Redwoods	69,097	1,392	1,392	0	B	93	93	0	N
29	C St Jean Richelieu	840	1,500	65,700	1,500	P	240	175	65	N
30	Camden County C	95,969 [1]	1,974	752	0 [1]	B	1,450	1,450 [1]	0	Y
31	Cape Fear CC	42,785	6,158	3,922	0	P	761	729	32	N
32	Capital CC	44,661	1,346	508	1,057	B	362	362	0	N
33	Carl Sandburg C	38,498	1,182	-220	839	P	440	420	20	N
34	Carroll Tech Inst	25,069	1,142	1,147	1,142	P	232	229	3	N
35	Carteret CC	20,438	-1	1,063	-1		115	115	0	N
36	Cedar Valley	53,227	1,266	992	0	P	455	455	0	Y
37	CEGEP Beauce-Appalach	90,505	1,107	455	1,107	P	141	106	35	Y
38	CEGEP Trois-Rivieres	78,824	2,307	6,134	1,595	P	325	240	85	Y
39	Central Alabama CC	40,320	814	660	593	B	237	196	41	N
40	Central Carolina Tech C	69,954	8,392	8,112	8,342	B	165	160	5	Y

1 -- See Footnotes   -1 -- Unavailable   -2 -- Not Applicable   B-Bibliographic   P-Physical

ACRL Library Data Tables 2005
COLLECTIONS

INSTITUTIONS GRANTING ASSOCIATE OF ARTS DEGREES (Carnegie Code A)

Microform Units	Gov't Documents	Computer Files	Manuscripts and Archives	Cartographic	Graphic	Audio	Film and Video	
6	7	8	9	10	11	12	13	Survey Question # Institution
24,800	667	69	0	17	0	527	1,176	A Baldwin Agrl C
41,810	0	97	32	0	0	2,189	2,441	Adirondack CC
-1	-1	-1	-1	32	108	126	1,672	Alpena CC
177	0	0	0	0	0	0	102	Alvin CC
-1 [1]	0	29	0	0	0	549	2,612	Am River C
0	0	3	0	0	0	100	1,000	Am Samoa CC
0	0	17	7	0	0	33	1,083	Andover C
8,000 [1]	0 [1]	287	0	0	0	1,535	6,411	Anne Arundel CC
25,906	-1	57	-1	2	76	22	1,949	Anoka-Ramsey CC
41,316	3,589	81	60	243	8,987	2,833	4,313	AR ST U Beebe
15,608	0	259	0	0	0	1,204	2,780	Athens Tech C
305,165	19,119 [1]	494	0	5,014	50	967	3,341	AZ Western C
0	0	275	0	0	0	190	1,934	Bellingham Tech C
0	0	26	0	4	193	11	2,114	Belmont Tech C
8,578	0	1,077	-1	-1	435	557	6,798	Bergen CC
8,342	130	0	0	0	0	0	111	Black Hawk C
0	122	52	0	0	95	0	5,104	Blackhawk Tech C
977	6,556	127	0	0	0	5	3,518	Blue Mountain CC
0	0	178	0	17	0	76	1,787	Blue Ridge CC
159,032	0	49	0	123	0	571	59	Brazosport C
5,624	0	249	60 [1]	108	264	156	981	Bunker Hill CC
371	0	55	4	7	0	250	1,673	Butler County CC
87,130	0	0	0	0	0	4,024	4,884	C Canyons
1,145	3,173	587	0	340	0	0	8,000	C Edouard Montpetit
0 [1]	0 [1]	104	0	199	0	1,339	5,133	C Lake Co
0	0	199	0	400	10,740	162	1,356	C Merici
0	0	1,178	0	0	351	981	5,803	C New Caledonia
54,550	6,378	0	108	0	0	797	1,320	C Redwoods
0	0	0	0	160	0	2,500	1,400	C St Jean Richelieu
8,110	0	60	0	0	0	733	2,861	Camden County C
26,401	0	0	0	0	0	603	5,475	Cape Fear CC
4,225	0	184	0	0	0	1,170	3,360	Capital CC
4,700	0	130	0	270	235	300	1,990	Carl Sandburg C
0	0	0	0	0	0	0	2,499	Carroll Tech Inst
951	0	43	0	17	0	608	1,439	Carteret CC
800	0	0	0	0	0	0	0	Cedar Valley
0	0	0	0	0	0	0	1,350	GEP Beauce-Appalaches
0	0	0	0	2,034	0	3,625	7,394	CEGEP Trois-Rivieres
3,397	0	0	0	0	1	15	375	Central Alabama CC
22,058	0	67	0	3	0	178	2,504	Central Carolina Tech C

1 -- See Footnotes   -1 -- Unavailable   -2 -- Not Applicable

5

ACRL Library Data Tables 2005
COLLECTIONS

INSTITUTIONS GRANTING ASSOCIATE OF ARTS DEGREES (Carnegie Code A)

Lib. No.	Survey Question # Institution	Volumes in Library 1	Volumes added (Gross) 1bi	Volumes added (Net) 1b	Monographs Purchased 2	Basis of Vol. Count 3	Total Serials Received 4	Serials Purchased 4a	Serials Received (not purchased) 4b	Gov Docs in Serial Count 5
41	Central ME Tech C	11,911	1,613	273	607	P	162	137	25	N
42	Central Piedmont CC	105,100	4,525	2,154	2,378	P	1,004	1,004	0	N
43	Central TX C	78,944	977	579	0	P	451	451	0	N
44	Centralia C	35,880	1,356 1	355	0	B	132	118 1	16	N
45	Chabot C	69,750	804	804	0	B	226	226	0	N
46	Chattahoochee Tech	28,721	4,252	347	4,252	P	262	1	1	N
47	Chippewa V Tech C	18,256	498	926 1	498	B	418	398	20	N
48	Clackamas CC	4,254	619	42	722	B	305	305	0	N
49	Clark C-WA	66,804	2,349	1,527	1,731	B	353	326	27	Y
50	Clinton CC	32,787	1,376	1,200	1,376	P	101	101	0	N
51	Cloud Co CC	22,316	237	168	235	B	145	145	0	N
52	Coastal GA CC	51,211	1,431	1,357	1,018	B	344	344	0	N
53	Colby CC	25,442	870	386	870	B	200	200	0	N
54	Columbia Junior C	145,567	1,949	896	1,382	B	356	339	17	N
55	Columbia ST CC	71,734	2,988	919	3,254	B	335	301	34	N
56	Columbus ST CC	45,974	106	86	0		0	0	0	N
57	Compton CC	39,277	757	-1,073	223	B	144	144	5	N
58	Connors ST C	31,733	922	630	392	P	201	191	10	N
59	Corning CC	62,260	1,330	-1,114	1,017	P	183	183	0	N
60	Cosumnes River C	70,696	3,034 1	1,425	0	P	339	248	91	N
61	Crowder C	38,093	1,071	641	545	P	152	135	17	N
62	Cuesta C	79,147	2,217	1,730	1,091	B	330	230	100	N
63	Cumberland Co C	40,257	447	-739	40,107	B	88	85	3	Y
64	CUNY Borough Manhattan C	111,966	4,433	188	3,987	P	268	244	24	N
65	CUNY Bronx CC	97,809	1,207	488	1,207	B	327	327	0	N
66	CUNY Hostos CC	60,216	2,169	2,020	1,605	P	279	279	0	Y
67	CUNY LaGuardia CC	117,330	4,403	1,230	5,091	P	25,662	1,256 1	24,406 1	Y
68	CUNY Queensborough CC	155,527	924	32	309	P	337	337	0	N
69	D.S. Lancaster CC	45,324	698	634	692	P	246	218	28	Y
70	Darton C	93,604	970	572	0	P	5,356	5,356 1	0	N
71	Dawson CC	20,823	346	297	0	B	179	156	23	N
72	Del Mar C	185,506	3,190	1,571	3,190	P	762	762	0	N
73	Delaware Co CC	52,561	2,632	118	906	B	278	277	1	N
74	Diablo Valley C	92,402	1,633	1,169	1,220	B	305	253	52	N
75	Dodge City CC	35,033	1,400	1,400	45	B	162	154	8	N
76	Dyersburg ST CC	44,185	152	152	152	P	86	86	0	N
77	East Central C	39,145	839	282	737	B	270	270	0	N
78	East Georgia C	41,783	386	372	386	B	135	132	3	N
79	East Los Angeles C	99,704	4,135	969	1,770	B	134	134	0	N
80	El Paso CC	183,818	10,677	8,978	8,602	P	752	752	0	N

1 -- See Footnotes   -1 -- Unavailable   -2 -- Not Applicable   B-Bibliographic   P-Physical

ACRL Library Data Tables 2005
COLLECTIONS

INSTITUTIONS GRANTING ASSOCIATE OF ARTS DEGREES (Carnegie Code A)

Microform Units	Gov't Documents	Computer Files	Manuscripts and Archives	Cartographic	Graphic	Audio	Film and Video	
6	7	8	9	10	11	12	13	Survey Question # Institution
0	0	0	0	0	0	0	0	Central ME Tech C
24,750	0	6	0	0	0	1,317	5,913	Central Piedmont CC
659,243	0	0	0	0	0	0	3,298	Central TX C
7,429	180	0	793 [1]	97	0	1,018 [1]	3,338 [1]	Centralia C
24,253	0	0	0	132	138	9,312	2,554	Chabot C
0	0	5	0	0	0	1	2,627 [1]	Chattahoochee Tech
0	0	1,395	0	0	366	1,489	7,647	Chippewa V Tech C
22,011	0	0	0	294	0	1,498	0	Clackamas CC
9,510	481	4	0	0	0	143	2,146	Clark C-WA
910	0	4	0	75	0	904	3,547	Clinton CC
0	0	101	0	0	0	1,244	1,703	Cloud Co CC
38,977 [1]	0	0	1,501	0	0	0	1,468	Coastal GA CC
1,670	56,597	0	30	0	0	200	2,442	Colby CC
11,833	0	37	233	1	3,111	12,658	3,177	Columbia Junior C
33,601	0	15	68	515	4	589	3,967	Columbia ST CC
0	0	73	0	0	1,085	220	5,282	Columbus ST CC
40,004	0	0	150	0	0	484	0	Compton CC
37,457	0	173	0	10	0	381	4,244	Connors ST C
0	3,465	0	54	150	3,887	1,754	1,512	Corning CC
35,525	0	0	26	0	0	641	2,138	Cosumnes River C
171,649	0	23	12	0	2,500	3,542	391	Crowder C
3,690	0	439	100	364	0	1,366	1,787	Cuesta C
3,934	0	157	0	0	0	474	1,446	Cumberland Co C
20,615	0	1,357	80	0	33	300	1,320	Y Borough Manhattan CC
30,667	0	0 [1]	0	0	0	551	3,788	CUNY Bronx CC
6,716	0	392	155	0	81	28	936	CUNY Hostos CC
586,986	7,405	344	617	0	1,980	2,341	2,097	CUNY LaGuardia CC
184	0	449	370	0	349	30	1,443	UNY Queensborough CC
6,007	0	167	0	0	858	1,583	5,770	D.S. Lancaster CC
36,981	0	0	0	0	18,288	2,364	1,735	Darton C
39,000	0	28	6	1	97	477	526	Dawson CC
9,939	0	0	0	0	0	6,600	7,322	Del Mar C
7,948	-2	35	10	10	0	733	2,152	Delaware Co CC
59	0	0	260	3,331	0	1,282	5,670	Diablo Valley C
59,000	0 [1]	0	57	0	78	329	522	Dodge City CC
313	0	0	0	0	0	317	2,248	Dyersburg ST CC
5,148	0	0	85	0	0	626	974	East Central C
13,000	0	0	0	0	0	10	1,107	East Georgia C
4,594	0	72	0	0	0	72	963	East Los Angeles C
2,467	0	244	0	0	0	411	766	El Paso CC

1 -- See Footnotes   -1 -- Unavailable   -2 -- Not Applicable

ACRL Library Data Tables 2005
COLLECTIONS

INSTITUTIONS GRANTING ASSOCIATE OF ARTS DEGREES (Carnegie Code A)

Lib. No.	Survey Question # Institution	Volumes in Library 1	Volumes added (Gross) 1bi	Volumes added (Net) 1b	Monographs Purchased 2	Basis of Vol. Count 3	Total Serials Received 4	Serials Purchased 4a	Serials Received (not purchased) 4b	Gov Docs in Serial Count 5
81	Estrn Arizona C	49,723	1,738	120	1,584	P	143	143	0	N
82	Estrn Idaho Tech C	22,183	4,652	3,007	3,500	B	137	97	40	N
83	Estrn Maine Tech C	16,274	973	937	232	P	212	212	0	N
84	Fayetteville Tech CC	64,143	2,088	1,208	52,004 [1]	B	319	319	0	Y
85	Fergus Falls CC	37,183	745	291	745	B	125	88	37	N
86	Flor Dar Tech C	32,769	837	767	0	B	257	257	0	N
87	Floyd C	67,012	1,422	1,241	1,113	P	249	134	115	Y
88	Gadsden ST CC	115,232	2,181	2,015	918	B	234	223	11	N
89	Gainesville C	81,126	1,234	610	936	P	189	179	10	N
90	Gavilan C	68,939	3,737	3,712	3,039	B	104	91	13	Y
91	GC Wallace CC	19,650	400	-46	96	B	66	66	0	N
92	Glendale CC	86,244	4,344	3,604	3,837	P	597	597 [1]	0	Y
93	Gogebic CC	25,178	733	271	733	B	168	161	7	Y
94	Gordon C-GA	93,450 [1]	4,009	4,009	1,686	B	3,780	4 [1]	0	N
95	Grand Rapids CC	76,284	2,564	775	2,549	B	12,088	10,082 [1]	2,006 [1]	N
96	Harrisburg Area CC	158,350	14,607	10,423	6,789	P	779	769	10	Y
97	Hawaii Pacific U	107,361	3,518	2,903	1,818	P	1,201	1,201	0	N
98	Hawkeye CC	39,252	2,500	2,097	2,433	P	576	576	0	Y
99	Highland CC KS	24,198	282	250	121	B	157	112	45	N
100	Hillsborough CC	116,791	5,117	2,825	2,783	B	1,379	1,356	23	N
101	Hinds CC	181,609	3,073	988	1,777	B	1,069	1,069	0	N
102	Hiwassee C	32,297	476	-1,098	293	P	153	115	38	Y
103	Hocking Tech C	15,968	1	446	0 [1]	B	237	227	10	N
104	Hopkinsville CC	46,635	1,032	961	19,864	P	160	146	14	N
105	Horry GTown Tech	94,260 [1]	15,759 [1]	13,497	3,050	B	409	409	0	N
106	Howard C	41,196	4,360	2,427	542	B	92	68	24	Y
107	Hutch CC&Voc Sch	42,883	746	143	2,134 [1]	P	177	161	16	N
108	IL E CC Wabash Cntrl C	34,139	1,758	450	1,454	B	8,712	70	8,642	N
109	IL Estrn CC-Frontier	22,273	1,156	-2,953	1,108	B	111	100	11	N
110	IL Estrn CC-Lincoln Trail	17,853	2,429	1,224	2,429	B	72	58	14	N
111	IL Valley CC	76,880	2,429	404	790	B	466	164	302	Y
112	Independence CC	31,242	322	103	285	P	59	58	1	N
113	Inst Com PR Jr C Arecibo	8,248	140	119	0	B	29	28	1	N
114	Inst Native Culture	29,000	2,000	1,000	850	P	120	100	20	N
115	Isothermal CC	39,458	2,722	2,122	1,798	B	194	186	6	Y
116	J.F. Drake ST Tech C	16,590	1,083	0	0	P	109	55	54	N
117	Jacksonville C	27,475	590	513	257	B	73	63	10	N
118	Jefferson CC-NY	58,684	1,623	1,623 [1]	0	P	239	233 [1]	6	N
119	Jefferson C-MO	77,842	3,229	3,116	1,824	B	147	139	8	Y
120	JS Reynolds CC	82,105	3,137	1,751	3,083	P	364	360	4	N

1 -- See Footnotes   -1 -- Unavailable   -2 -- Not Applicable   B-Bibliographic P-Physical

ACRL Library Data Tables 2005
COLLECTIONS

INSTITUTIONS GRANTING ASSOCIATE OF ARTS DEGREES (Carnegie Code A)

Microform Units	Gov't Documents	Computer Files	Manuscripts and Archives	Cartographic	Graphic	Audio	Film and Video	
6	7	8	9	10	11	12	13	Survey Question # Institution
24,240	0	188	0	15	0	466	1,827	Estrn Arizona C
30,630	0	105	0	0	0	57	285	Estrn Idaho Tech C
0 [1]	1,664	41	38	15	12	167	506	Estrn Maine Tech C
3,103	0	0	55	2	0	120	7,738	Fayetteville Tech CC
19,400	0	0	0	0	0	1,561	908	Fergus Falls CC
0	0	0	0	0	0	0	81	Flor Dar Tech C
19,397	0	175	10	329	2,355	5,097	1,958	Floyd C
7,820	0	0	0	0	0	0	0	Gadsden ST CC
30,330	0	5	0	0	156	145	432	Gainesville C
5,441	0	0	0	0	0	56	5,190	Gavilan C
0	0	56	0	0	0	20	300	GC Wallace CC
2,596	0	0	0	0	0	0	406	Glendale CC
0	0	0	0	0	0	57	1,287	Gogebic CC
8,564	0	78	801	116	661	3,070	1,542	Gordon C-GA
127,020	0	2	300	0	0	261	1,649	Grand Rapids CC
6,827	0	2,228	63	100	10,510	944	7,650	Harrisburg Area CC
390,651	0	0	0	0	0	0	0	Hawaii Pacific U
3,739	0	27	0	0	0	108	2,159	Hawkeye CC
272	0	0	0	6	0	0	1,801	Highland CC KS
38,100	0	207 [1]	0	0	30,003 [1]	361 [1]	7,918 [1]	Hillsborough CC
155,101	0	1,796	802	620	82,768	10,924	8,437	Hinds CC
54,133	0	62	0	0	2,843	2,361	262	Hiwassee C
44,011	0	85	0	2	0	430	3,587	Hocking Tech C
25,978	0	180	0	0	1,500	1,881	2,484	Hopkinsville CC
12,550	0	0	0	0	0	0	0	Horry GTown Tech
97,566	0	4	6	0	32	221	2,146	Howard C
1,212	0	0	0	1	1,212	410	2,389	Hutch CC&Voc Sch
0	0	0	0	0	0	29	1,679	IL E CC Wabash Cntrl C
0	0	28	0	3	205	263	2,221	IL Estrn CC-Frontier
0	0	41	0	5	0	126	1,506	IL Estrn CC-Lincoln Trail
139,775	0	275	0	0	0	216	1,639	IL Valley CC
2,028	0	0	0	2	0	0	0	Independence CC
0	0	0	0	0	0	0	0	Inst Com PR Jr C Arecibo
0	0	45	1,333	0	3,500	350	1,500	Inst Native Culture
3,349	0	0	100	68	763	1,580	1,596	Isothermal CC
0	0	0	0	0	0	0	3,821	J.F. Drake ST Tech C
0	0	0	0	0	0	225	591	Jacksonville C
27,854 [1]	0 [1]	122	36	430	120	285	4,421	Jefferson CC-NY
45,430	313	0	709	0	0	423	2,803	Jefferson C-MO
10,631	0	2	0	0	0	0	2,069	JS Reynolds CC

1 -- See Footnotes   -1 -- Unavailable   -2 -- Not Applicable

INSTITUTIONS GRANTING ASSOCIATE OF ARTS DEGREES (Carnegie Code A)

Lib. No.	Survey Question # Institution	Volumes in Library 1	Volumes added (Gross) 1bi	Volumes added (Net) 1b	Monographs Purchased 2	Basis of Vol. Count 3	Total Serials Received 4	Serials Purchased 4a	Serials Received (not purchased) 4b	Gov Docs in Serial Count 5
121	Justice Inst BC	20,799	-1	-1	-1	B	190	182	8	N
122	Kaskaskia C	23,950	610	24,082	-1	P	168	158	10	N
123	Kent St U E Liverpool	37,036	383	0 [1]	203	B	57	55	2	N
124	Kent St U Tuscarawas	63,433	1,124	650	764	P	199	196	3	N
125	Kilgore C	55,563	1,400	1,316	510	P	17,235	17,221	14	N
126	Kirkwood CC	65,975	3,182	586	2,078	B	334	297	37	N
127	Kirtland CC	45,092	1,116	924	1,000	B	206	195	11	N
128	Labette CC	23,878	618	60	377	P	80	73	7	N
129	Laboure C	10,357	275	117	0	P	150	150	0	N
130	Lake City CC	44,883	1,252	586	1,115	B	125	107	18	N
131	Lakeland CC-OH	57,480	2,902	627	2,902	B	429	395	34	N
132	Lane CC-OR	63,947	3,433	-957	4,080	B	474	469	5	N
133	Lansdale Sch of Bus	2,536	77	74	52 [1]	B	69	29	40	N
134	Laramie Co CC	53,075	2,232 [1]	1,203 [1]	1,203	B	251	242	9	N
135	Lassen CC	23,146	280	128	269	P	113	102	11	N
136	Lexington CC	42,263	2,881	1,473	2,711 [1]	B	217 [1]	211 [1]	6 [1]	Y
137	Linn ST Tech C	14,072	2,990	2,990	414	P	151	145	6	N
138	Lord Fairfax CC	61,528	3,657	2,148	3,302	B	364	364	0	N
139	Los Angeles Valley C	129,574	3,408	1,408	2,162	P	359	359	0	Y
140	Luzerne County CC	59,764	541	-1,141	541	P	230	221	9	N
141	Manatee CC	80,380	3,335	1,756	3,217	B	358	355	3	N
142	Maple Woods CC	32,815	1,269	-91	-1	B	210	203	7	N
143	Marymount C CA	21,338	1,242	1,120	1,242	B	165	160	5	N
144	Massasoit CC	63,764	2,800	1,184	2,800	P	175	175	0	N
145	McDowell Tech CC	28,376	829	522	829	B	219	212	7	N
146	Mesa CC	82,796	4,166	1,597	3,791	P	751	737	14	Y
147	Middlesex Co C-NJ	86,450	500	450	500	P	560	560	0	N
148	Midland C	72,286 [1]	1,466	1,325	5,793 [1]	B	360	347	13	N
149	Miles CC	325	529	-9,947	0	P	59	59	0	N
150	MiraCosta C	71,410	2,386	1,608	1,970	B	215	215	0	N
151	Monroe CC	105,816	4,090	3,585	4,200	P	625	625	0	Y
152	Mountain Empire CC	39,907	1,266	1,087	1,246	P	179	176	3	N
153	MS County CC	17,100	1,084	16,016	1,084	B	183	173	10	N
154	MS Delta CC	41,367	733	675	0	P	361	361	0	N
155	Mt Hood CC	52,344	3,211	2,764	3,110	P	462	437	25	N
156	N Alberta Inst	65,262	1,531	-5,079	1,531	P	453	453 [1]	1	Y
157	National Hispanic U	14,807	1,559	1,409	1,211	P	0	66	5	N
158	ND ST C Science	68,936	1,406	14	0 [1]	B	357	348	9	N
159	NE WI Tech C	24,446	4,191 [1]	3,608	3,800 [1]	B	684	628	56	N
160	NH CC-Berlin	14,523	953	765	413	B	68	63	5	N

1 -- See Footnotes   -1 -- Unavailable   -2 -- Not Applicable   B-Bibliographic   P-Physical

ACRL Library Data Tables 2005
COLLECTIONS

INSTITUTIONS GRANTING ASSOCIATE OF ARTS DEGREES (Carnegie Code A)

Microform Units	Gov't Documents	Computer Files	Manuscripts and Archives	Cartographic	Graphic	Audio	Film and Video	Survey Question #
6	7	8	9	10	11	12	13	Institution
6	0	0	0	0	61	208	4,723	Justice Inst BC
2,642	-1	0	-1	-1	-1	-1	250	Kaskaskia C
0	0	56	0	14	568	6	732	Kent St U E Liverpool
2,200	0	2	100	200	130	35	1,150	Kent St U Tuscarawas
67,881	0	66	0	171	400	194	3,702	Kilgore C
53,700	0	59	180	2	79	577	845	Kirkwood CC
13,147	0	31	9	0	0	420	1,075	Kirtland CC
2,015	0	0	0	0	0	218	689	Labette CC
20	0	70	0	0	0	0	650	Laboure C
39,689	0	0	0	0	0	896	2,539	Lake City CC
0	0	19	0	0	0	253	3,768	Lakeland CC-OH
157,141	-2	1	-2	-2	-2	2,267	4,003	Lane CC-OR
0	0	4	0	0	0	0	10	Lansdale Sch of Bus
9,826	777	0	0	0	24,679	1,321	5,438	Laramie Co CC
61,356	-1	50 [1]	-1	-1	-1	209	15	Lassen CC
2,283 [1]	0	56 [1]	0	0	90 [1]	1,041 [1]	1,735 [1]	Lexington CC
0	0	0	0	0	0	31	106	Linn ST Tech C
44,789	0	0	30	155	0	1,439	4,175	Lord Fairfax CC
8,023	0	0	0	0	0	0	0	Los Angeles Valley C
11,448	0	53	0 [1]	407	97	471	2,066 [1]	Luzerne County CC
-1	-1	120	137	7	0	771	6,698	Manatee CC
5,153	0	62	21	0	0	701	64	Maple Woods CC
11,234	0	0	0	0	0	0	685	Marymount C CA
7,025	0	0	0	0	0	0	2,104	Massasoit CC
3,009	0	0	0	0	9,361	1,661	1,093	McDowell Tech CC
587,181	0	0	545	1,056	0	233	639	Mesa CC
900	0	0	0	0	0	50	2,000	Middlesex Co C-NJ
92,976	0	40	0	3	12	4	371	Midland C
0	0	0	0	0	0	0	714	Miles CC
137,951	0	0	0	0	0	2,142	4,687	MiraCosta C
10,257	0	339	232	33	0	3,393	1,466	Monroe CC
8,178	0	30	66	0	0	89	1,720	Mountain Empire CC
3,561	0	0	0	0	0	0	95	MS County CC
4,332	0	0	0	12	5,325	2,570	4,654	MS Delta CC
20,024	0	165	200	157	1	126	2,955	Mt Hood CC
46	1	1	1	1	1	1	8,240 [1]	N Alberta Inst
7,200	0	6	10	1	0	5	30	National Hispanic U
0 [1]	0	0	0 [1]	0	0	0 [1]	0 [1]	ND ST C Science
644	0	786	0	0	96	644	7,253	NE WI Tech C
17,610	500	0	0	109	74	284	167	NH CC-Berlin

1 -- See Footnotes   -1 -- Unavailable   -2 -- Not Applicable

ACRL Library Data Tables 2005
COLLECTIONS

INSTITUTIONS GRANTING ASSOCIATE OF ARTS DEGREES (Carnegie Code A)

Lib. No.	Survey Question # Institution	Volumes in Library 1	Volumes added (Gross) 1bi	Volumes added (Net) 1b	Monographs Purchased 2	Basis of Vol. Count 3	Total Serials Received 4	Serials Purchased 4a	Serials Received (not purchased) 4b	Gov Docs in Serial Count 5
161	NH CC-Laconia	11,724	84	84	105	B	90	90	0	N
162	Nicolet Area Tech C	42,241	1,012 [1]	712	1,000	B	213	187	26	N
163	NM St U-Carlsbad	16,189	155	155	155	B	162	159	3	N
164	Normandale CC	88,205	5,116	-483	5,116	B	523	514	9	Y
165	North AR C	35,263	1,995	-301 [1]	1,995	B	410	398	12	Y
166	Northeast ST Tech CC	47,334	2,877	2,337	2,877	P	443	427	16	N
167	Northeastern JC	26,946	912	814	679	B	267	267	0 [1]	N
168	Northwest C	49,424	0	3,182	1,795	B	532	463	69	Y
169	Nwestern Business C	9,926	1,581	757	857	P	159	146	13	N
170	Nwestern CT Tech CC	42,370	834	148	0	B	172	146	26	N
171	OH ST U Ag Tech Inst	18,931	312	42	251 [1]	B	418	408	10	Y
172	Ohlone C	69,623	507	0	507	B	187	184	3	Y
173	Okaloosa-Walton CC	93,636	2,558	2,159	2,135	B	435	366	69	Y
174	Orange County CC	101,146	1,087	843	0	P	345	0	0	Y
175	Owensboro	23,396	837	675	0 [1]		148	128	20	Y
176	Owensboro Jr C Bus	4,210	280	210	150	P	90	90	0	Y
177	Oxnard C	33,455	806	806	0	P	87	84	3	Y
178	Passaic County CC	58,789	3,837	3,642	2,694	B	256	256	0	N
179	Paul D. Camp CC	26,360	231	723	233	B	208	208	0	N
180	Pellissippi ST Tech CC	112,756	55,077 [1]	53,365 [1]	4,236 [1]	B	336	325	11	N
181	Pensacola Jr C	155,002	6,223	5,330	4,954	B	361	350	11	N
182	Petit Jean C	16,123	887	0	0	P	40	40	0	N
183	Piedmont Tech C	27,259	1,734	1,298	1,478 [1]	B	423	404	19	N
184	Pittsburgh Tech Inst	8,057	328 [1]	328	328	B	125	108	17	N
185	Portland CC	130,501	6,702	59	6,702	P	1,396	1,268	128	Y
186	Potomac St C-WVU	43,361	484	-952	610	P	5,971	5,949	22	N
187	Prairie ST C	46,618	4,110	2,931	1,697	B	490	290	200	Y
188	Prince George CC	94,606	1,423	1,106	1,423	P	205	203	2	N
189	Pueblo CC	21,983	386	171	123	P	109 [1]	56	53	Y
190	Pulaski Tech C	16,138	4,772	4,300	4,744 [1]	B	250	245	5	N
191	Quinebaug Vally Comm TC	28,123	950	692	950	P	125	125	0	N
192	Quinsigamond CC	45,641	3,217	3,217	3,217	B	294	268	26	N
193	Reading Area CC	40,213	3,704	1,482	0	P	240	230	10	Y
194	Red Deer C	134,963	2,711	1,896	1,175	P	581	581	0	N
195	Redlands CC	11,029	643	290	278	B	97	79	18	N
196	Rend Lake C	29,821	849	596	750	P	223	223	0	N
197	Renton Tech C	23,292	4,331	4,212	2,474	B	212	190	22	Y
198	Robeson CC	43,433	1,724	1,322	1,724	B	123	123	0	N
199	Rogue CC	49,830	3,217	1,267	1,130	B	165	165	0	N
200	Sacramento City C	78,090	3,232	785	0	B	416	402	14	Y

1 -- See Footnotes   -1 -- Unavailable   -2 -- Not Applicable   B-Bibliographic   P-Physical

ACRL Library Data Tables 2005
COLLECTIONS

INSTITUTIONS GRANTING ASSOCIATE OF ARTS DEGREES (Carnegie Code A)

Microform Units	Gov't Documents	Computer Files	Manuscripts and Archives	Cartographic	Graphic	Audio	Film and Video	
6	7	8	9	10	11	12	13	Survey Question # Institution
5,000	0	0	0	79	0	0	523	NH CC-Laconia
3,061	4,020	10	0	11	60	1,936	10,756	Nicolet Area Tech C
370	0	0	0	0	0	0	1,607	NM St U-Carlsbad
5,843	0	867	48	371	30,241 [1]	6,214	5,589	Normandale CC
7,393	0	56	5	0	0	45	7,192	North AR C
54,937	0	416	0	78	160	1,437	7,013	Northeast ST Tech CC
143 [1]	0	0	0	0	0	582	2,778	Northeastern JC
18,446	13,291	648	220	4,383	978	1,053	768	Northwest C
0	0	0	0	0	0	41	329	Nwestern Business C
2,937	0	0	54	0	0	1,287	888	Nwestern CT Tech CC
34,583	0	70	0	8	0	23	286	OH ST U Ag Tech Inst
47,168	0	868	14	70	200	5,961	2,289	Ohlone C
149,605	0	407	0	1,132	107	3,514	1,897	Okaloosa-Walton CC
71,137	0	36	60	0	165	333	1,433	Orange County CC
52,001	0	0	0	0	0	346	2,029	Owensboro
0	2	375	0	5	6	1	127	Owensboro Jr C Bus
925	0	0	0	0	0	0	0	Oxnard C
0	0	82	0	0	0	531	1,143	Passaic County CC
0	0	0	0	0	33	92	99	Paul D. Camp CC
9,910	0	84	0	0	0	131	0 [1]	Pellissippi ST Tech CC
10,738	0	0 [1]	0	17	49	810	3,615	Pensacola Jr C
0	0	0	0	0	0	0	417	Petit Jean C
4,606 [1]	0 [1]	331 [1]	34	15 [1]	17 [1]	768 [1]	2,301 [1]	Piedmont Tech C
534	-2	-1	-2	-1	-2	-1	-1	Pittsburgh Tech Inst
277	0	426	0	336	3	1,725	11,492	Portland CC
63,615	0	84	39	22	7,693	591	1,694	Potomac St C-WVU
66,000	0	0	40	0	0	100	850	Prairie ST C
0	0	0	0	15	0	476	88	Prince George CC
1,316	0	12,775	176	1	747	2,402	11,749	Pueblo CC
0	0	0	0	2	0	120	1,346	Pulaski Tech C
17,941	0	0	18	0	0	116	750	uinebaug Vally Comm TC
4,900	0	0	0	0	0	0	2,899	Quinsigamond CC
9,953	0	1	100	1,110	1,552	1,268	3,286	Reading Area CC
0	0	0	0	288 [1]	0	962 [1]	3,447 [1]	Red Deer C
0	0	0	0	292	44	182	988	Redlands CC
60,974	0	51	0	42	24,723	1,547	1,964	Rend Lake C
0	0	0	0	50	60	158	1,523	Renton Tech C
2,145	0	0	0	0	0	100	1,973	Robeson CC
0	0	0	0	41	0	788 [1]	3,957 [1]	Rogue CC
4,680	0	16	0	0	0	525	8,060	Sacramento City C

1 -- See Footnotes   -1 -- Unavailable   -2 -- Not Applicable

INSTITUTIONS GRANTING ASSOCIATE OF ARTS DEGREES (Carnegie Code A)

Lib. No.	Survey Question # Institution	Volumes in Library 1	Volumes added (Gross) 1bi	Volumes added (Net) 1b	Monographs Purchased 2	Basis of Vol. Count 3	Total Serials Received 4	Serials Purchased 4a	Serials Received (not purchased) 4b	Gov Docs in Serial Count 5
201	San Antonio C	198,807	12,546	357	7,130	B	570	570	0	Y
202	San Jacinto C South	71,222 [1]	1,862	1,862	-1	B	134	134	0	N
203	San Joaquin Delta C	94,640	1,888	1,326	1,888	B	501	496	5	Y
204	Santa Fe CC-NM	89,273	5,544	2,803	3,287	B	504	504	0	N
205	Santa Monica C	99,855	2,303	1,855	1,622	B	150	150	0	Y
206	Selkirk C	73,159	1,402	942	1,000 [1]	P	447	440	7 [1]	N
207	Seward County CC	42,158	669	669	0	P	314	314	0	N
208	South AR CC	22,274	1,382	1,421	214	B	216	173	43	N
209	South Florida CC	48,138	1,598	953	1,114	B	354	338	16	N
210	South Puget Sound CC	57,156	2,005	362	2,005	P	55	55	0	N
211	Southeast CC	53,440	3,041	2,672	1,618	B	265	198	67	N
212	Southwest VA CC	42,352	2,122	989	2,047	P	176	176	0	N
213	Spartanburg Tech C	35,624	2,306	985	2,306	B	284	272	12	N
214	Spoon River C	39,785	1,502	1,361	1,502	B	33	30	3	Y
215	St Charles County CC	61,228	2,150	1,954	2,115	P	300	266	34	Y
216	Sthrn U-Shreveport/Bossier	51,249	701	606	554	P	235	213	22	N
217	Tacoma CC	65,966	1,012	411	703	B	187	167	20	N
218	Tallahassee CC	106,324	5,253	5,051	5,118	B	731	633	98	Y
219	Tech C Lowcountry	23,576	739	320	14,759 [1]	P	215	0 [1]	0 [1]	N
220	Temple C	56,659	0	981	1,257	B	324	316	8	N
221	Tri County Tech C	33,726 [1]	2,764	1,950	942	B	246	220	26	N
222	Trocaire C	14,976	1,014	167	373	B	259	240	19	Y
223	Tunxis CC Tech	52,145	3,385	3,094	3,025	B	239	236	3	Y
224	TX ST Tech C Waco	48,251	793	105	543	P	289	289	0	N
225	U Akron Wayne C	23,091	912	508	724 [1]	P	201	0	0	N
226	U HI-Kapiolani CC	73,359	1,415	1,385	303	B	276	239	37	N
227	U HI-Kauai CC	58,842	1,310	1,103	76	B	166	156	10	N
228	U HI-Windward CC	48,552	588	424	390	B	167	151	16	N
229	U NM Gallup Branch	38,330	1,190	990	1,136	B	296	284	12	N
230	VA Western CC	72,208	1,527	1,492	1,523	B	181	175	6	Y
231	W.Rainey Harper C	127,160	5,848	136	5,157	B	279	8,473	0	N
232	Walsh U	139,589	2,981	2,284	2,446	B	5,424	5,412	12	Y
233	Walters ST CC	49,225	115	115	115	P	128	116	12	N
234	Waycross C	33,738	785	517	540	P	185	165	20 [1]	N
235	Weatherford C	65,496	1,916	1,616	1,916	B	435	387	38	N
236	Western IA Tech CC	24,742	1,112	1,006	986	P	261	244	17	N
237	Wharton Co Jr C	50,937	510	-589	465	B	295	295	0	N
238	Whatcom CC	28,440 [1]	0	0	1,412	B	244	224	20	Y
239	Wytheville CC	30,121	978	466	916	B	243	219	24	Y
240	Yakima Valley CC	39,491	1,347	1,160	0	P	81	81	0	N

1 -- See Footnotes   -1 -- Unavailable   -2 -- Not Applicable   B-Bibliographic   P-Physical

ACRL Library Data Tables 2005
COLLECTIONS

INSTITUTIONS GRANTING ASSOCIATE OF ARTS DEGREES (Carnegie Code A)

Microform Units	Gov't Documents	Computer Files	Manuscripts and Archives	Cartographic	Graphic	Audio	Film and Video	
6	7	8	9	10	11	12	13	Survey Question # Institution
6,788	8,667	1,253	0	1,980	174	847	5,792	San Antonio C
11,962	0	0	45	0	0	0	0	San Jacinto C South
145,723	0	76	252	81	0	2,175	4,954	San Joaquin Delta C
2,954	0	0	0	12	0	66	3,704	Santa Fe CC-NM
3,625	0	0	0	0	178	49	1,877	Santa Monica C
5,000 [1]	12,000 [1]	275 [1]	250 [1]	300 [1]	100 [1]	459	3,262	Selkirk C
874	0	0	0	0	0	0	0	Seward County CC
41,768	0	21	60	0	0	63	1,022	South AR CC
0	0	0	0	0	25	311	1,354	South Florida CC
0	0	0	0	0	0	0	9,594 [1]	South Puget Sound CC
19,480	0	150	0	734	0	218	4,047	Southeast CC
0	0	1	0	0	0	110	133	Southwest VA CC
0	0	0	0	0	0	0	3,752	Spartanburg Tech C
4	0	20	0	3	53	5	3,507	Spoon River C
39,038	0	298	0	72	65	925	6,761	St Charles County CC
29,193	525	92	500	5	24,093	1,414	735	thrn U-Shreveport/Bossier
4,765	0	75	0	130	0	1,407	2,567	Tacoma CC
54,706	0	159	0	1	0	2,287	6,807	Tallahassee CC
9,978	0	0 [1]	0	0 [1]	0 [1]	0 [1]	3,045	Tech C Lowcountry
44,148	0	3	0	2	0	853	1,722	Temple C
56,695	0	0	0	0	0	0	891 [1]	Tri County Tech C
0	0	51	0	3	0	185	691	Trocaire C
78,959	0	0	9	0	10 [1]	1,322	4,199	Tunxis CC Tech
1,123,437	0	300	30 [1]	250	3,001	20	2,922	TX ST Tech C Waco
33,761	0	0	0	0	0	39	884	U Akron Wayne C
18,424	0	0	0	0	0	0	972	U HI-Kapiolani CC
6,611	0	169	106	312	1,533	1,890	1,551	U HI-Kauai CC
1,898	0	49	0	411	261	2,624	1,303	U HI-Windward CC
84,214	3,100 [1]	600	1 [1]	0	0	190	2,632	U NM Gallup Branch
55,885	0	0	0	30	0	2,566	198	VA Western CC
49,379	0	1,233	207	0	6,575	6,752	14,162	W.Rainey Harper C
3,191	0	70	116	0	0	341	1,843	Walsh U
0	0	0	0	6	348	2,248	4,575	Walters ST CC
17,012	0	17	0	162	7,307	1,843	821	Waycross C
194,842	0	980	121	0	0	0	3,182	Weatherford C
0	0	507	0	103	282	257	3,572	Western IA Tech CC
6,946	-2	-2	-2	0	18	31	1,870	Wharton Co Jr C
11	0	105	20	268	9	628	2,695	Whatcom CC
1,916	0	12	122	323	2,844	446	990	Wytheville CC
430	0	55	0	4	0	651	4,078	Yakima Valley CC

1 -- See Footnotes   -1 -- Unavailable   -2 -- Not Applicable

ACRL Library Data Tables 2005
COLLECTIONS

INSTITUTIONS GRANTING ASSOCIATE OF ARTS DEGREES (Carnegie Code A)

Lib. No.	Survey Question # Institution	Volumes in Library 1	Volumes added (Gross) 1bi	Volumes added (Net) 1b	Monographs Purchased 2	Basis of Vol. Count 3	Total Serials Received 4	Serials Purchased 4a	Serials Received (not purchased) 4b	Gov Docs in Serial Count 5
241	Yavapai C	61,056	1,507	-307 [1]	1,507	P	774	603	171	Y

ACRL Library Data Tables 2005
COLLECTIONS

INSTITUTIONS GRANTING ASSOCIATE OF ARTS DEGREES (Carnegie Code A)

Microform Units	Gov't Documents	Computer Files	Manuscripts and Archives	Cartographic	Graphic	Audio	Film and Video	
6	7	8	9	10	11	12	13	Survey Question # Institution
151,756	56,066	1,395	92	3,500	0	2,384	4,658	Yavapai C

1 -- See Footnotes   -1 -- Unavailable   -2 -- Not Applicable

ACRL LIBRARY DATA TABLES 2005

SUMMARY DATA: EXPENDITURES

INSTITUTIONS GRANTING ASSOCIATE OF ARTS DEGREES (Carnegie Code A)

(Survey Question #)	Total Library Materials 15	Monographs 15a	Current Serials 15b	Other Library Materials 15c	Misc. Materials 15d	Contract Binding 16
High	543,276	342,119	284,290	128,700	253,359	15,510
Mean	111,673	55,261	34,778	12,689	10,279	858
Median	76,164	42,139	21,310	7,010	1,000	0
Low	718	0	718	0	0	0
Total	26,689,893	13,096,809	8,207,592	2,892,999	2,209,927	187,010
Libraries Reporting	239	237	236	228	215	218

ACRL LIBRARY DATA TABLES 2005

SUMMARY DATA: EXPENDITURES

INSTITUTIONS GRANTING ASSOCIATE OF ARTS DEGREES (Carnegie Code A)

Total Salaries & Wages*	Salaries & Wages Professional Staff*	Salaries & Wages Support Staff*	Salaries & Wages Student Assistants	Other Operating Expend.	Total Library Expend.	
17	17a	17b	17c	19	20	(Survey Question #)
1,798,824	981,436	853,825	191,844	684,361	2,515,658	High
397,026	219,682	152,566	17,878	56,680	558,842	Mean
283,576	160,085	101,299	8,790	23,033	409,385	Median
3,721	19,200	0	0	0	29,953	Low
94,492,073	49,867,865	34,327,306	3,933,071	12,753,044	134,122,017	Total
238	227	225	220	225	240	Libraries Reporting

ACRL Library Data Tables 2005
EXPENDITURES

INSTITUTIONS GRANTING ASSOCIATE OF ARTS DEGREES (Carnegie Code A)

Survey Question #	Reported in Canadian $ 14	Total Library Materials 15	Monographs 15a	Current Serials 15b	Other Library Materials 15c	Misc. Materials 15d	Contract Binding 16
Lib. No. Institution							
1 A Baldwin Agrl C		37,474	5,256	21,493	7,799	2,926	1,173
2 Adirondack CC		163,293	75,137	60,103	17,000	11,053	1,000
3 Alpena CC		68,700	18,500	44,100	6,100	0	0
4 Alvin CC		24,709	20,097	4,362	0	250	294
5 Am River C		504,614	225,130	272,253	7,231	0	0
6 Am Samoa CC		61,500	60,000	1,500	0	0	0
7 Andover C		22,014	13,316	6,639	1,551	508 [1]	0
8 Anne Arundel CC		134,081	72,088	50,278	11,715	0	6,398
9 Anoka-Ramsey CC		78,334	29,558	42,704	6,072	0 [1]	308
10 AR ST U Beebe		101,769	67,143	20,590	14,036	0	1,018
11 Athens Tech C		125,167	58,193 [1]	62,219	4,745	10	0 [1]
12 AZ Western C		179,146	68,410	45,184	23,452	42,100	902
13 Bellingham Tech C		36,885	34,822 [1]	2,063	0	0	0
14 Belmont Tech C		63,440	26,523	22,554	14,363	0	0
15 Bergen CC		369,000	270,000	55,000	44,000	0	0
16 Black Hawk C		119,220	54,950	15,270	45,000	4,000	870
17 Blackhawk Tech C		73,014	18,897 [1]	25,457	23,400	5,260	0
18 Blue Mountain CC		66,767	32,000	18,000	8,000	8,767 [1]	0
19 Blue Ridge CC		94,886	50,742	22,561	13,999	7,584	220
20 Brazosport C		155,488	104,988	23,000	27,500	0	3,000
21 Bunker Hill CC		217,202	34,988	32,565	28,389	121,260 [1]	0
22 Butler County CC		42,290	30,186	5,999	3,836	2,269	118
23 C Canyons		34,166	17,579	13,379	3,208	0	0
24 C Edouard Montpetit	Y	132,000	63,500	48,500	20,000	0	15,000
25 C Lake Co		454,540	230,592	77,112	34,160	112,676	0 [1]
26 C Merici	Y	40,000	21,000	15,000	4,000	0	8,000
27 C New Caledonia	Y	131,832	84,713	47,119	0	0	1,000
28 C Redwoods		76,164	68,552	7,612	0	0	0
29 C St Jean Richelieu	Y	70,800	50,000	13,800	3,000	4,000	2,542
30 Camden County C		110,729	42,242	66,289	2,198	0	3,585
31 Cape Fear CC		205,059	83,875	81,556	24,108	15,520	7,644
32 Capital CC		125,051	19,000	72,661	8,254	25,136	0
33 Carl Sandburg C		72,070	41,080	24,540	6,450	0	0
34 Carroll Tech Inst		89,000	60,000	21,000	8,000	0	0
35 Carteret CC		37,375	13,114	15,772	6,064	2,425	0
36 Cedar Valley		46,190	29,682	13,310	3,198	0	981
37 CEGEP Beauce-Appalaches	Y	40,478	34,450	6,028	0	0	1,600
38 CEGEP Trois-Rivieres	Y	121,270	42,789	32,235	28,526	17,720	5,000
39 Central Alabama CC		52,018	10,201	26,515	3,047	12,255	2,473
40 Central Carolina Tech C		93,246	23,021	47,532	3,008	19,685	0

1 -- See Footnotes   -1 -- Unavailable   -2 -- Not Applicable

ACRL Library Data Tables 2005
EXPENDITURES

INSTITUTIONS GRANTING ASSOCIATE OF ARTS DEGREES (Carnegie Code A)

Total Salaries & Wages* 17	Salaries & Wages Prof. Staff* 17a	Salaries & Wages Suppt. Staff* 17b	Salaries & Wages Stud. Ass'ts* 17c	Fringe Benefits Included 18	Other Operating Expenditures 19	Total Library Expenditures 20	Survey Question #
							Institution
171,017	80,701	90,316	0	Y	31,865	241,529	A Baldwin Agrl C
409,333	292,078	93,547	23,708	N	13,749	587,375	Adirondack CC
1,798,824	0 [1]	174,824 [1]	5,000 [1]	Y	91,799 [1]	1,959,323	Alpena CC
140,048	66,031	45,835	28,182	N	0	165,051	Alvin CC
785,091	472,337	230,762	81,992	N	77,926	1,367,631	Am River C
138,500	71,000	62,000	5,500	Y	0	200,000	Am Samoa CC
45,048	39,288	0	5,760	N	0	67,062	Andover C
810,269	383,361	426,907	0 [1]	N	4,268	955,016	Anne Arundel CC
150,749	116,912	33,838	-1	N	200	229,591	Anoka-Ramsey CC
310,185	127,735	167,980	14,470	Y	31,899	444,871	AR ST U Beebe
244,785	166,611	40,443	37,731	N	23,423	393,375	Athens Tech C
381,571	220,087	127,193	34,291	N	69,522	631,141	AZ Western C
126,286	50,196	76,090	0 [1]	N	53,284	216,455	Bellingham Tech C
219,501	124,891	88,550	6,060	N	13,287	296,228	Belmont Tech C
0	-1	-1	-1	N	420,000	789,000	Bergen CC
290,500	201,840	88,660	0	N	0	410,590	Black Hawk C
129,444	67,347	62,097	0	N	1,344 [1]	203,802	Blackhawk Tech C
152,832	87,561	56,383	8,888 [1]	N	28,792	248,391 [1]	Blue Mountain CC
258,649	142,907	115,742	0	Y	15,181	368,936	Blue Ridge CC
284,125	181,357	85,258	17,510	N	21,652	464,265	Brazosport C
370,291	239,872	108,751	21,668	N	7,169	594,662	Bunker Hill CC
267,320	102,541	146,068	18,711	N	23,228 [1]	332,956 [1]	Butler County CC
759,625	239,386	279,915	58,569	Y	72,585	866,376	C Canyons
771,080	153,700	615,330	2,050	Y	0	918,080	C Edouard Montpetit
1,005,740	560,840	431,941	12,959	N	61,450	1,521,730	C Lake Co
155,930	62,475	91,355	2,100	N	12,162	216,092	C Merici
703,609	0	0	0	Y	83,157	919,598	C New Caledonia
310,041	280,041 [1]	0	30,000	N	78,269	464,474	C Redwoods
245,888	62,715	177,000	6,173	Y	0	319,230	C St Jean Richelieu
562,113	289,567	269,696	2,850	N	96,755	773,182	Camden County C
712,606	317,636	368,940	26,030	N	684,361	1,609,670	Cape Fear CC
389,548	316,931	34,409	38,208	N	16,781	531,380	Capital CC
259,820	122,450	132,370	5,000	N	42,570	374,460	Carl Sandburg C
228,500	144,000	74,500	10,000	N	0	317,500	Carroll Tech Inst
180,600	91,656	88,944	0	N	7,860	225,835	Carteret CC
182,183	175,924	4,665	1,594	N	74,599	303,953	Cedar Valley
238,214	65,132	173,082	0	N	17,990	298,282	EGEP Beauce-Appalaches
482,089	117,591	364,488	0	Y	0	608,359	CEGEP Trois-Rivieres
219,830	82,594	116,058	21,178	Y	1,820	276,141	Central Alabama CC
85,557 [1]	0	0	0	Y	0	178,803	Central Carolina Tech C

1 -- See Footnotes   -1 -- Unavailable   -2 -- Not Applicable

ACRL Library Data Tables 2005
EXPENDITURES

INSTITUTIONS GRANTING ASSOCIATE OF ARTS DEGREES (Carnegie Code A)

Survey Question #	Reported in Canadian $ 14	Total Library Materials 15	Monographs 15a	Current Serials 15b	Other Library Materials 15c	Misc. Materials 15d	Contract Binding 16
Lib. No. **Institution**							
41 Central ME Tech C		47,534	21,244	26,290	0	0	0
42 Central Piedmont CC		171,667	52,032	107,251	10,086	2,298	0
43 Central TX C		163,426	101,151	62,275	0	0	0
44 Centralia C		68,530 [1]	25,000 [1]	15,330 [1]	14,000 [1]	14,200 [1]	0
45 Chabot C		76,474	0	32,111	44,363	0	0
46 Chattahoochee Tech		87,098	69,098	18,000	0	0	0
47 Chippewa V Tech C		129,219	44,699	54,392	30,128	0	0
48 Clackamas CC		84,679	44,104	25,988	11,658	2,929	432
49 Clark C-WA		108,114	66,358	38,164	3,592	0	474
50 Clinton CC		56,164	29,042	16,163	10,959	0	0
51 Cloud Co CC		28,413	9,840	11,316	7,019 [1]	238 [1]	0
52 Coastal GA CC		75,962	19,334	27,177	21,163	8,288	0
53 Colby CC		36,500	21,000	7,500	5,000	3,000	800
54 Columbia Junior C		147,684	80,196	33,554	28,085	5,849	2,360
55 Columbia ST CC		162,000	125,000	16,500	20,000	500	4,500
56 Columbus ST CC		0	0	0	0	0	0
57 Compton CC		89,533	15,735	7,682	2,310	63,806 [1]	0
58 Connors ST C		84,780	31,454	27,240	26,085	0	0
59 Corning CC		38,095	20,497	14,860	2,238	500	1,073
60 Cosumnes River C		110,130	72,114	14,221	23,795	0	0
61 Crowder C		43,485	12,139	8,740	15,141	7,465	0
62 Cuesta C		115,669	56,082	37,577	0 [1]	22,010	0
63 Cumberland Co C		73,400	42,750	6,400	24,250	0	200
64 CUNY Borough Manhattan CC		254,802	107,674	72,575	41,382	33,171	0
65 CUNY Bronx CC		107,693	32,500	65,461	3,281	6,451	0
66 CUNY Hostos CC		141,124	56,069	75,240	5,460	4,355	6,551
67 CUNY LaGuardia CC		477,890	100,000	73,531	51,000	253,359	0
68 CUNY Queensborough CC		49,448	17,448	21,000	11,000	0	0
69 D.S. Lancaster CC		31,374	9,542	19,983	1,849	0	74
70 Darton C		0	0	0	0	0	0
71 Dawson CC		23,600	10,450	12,060	1,090	0	0
72 Del Mar C		365,990	144,007	96,210	115,783	9,990	861
73 Delaware Co CC		133,914	80,055	44,060	9,800	-1	0
74 Diablo Valley C		90,000	57,032	27,391	5,577	0	0
75 Dodge City CC		30,027	10,548 [1]	14,979 [1]	0 [1]	4,500 [1]	0
76 Dyersburg ST CC		58,319	10,654	5,540	3,629	38,496	0
77 East Central C		55,589	25,255	17,421	12,913	0	0
78 East Georgia C		45,781	17,938	14,962	1,751	11,130	0
79 East Los Angeles C		104,211	88,211	13,000	3,000	0	0
80 El Paso CC		419,997	342,119	77,878	0	0	0

1 -- See Footnotes   -1 -- Unavailable   -2 -- Not Applicable

ACRL Library Data Tables 2005
EXPENDITURES

INSTITUTIONS GRANTING ASSOCIATE OF ARTS DEGREES (Carnegie Code A)

Total Salaries & Wages* 17	Salaries & Wages Prof. Staff* 17a	Salaries & Wages Suppt. Staff* 17b	Salaries & Wages Stud. Ass'ts* 17c	Fringe Benefits Included 18	Other Operating Expenditures 19	Total Library Expenditures 20	Survey Question #
							Institution
140,519	103,698	36,821	0	N	30,843	218,896	Central ME Tech C
1,107,294	628,190	479,104	0	Y	26,755	1,305,716	Central Piedmont CC
377,358 [1]	0	0	0	N	339,701	880,485	Central TX C
228,024 [1]	155,679	49,308	23,037 [1]	N	40,282 [1]	336,836	Centralia C
692,284	379,171	255,139	57,974	N	61,229	829,987	Chabot C
364,624	188,933	166,861	8,830	Y	34,984	486,706	Chattahoochee Tech
226,122	65,001	145,121	16,000	N	127,082	482,423	Chippewa V Tech C
296,245	168,972	121,003	6,270	N	227,691	609,047	Clackamas CC
777,356	353,418	418,967	4,971	N	99,074	985,018	Clark C-WA
228,432	159,363	69,069	0	N	27,334	311,930	Clinton CC
111,503	59,064	44,534	7,905 [1]	N	13,534	153,450	Cloud Co CC
323,837	233,748	83,676	6,413	N	77,026	476,825	Coastal GA CC
97,000	39,000	55,000	3,000	N	11,000	145,300	Colby CC
385,684	250,058	101,299	34,327	N	40,841	576,569	Columbia Junior C
295,000	187,000	103,000	5,000	N	50,000	511,500	Columbia ST CC
0	0	0	0	(N	0	0	Columbus ST CC
361,146	266,679	70,916	23,551	N	0	450,679	Compton CC
238,094	134,981	78,308	24,805	Y	50,510	373,384	Connors ST C
572,432	309,574	254,458	8,400 [1]	N	25,215	636,815	Corning CC
485,187	295,645	184,820	4,722	N	13,157 [1]	608,474	Cosumnes River C
89,335	44,664	33,487	11,184	N	17,730	150,550	Crowder C
613,305	341,428	250,609	21,268	N	47,387	776,361	Cuesta C
174,266	127,054	40,445	6,767	N	21,808	269,674	Cumberland Co C
1,345,162	843,048	310,270	191,844	Y	0	1,599,964	NY Borough Manhattan CC
1,113,404	724,683	377,221	11,500	N	116,000	1,337,097	CUNY Bronx CC
788,365	656,420	106,798	25,147	N	39,890	975,930	CUNY Hostos CC
1,608,911	981,436 [1]	530,941	96,535	N	350,000	2,436,801	CUNY LaGuardia CC
1,045,210	753,676	280,934	15,000	Y	0	1,094,658	CUNY Queensborough CC
138,050	57,329	76,311	4,410	N	4,616	174,114	D.S. Lancaster CC
0	0	0	0	Y	0	0	Darton C
78,313	51,323	24,490	2,500	N	12,487	114,400	Dawson CC
1,239,418	531,122	616,292	92,004	N	189,043	1,795,312	Del Mar C
602,501	433,433	169,068	0	N	274,495	1,010,910	Delaware Co CC
809,869	455,689	310,925	43,255	N	80,712	980,581	Diablo Valley C
73,017	44,768	26,249	2,000	N	9,876	112,920	Dodge City CC
214,820	163,810	30,810	20,200	N	56,625	329,764	Dyersburg ST CC
121,438	78,614	42,824	0	N	83,973	261,000	East Central C
94,061	47,994	44,149	1,918	N	12,329	152,171	East Georgia C
496,877	275,500	213,377	8,000	N	4,751	605,839	East Los Angeles C
1,515,866	951,356	548,901	15,609	Y	86,613 [1]	2,022,476	El Paso CC

1 -- See Footnotes   -1 -- Unavailable   -2 -- Not Applicable

23

ACRL Library Data Tables 2005
EXPENDITURES

INSTITUTIONS GRANTING ASSOCIATE OF ARTS DEGREES (Carnegie Code A)

Lib. No.	Institution	Reported in Canadian $ 14	Total Library Materials 15	Monographs 15a	Current Serials 15b	Other Library Materials 15c	Misc. Materials 15d	Contract Binding 16
81	Estrn Arizona C		71,354	34,701	12,234	819	23,600	400
82	Estrn Idaho Tech C		48,248	25,640	6,661	11,447	4,500	0
83	Estrn Maine Tech C		55,022	18,737	25,673	0	10,612	0
84	Fayetteville Tech CC		225,268	133,589	71,654	20,025	0	0
85	Fergus Falls CC		42,608	25,602	6,034	0	10,972	0
86	Flor Dar Tech C		136,750	0	0	0	0	0
87	Floyd C		115,039	84,354	30,685	0 [1]	0	805
88	Gadsden ST CC		61,200	36,033	15,603	9,564	0	850
89	Gainesville C		65,158	39,682	19,744	5,732	0	837
90	Gavilan C		54,770	43,224	10,315	1,231	0	0
91	GC Wallace CC		10,000	5,000	5,000	0	0	0
92	Glendale CC		285,472	148,528	32,203 [1]	104,741 [1]	0	1,217
93	Gogebic CC		42,207	16,569	23,577	2,061	0	0
94	Gordon C-GA		49,174	11,361	37,595	218	0	12,515
95	Grand Rapids CC		389,970	147,929	107,597	23,158	111,286 [1]	0
96	Harrisburg Area CC		543,276	242,812	250,992	10,341	39,131	2,687
97	Hawaii Pacific U		508,350	224,060	284,290	0	0	0
98	Hawkeye CC		139,571	52,372	84,504	2,695	0	561
99	Highland CC KS		15,258	3,181	8,752	3,325	0	0
100	Hillsborough CC		208,416	60,910	146,037	1,469	0	0
101	Hinds CC		278,485	77,670	112,391	33,233	55,191	2,023
102	Hiwassee C		20,795	11,213	7,345	2,237	0	1,298
103	Hocking Tech C		62,277	6,941	33,081	5,346	16,909	981
104	Hopkinsville CC		76,498	46,715	10,175	16,682	2,926	115
105	Horry GTown Tech		173,820	75,484	39,375	0	58,961	1,435
106	Howard C		31,900	13,570	14,100	230	4,000	0
107	Hutch CC&Voc Sch		36,725	18,462	15,853	0	2,410 [1]	0
108	IL E CC Wabash Cntrl C		28,091	14,639	5,000	8,193	259	0
109	IL Estrn CC-Frontier		19,303	11,968	3,107	4,228	0	0
110	IL Estrn CC-Lincoln Trail		50,888	40,997	5,797	1,830	2,264	0
111	IL Valley CC		62,753	29,357	22,570	8,755	2,070	0
112	Independence CC		20,480	9,563	4,483	5,562	872	0
113	Inst Com PR Jr C Arecibo		718	0	718	0	0	0
114	Inst Native Culture		63,000	46,000	12,000	0	5,000	1,000
115	Isothermal CC		55,133	38,004	12,349	4,780	0	0
116	J.F. Drake ST Tech C		41,942	0	7,500	21,278	13,164	0
117	Jacksonville C		5,438	1,082	4,356	0	0	0
118	Jefferson CC-NY		156,368	50,968 [1]	86,400 [1]	18,000 [1]	1,000 [1]	0
119	Jefferson C-MO		93,361	45,488	20,330	26,215	1,328	0
120	JS Reynolds CC		122,265	74,985	32,909	14,371	0	0

1 -- See Footnotes   -1 -- Unavailable   -2 -- Not Applicable

ACRL Library Data Tables 2005
EXPENDITURES

INSTITUTIONS GRANTING ASSOCIATE OF ARTS DEGREES (Carnegie Code A)

Total Salaries & Wages* 17	Salaries & Wages Prof. Staff* 17a	Salaries & Wages Suppt. Staff* 17b	Salaries & Wages Stud. Ass'ts* 17c	Fringe Benefits Included 18	Other Operating Expenditures 19	Total Library Expenditures 20	Survey Question #
							Institution
219,781	60,368	100,106	59,307	N	22,235	313,770	Estrn Arizona C
66,122	53,222	28,200	10,080	Y	24,676	139,046	Estrn Idaho Tech C
112,662	87,211	13,775	11,676	N	0	167,684	Estrn Maine Tech C
302,471	136,806	165,665	0	Y	92,564	620,303	Fayetteville Tech CC
133,801	60,500	49,557	23,744	N	0	176,409	Fergus Falls CC
211,316	0	0	0	N	67,030	415,096	Flor Dar Tech C
355,162	277,346	65,304	12,512	N	291,108	762,114	Floyd C
416,057	235,433	180,624	0	N	0	478,106	Gadsden ST CC
355,264	247,241	97,023	11,000	N	42,000	463,259	Gainesville C
406,538	196,227	210,311	0	Y	16,677	477,985	Gavilan C
105,632	64,705	28,927	12,000	Y	12,460	128,092	GC Wallace CC
1,091,325	544,994	487,936 [1]	58,395 [1]	N	50,766 [1]	1,428,780	Glendale CC
121,966	77,445	34,221	10,300	N	68,893	233,066	Gogebic CC
252,892	174,527	75,136	3,229	N	41,213	355,794	Gordon C-GA
911,891	614,101 [1]	243,146	54,644	N	0	1,301,861	Grand Rapids CC
1,393,448	906,138	392,946	94,364	N	547,040	2,486,451	Harrisburg Area CC
0	0	0	0	N	155,580	663,930	Hawaii Pacific U
187,162	107,372	78,629	1,161	N	29,640	356,934	Hawkeye CC
76,107	42,204	27,058	6,845	Y	1,980	93,345	Highland CC KS
1,064,455	508,741	534,209	21,505	N	91,807	1,364,678	Hillsborough CC
841,581	436,653	393,096	11,832	N	55,506	1,177,595	Hinds CC
85,436	54,636	26,400	4,400	N	4,700	112,229	Hiwassee C
244,505	176,112	59,669	8,724	Y	104,061	411,824	Hocking Tech C
211,731	135,986	68,667	7,078	Y	22,062	310,406	Hopkinsville CC
349,828	169,387	165,979	14,462	N	71,257	596,340	Horry GTown Tech
151,943	80,565	69,378	2,000	N	48,083	231,926	Howard C
152,335	102,605	44,110	5,620	N	0	189,060	Hutch CC&Voc Sch
105,068	51,655	48,572	4,841	N	3,946	137,105	IL E CC Wabash Cntrl C
85,069	44,889	32,273	7,907	N	7,437	111,809	IL Estrn CC-Frontier
74,770	35,905	34,484	4,381	N	1,645	127,303	IL Estrn CC-Lincoln Trail
165,094	108,597	39,468	17,029	N	33,537	261,384	IL Valley CC
117,129	95,515	21,614	0	Y	0	137,609	Independence CC
35,160	19,200	14,400	1,560	N	0	35,878	Inst Com PR Jr C Arecibo
238,000	182,500	38,500	17,000	N	81,700	383,700	Inst Native Culture
213,554	97,056	112,249	4,249	Y	5,529	274,216	Isothermal CC
92,843	89,629 [1]	0	3,214	Y	9,447	144,232	J.F. Drake ST Tech C
59,870	25,416	32,560	1,894	N	22,713	88,021	Jacksonville C
316,861	189,178	107,583	20,100	N	14,566	487,795	Jefferson CC-NY
294,682	169,720	119,900	5,062	N	59,280	447,323	Jefferson C-MO
666,457	405,107	261,350	0	Y	28,500	817,222	JS Reynolds CC

1 -- See Footnotes   -1 -- Unavailable   -2 -- Not Applicable

ACRL Library Data Tables 2005
EXPENDITURES

INSTITUTIONS GRANTING ASSOCIATE OF ARTS DEGREES (Carnegie Code A)

Survey Question #	Reported in Canadian $ 14	Total Library Materials 15	Monographs 15a	Current Serials 15b	Other Library Materials 15c	Misc. Materials 15d	Contract Binding 16
Lib. No. Institution							
121 Justice Inst BC	Y	52,449	12,526	18,075	8,939	12,909	0
122 Kaskaskia C		33,900	9,900	14,700	100	9,200	-1
123 Kent St U E Liverpool		25,336	7,079	18,128	129	0	0
124 Kent St U Tuscarawas		76,423	28,633	41,639	1,500	4,651	5,231
125 Kilgore C		65,883	18,911	38,039	7,192	1,741	0
126 Kirkwood CC		106,512	56,266	36,919	4,738	8,589	546
127 Kirtland CC		47,247	26,528	18,949	1,635	135	0
128 Labette CC		66,363	22,074	6,809	31,873	5,607	0
129 Laboure C		53,172	15,000	16,500	3,000	18,672	0
130 Lake City CC		33,336	18,243	4,418	10,675	0	471
131 Lakeland CC-OH		155,690	98,807	31,961	1,437	23,485	0
132 Lane CC-OR		220,522	153,401	65,570	0	1,551	0
133 Lansdale Sch of Bus		5,953	1,624	1,897	116	2,316 [1]	0
134 Laramie Co CC		109,153	51,251	21,733	19,428	16,741 [1]	258
135 Lassen CC		23,668	8,933	10,620	4,115	0	0
136 Lexington CC		155,982	85,086	28,414 [1]	20,491 [1]	21,991 [1]	835
137 Linn ST Tech C		39,719	17,951	17,244	3,524	1,000	0
138 Lord Fairfax CC		136,157	100,587	23,534	8,069	3,967	0
139 Los Angeles Valley C		171,067	124,144	34,071	12,852	0	2,350
140 Luzerne County CC		128,910	55,608	37,000	19,960	16,342	1,700
141 Manatee CC		206,328	107,861	56,986	21,067	20,414	404
142 Maple Woods CC		88,444	55,521	17,858	15,065	0	0
143 Marymount C CA		127,690	50,000	52,000	3,000	22,690	0
144 Massasoit CC		144,815	109,287	10,976	24,552	0	506
145 McDowell Tech CC		36,185	19,308	12,703	4,174	0	397
146 Mesa CC		303,066	150,528	128,895	23,643	0	15,510
147 Middlesex Co C-NJ		225,000	120,000	98,000	7,000	0	100
148 Midland C		82,679	37,269	41,922	3,488	0	253
149 Miles CC		15,342	382	5,983	587	8,390 [1]	0
150 MiraCosta C		157,976	97,393	25,521	35,062	0	0
151 Monroe CC		273,009	149,118	123,891	0	0	3,505
152 Mountain Empire CC		73,211	31,463	14,215	27,533	0	484
153 MS County CC		37,085	14,345	13,062	9,678	0	0
154 MS Delta CC		25,664	0	6,623	18,570	471	1,000
155 Mt Hood CC		186,845	129,779 [1]	42,548	14,518 [1]	0	422
156 N Alberta Inst	Y	319,558	79,998	51,140	55,089	133,331 [1]	1
157 National Hispanic U		63,900	50,000	5,900	500	7,500	0
158 ND ST C Science		145,820 [1]	0	0	0	0	0
159 NE WI Tech C		117,855	64,236	52,319	1,300	0	0
160 NH CC-Berlin		22,117	4,314	7,233	88	10,482	0

1 -- See Footnotes   -1 -- Unavailable   -2 -- Not Applicable

ACRL Library Data Tables 2005
EXPENDITURES

INSTITUTIONS GRANTING ASSOCIATE OF ARTS DEGREES (Carnegie Code A)

Total Salaries & Wages* 17	Salaries & Wages Prof. Staff* 17a	Salaries & Wages Suppt. Staff* 17b	Salaries & Wages Stud. Ass'ts* 17c	Fringe Benefits Included 18	Other Operating Expenditures 19	Total Library Expenditures 20	Survey Question #
							Institution
313,057	-1	-1	-1	Y	53,183	418,689	Justice Inst BC
106,750	42,850	56,600	7,300	N	4,500	145,149	Kaskaskia C
92,232	60,978	24,466	6,788	N	689	118,257	Kent St U E Liverpool
125,090	51,398	48,692	25,000	N	8,772	215,516	Kent St U Tuscarawas
232,210	172,266	39,723	20,221	N	22,884	320,977	Kilgore C
473,023	283,194	171,643	18,186	N	8,479	588,560	Kirkwood CC
149,380	127,310	17,821	4,249	N	17,168	213,795	Kirtland CC
84,415	36,571	41,586	6,258	Y	1,189	151,967	Labette CC
71,676	44,286	0	27,390	N	0	124,848	Laboure C
197,689	80,214	112,528	4,947	N	22,680	254,176	Lake City CC
492,643	241,746	229,846	21,051	N	142,865	791,198	Lakeland CC-OH
533,908	241,882	278,729	13,297	N	428,147	1,182,577	Lane CC-OR
24,000	24,000	0	0	N	0	29,953	Lansdale Sch of Bus
390,503	208,019	175,349	7,135	Y	23,033 [1]	522,947	Laramie Co CC
157,060	79,852	72,695	4,513	N	41,306	222,034	Lassen CC
503,464	354,594 [1]	103,879	44,991	N	22,339	682,620	Lexington CC
136,602	65,094	71,508	0	Y	10,361	186,682	Linn ST Tech C
465,667	0	0	10,080	Y	48,874	650,698	Lord Fairfax CC
731,717	429,708	283,390	18,619	N	54,190	959,324	Los Angeles Valley C
512,093	251,606	260,487	0	N	5,130	647,833	Luzerne County CC
641,193	427,617	194,008	19,568	N	8,457	856,382	Manatee CC
242,358	134,545	107,813	0	N	12,180	342,982	Maple Woods CC
196,489	153,541	28,748	14,200	N	45,306	369,485	Marymount C CA
359,494	283,065	67,679	8,750	Y	30,882	535,697	Massasoit CC
118,834	91,428	27,406	0	N	5,952	161,368	McDowell Tech CC
862,784	249,224	485,536	128,024	N	0	1,181,360	Mesa CC
1,024,000	500,000	500,000	24,000	N	0	1,249,100	Middlesex Co C-NJ
322,762	214,191	107,462	1,109	N	42,918	448,612	Midland C
107,575	44,000	57,002 [1]	6,573 [1]	Y	0	122,917	Miles CC
1,095,986	661,516	341,780	92,690	N	0	1,253,962	MiraCosta C
994,591	678,340	285,209	31,042	N	445,854	1,716,959	Monroe CC
171,698	70,003	99,404	2,291	N	67,003 [1]	312,396	Mountain Empire CC
147,139	62,183	82,956	2,000	N	0	184,224	MS County CC
479,300	222,000	237,000	20,300	N	13,550	519,514	MS Delta CC
594,413	253,866 [1]	288,843 [1]	51,704 [1]	N	265,685 [1]	1,047,365	Mt Hood CC
1,392,210	0	0	0	Y	114,908	1,826,677	N Alberta Inst
127,000	60,000	60,000	7,000	N	60,000	250,900	National Hispanic U
253,088	0 [1]	0 [1]	0 [1]	Y	0	398,907	ND ST C Science
251,366	117,202	134,164	0	N	17,405	386,626	NE WI Tech C
84,208	51,976	23,532	8,700	N	3,636	109,961	NH CC-Berlin

1 -- See Footnotes   -1 -- Unavailable   -2 -- Not Applicable

27

ACRL Library Data Tables 2005
EXPENDITURES

INSTITUTIONS GRANTING ASSOCIATE OF ARTS DEGREES (Carnegie Code A)

Lib. No.	Institution	Reported in Canadian $ 14	Total Library Materials 15	Monographs 15a	Current Serials 15b	Other Library Materials 15c	Misc. Materials 15d	Contract Binding 16
	Survey Question #							
161	NH CC-Laconia		27,162	9,575	6,447	10,941	199	0
162	Nicolet Area Tech C		192,599	82,186	37,181	46,325	26,907	0
163	NM St U-Carlsbad		34,254	9,863	18,720	5,671	0	23
164	Normandale CC		410,419	158,827	85,395	43,910	122,287 [1]	848
165	North AR C		80,838	42,139	32,287 [1]	6,055 [1]	357	0
166	Northeast ST Tech CC		134,516	80,526	40,942	10,780	2,268	988
167	Northeastern JC		42,833	22,301	12,399	8,133	0	86
168	Northwest C		95,331	31,657	40,081	20,433	3,160	128
169	Nwestern Business C		73,070	32,232	14,668	26,170	0	0
170	Nwestern CT Tech CC		34,101	16,373	14,215	2,460	1,053 [1]	0
171	OH ST U Ag Tech Inst		40,976	17,792	22,550	579	55 [1]	0
172	Ohlone C		56,000	25,000	25,000	5,000	1,000	0
173	Okaloosa-Walton CC		165,909	78,055	41,974	19,369	26,511	2,398
174	Orange County CC		152,804	59,650	45,900	0	47,254	5,800
175	Owensboro		49,792	30,795	14,930	4,067	0	145
176	Owensboro Jr C Bus		10,160	860	1,200	8,000	100	0
177	Oxnard C		28,143	20,000	8,143	0	0	0
178	Passaic County CC		130,696	100,000	30,696	0	0	0
179	Paul D. Camp CC		33,126	15,204	17,922	0	0	0
180	Pellissippi ST Tech CC		171,952	103,848	59,833	8,271	0	293
181	Pensacola Jr C		246,583	171,212	43,602	24,184	7,584	2,298
182	Petit Jean C		26,089	0	12,711	0	13,378 [1]	0
183	Piedmont Tech C		68,765	30,965	27,264	2,378 [1]	8,158 [1]	0
184	Pittsburgh Tech Inst		26,772	19,155 [1]	7,618	-1	0	-2
185	Portland CC		216,352	83,519	105,713	27,120	0	0
186	Potomac St C-WVU		118,774	45,281	17,991	19,017	36,485	776
187	Prairie ST C		75,538	35,006	32,102	2,443	5,987	0
188	Prince George CC		105,951	56,464	20,000	29,487	0	1,500
189	Pueblo CC		45,412	8,108	8,910	1,274	27,120 [1]	0
190	Pulaski Tech C		40,414	14,008	20,760	2,244	3,402	0
191	Quinebaug Vally Comm TC		53,500	53,500	0 [1]	0 [1]	0	0
192	Quinsigamond CC		227,340	156,158	56,729	14,453	0	0
193	Reading Area CC		69,738	45,679	20,020	4,039	0	0
194	Red Deer C	Y	399,700 [1]	75,000 [1]	196,000 [1]	128,700 [1]	0	0
195	Redlands CC		10,662	5,438	3,997	1,227	0	0
196	Rend Lake C		69,321	34,138	24,198	10,985	0	0
197	Renton Tech C		89,700	53,500	10,700	25,500	0	0
198	Robeson CC		54,333	47,333	7,000	0	0	0
199	Rogue CC		67,143	47,433	19,700	10	0	0
200	Sacramento City C		153,761	111,310	36,351	5,000	1,100	3,499

1 -- See Footnotes   -1 -- Unavailable   -2 -- Not Applicable

ACRL Library Data Tables 2005
EXPENDITURES

INSTITUTIONS GRANTING ASSOCIATE OF ARTS DEGREES (Carnegie Code A)

Total Salaries & Wages* 17	Salaries & Wages Prof. Staff* 17a	Salaries & Wages Suppt. Staff* 17b	Salaries & Wages Stud. Ass'ts* 17c	Fringe Benefits Included 18	Other Operating Expenditures 19	Total Library Expenditures 20	Survey Question #
							Institution
74,169	41,000	25,000	8,169	N	0	101,331	NH CC-Laconia
491,494	292,450	185,072	13,972	N	215,487	899,580	Nicolet Area Tech C
116,345	44,015	66,603	5,727	N	11,175 [1]	161,797	NM St U-Carlsbad
519,170	257,644	227,817	33,709	N	11,104	941,541	Normandale CC
116,943 [1]	66,706 [1]	38,265 [1]	11,972 [1]	N	39,877 [1]	237,658	North AR C
366,114	252,220	111,260	2,634	N	98,420	600,038	Northeast ST Tech CC
178,476	46,745	131,731	0 [1]	N	28,956	250,351	Northeastern JC
146,144	81,218	51,632	13,294	N	10,744	252,346	Northwest C
148,921	117,244	18,237	13,440	Y	20,903	242,894	Nwestern Business C
286,823	158,135	121,888	6,800	N	16,725 [1]	337,649	Nwestern CT Tech CC
166,082	91,164	54,009	20,909	N	14,364	221,422	OH ST U Ag Tech Inst
555,878	330,327	211,371	14,180	N	108,369	720,247	Ohlone C
647,931	269,452	378,479	0	N	62,554	878,792	Okaloosa-Walton CC
542,698	325,203	217,495	0	Y	0	701,302	Orange County CC
280,492	275,871 [1]	0	4,621	Y	18,434	348,863	Owensboro
35,000	29,000	0	6,000	N	0	45,160	Owensboro Jr C Bus
361,962	229,730	128,729	3,503	Y	59,212	449,317	Oxnard C
586,090	319,120	186,970	80,000 [1]	N	33,800	750,586	Passaic County CC
177,374	116,228	61,146	0	N	0	210,500	Paul D. Camp CC
528,157	413,806 [1]	92,461	21,890	N	147,482	847,884	Pellissippi ST Tech CC
987,109	557,841	420,368	8,900	N	23,743	1,259,733	Pensacola Jr C
93,319	66,082	27,237	0	Y	3,321	122,729	Petit Jean C
160,822	110,961	47,905	1,956 [1]	N	7,931 [1]	237,518 [1]	Piedmont Tech C
138,298	113,000	-2	25,300	N	6,457	171,525	Pittsburgh Tech Inst
1,654,765	784,776	853,825	16,164	N	644,541	2,515,658	Portland CC
160,922	72,530	76,109	12,283	N	4,966	285,438	Potomac St C-WVU
405,521	194,813	210,708	0	N	54,140	535,199	Prairie ST C
1,046,860	660,484	266,188	120,188 [1]	Y	301,932	1,456,243	Prince George CC
233,848	120,993	112,855	-1 [1]	Y	35,769	315,029	Pueblo CC
145,542	83,765	59,240	2,537	N	42,960	228,916	Pulaski Tech C
300,000	260,000	0	40,000	Y	0	353,500	Quinebaug Vally Comm TC
300,900	185,926	114,974	0	N	56,815	585,055	Quinsigamond CC
298,714	160,085	138,629	0	N	96,377	464,829	Reading Area CC
908,067 [1]	0	0	0	N	241,764 [1]	1,549,531 [1]	Red Deer C
55,138	38,500	14,784	1,854	N	2,900	68,700	Redlands CC
141,356	75,727	53,341	12,288	N	15,909	226,586	Rend Lake C
397,780	254,708	131,223	118,849	Y	14,000	501,480	Renton Tech C
299,698	157,164	137,574	4,960	N	54,590	408,621	Robeson CC
474,035	270,556	178,653	24,826	N	122,377	663,555	Rogue CC
1,289,859	542,120	676,468	71,271	N	6,225	1,453,344	Sacramento City C

1 -- See Footnotes   -1 -- Unavailable   -2 -- Not Applicable

ACRL Library Data Tables 2005
EXPENDITURES

INSTITUTIONS GRANTING ASSOCIATE OF ARTS DEGREES (Carnegie Code A)

Survey Question #	Reported in Canadian $ 14	Total Library Materials 15	Monographs 15a	Current Serials 15b	Other Library Materials 15c	Misc. Materials 15d	Contract Binding 16
Lib. No. Institution							
201 San Antonio C		320,425	178,183	84,772	57,470	0	0
202 San Jacinto C South		289,167	223,717	11,324	39,918	14,208	245
203 San Joaquin Delta C		181,786	100,000	66,986	14,800	0	1,300
204 Santa Fe CC-NM		239,672	158,229	69,415	7,428	4,600	408
205 Santa Monica C		149,081	48,000	20,593	3,088	77,400	1,000
206 Selkirk C	Y	65,341	29,942	31,390	4,009	0	2,282
207 Seward County CC		37,832	20,000	15,000	0	2,832	0
208 South AR CC		55,739	46,539	5,434	2,293	1,473	0
209 South Florida CC		58,984	44,367	10,335	2,203	2,079	0
210 South Puget Sound CC		67,821	37,347	13,227	17,247	0	0
211 Southeast CC		72,794 [1]	44,046	11,317	7,809	9,622	0
212 Southwest VA CC		104,911	67,971	17,930	17,309	1,701	0
213 Spartanburg Tech C		105,000	67,529	26,650	10,821	0	0
214 Spoon River C		31,680	13,830	2,000	6,000	9,850	0
215 St Charles County CC		138,783	81,603	52,326	4,854	0	359
216 Sthrn U-Shreveport/Bossier		57,604	24,590	32,186	828	0	0
217 Tacoma CC		59,172	33,650	21,022	0	4,500	0
218 Tallahassee CC		319,408	159,029	111,435	40,495	8,449	5,532
219 Tech C Lowcountry		52,215	31,568	18,994	1,653	0	0
220 Temple C		106,646	44,185	33,261	12,862	16,338	3,088
221 Tri County Tech C		103,964	58,827	18,673	0	26,464	0
222 Trocaire C		28,535	14,561	8,329	5,645 [1]	0	0
223 Tunxis CC Tech		135,421	94,306	20,194	20,921	0	297
224 TX ST Tech C Waco		117,389	44,036	50,094	625	22,634	0
225 U Akron Wayne C		59,329	37,050	18,804	3,475	0	0
226 U HI-Kapiolani CC		62,099	10,372	37,851	13,876	0	0
227 U HI-Kauai CC		54,610	13,110	15,200	24,700	1,600	500
228 U HI-Windward CC		36,801	12,685	14,713	9,403	0	2,202
229 U NM Gallup Branch		134,457	80,920 [1]	34,449	19,088	0	0
230 VA Western CC		75,187	55,189	19,998	0	0	300
231 W.Rainey Harper C		451,817	223,952	150,314 [1]	69,747	7,804 [1]	0
232 Walsh U		182,412	61,665	83,889	36,858	0	7,411
233 Walters ST CC		45,583	25,236	17,001	3,346	0	0
234 Waycross C		52,460	17,885	21,426	8,759	4,390	342
235 Weatherford C		131,480	65,359	43,390	22,331	400	250
236 Western IA Tech CC		83,534	28,033	25,927	27,435	2,140	30
237 Wharton Co Jr C		82,601	27,063	30,340	7,275	17,923	0
238 Whatcom CC		56,256	41,227	15,029	0	0	0
239 Wytheville CC		92,036	57,815	21,194	9,776	3,251	0
240 Yakima Valley CC		85,225	66,696	1,757	7,437	9,335	0

1 -- See Footnotes   -1 -- Unavailable   -2 -- Not Applicable

ACRL Library Data Tables 2005
EXPENDITURES

INSTITUTIONS GRANTING ASSOCIATE OF ARTS DEGREES (Carnegie Code A)

Total Salaries & Wages* 17	Salaries & Wages Prof. Staff* 17a	Salaries & Wages Suppt. Staff* 17b	Salaries & Wages Stud. Ass'ts* 17c	Fringe Benefits Included 18	Other Operating Expenditures 19	Total Library Expenditures 20	Survey Question #
							Institution
1,793,850	915,801	821,114	56,935	N	0	2,114,275	San Antonio C
255,593	161,094	72,730	21,769	N	13,531	558,536	San Jacinto C South
1,039,536	566,286	429,760	43,490	N	0	1,222,622	San Joaquin Delta C
755,752	545,715	116,944	93,093	Y	3,554	999,386	Santa Fe CC-NM
910,784	669,071	193,713	48,000	N	0	1,060,865	Santa Monica C
469,209	258,139	211,070	0	Y	0	536,832	Selkirk C
100,169	55,364	44,805	0	N	37,832	175,833	Seward County CC
98,335	50,162	48,173	0	N	2,348	156,422	South AR CC
246,683	106,177	136,480	4,026	N	9,874	315,541	South Florida CC
396,414	193,812	187,834	14,768	N	40,116	504,351	South Puget Sound CC
337,296	236,010	101,286	0 [1]	N	0 [1]	410,090	Southeast CC
207,677	114,253	88,138	5,286	N	13,700	326,288	Southwest VA CC
262,332	152,367	109,965	0	N	41,348	408,680	Spartanburg Tech C
127,584	49,164	75,420	3,000	Y	26,400	185,664	Spoon River C
394,243	241,526	151,553	1,164	N	65,123	598,508	St Charles County CC
316,523	152,350	150,637	13,536	Y	3,724	377,851	Sthrn U-Shreveport/Bossier
504,000	339,000	165,000	0	Y	0	563,172	Tacoma CC
775,523	368,981	352,657	53,885	N	185,580	1,286,043	Tallahassee CC
185,762	117,811	60,502	7,449	N	79,689	317,666	Tech C Lowcountry
213,717	181,695	21,857	10,165	N	33,826	357,277	Temple C
3,721	0	0	3,721	N	0	107,685	Tri County Tech C
100,540	93,260	0	7,280	N	3,407	132,482	Trocaire C
584,232	502,959	49,426	31,847	N	21,812	741,762	Tunxis CC Tech
311,960	225,204	84,756	2,000	Y	5,831	435,180	TX ST Tech C Waco
122,044	40,394	61,639	20,011	N	9,053	190,426	U Akron Wayne C
642,017	342,253	252,941	46,824	Y	39,092	743,208	U HI-Kapiolani CC
282,000	189,000	91,000	2,000	N	0	337,110	U HI-Kauai CC
289,011	176,070	88,419	24,522	Y	33,845	361,859	U HI-Windward CC
229,801	109,000	107,801	13,000	N	9,236	373,494	U NM Gallup Branch
282,311	162,113	110,273	9,925	N	31,332	389,130	VA Western CC
928,890 [1]	391,930 [1]	515,532	21,428	N	44,804	1,425,511	W.Rainey Harper C
283,026	157,381	84,545	41,100	N	110,162	583,011	Walsh U
317,504	227,885	85,119	4,500	N	22,568	385,655	Walters ST CC
156,284	93,123	51,882	11,279	N	22,693	231,779 [1]	Waycross C
320,382	147,790	170,302	2,290	N	64,897	517,009	Weatherford C
690,307	74,531	609,191	6,585	N	3,387	777,258	Western IA Tech CC
301,364	169,533	121,942	9,889	Y	30,550	414,515	Wharton Co Jr C
357,938	172,619	173,653	11,666 [1]	N	11,634	425,828	Whatcom CC
181,121	138,978	33,184	8,959	N	4,138	277,295	Wytheville CC
344,340	219,689	123,571	1,080	N	8,975	438,540	Yakima Valley CC

1 -- See Footnotes   -1 -- Unavailable   -2 -- Not Applicable

ACRL Library Data Tables 2005
EXPENDITURES

INSTITUTIONS GRANTING ASSOCIATE OF ARTS DEGREES (Carnegie Code A)

Survey Question #		Reported in Canadian $ 14	Total Library Materials 15	Monographs 15a	Current Serials 15b	Other Library Materials 15c	Misc. Materials 15d	Contract Binding 16
Lib. No.	Institution							
241	Yavapai C		87,430 [1]	50,977	34,712	1,741	0	1,534

1 -- See Footnotes   -1 -- Unavailable   -2 -- Not Applicable

ACRL Library Data Tables 2005
EXPENDITURES

INSTITUTIONS GRANTING ASSOCIATE OF ARTS DEGREES (Carnegie Code A)

Total Salaries & Wages* 17	Salaries & Wages Prof. Staff* 17a	Salaries & Wages Suppt. Staff* 17b	Salaries & Wages Stud. Ass'ts* 17c	Fringe Benefits Included 18	Other Operating Expenditures 19	Total Library Expenditures 20	Survey Question #
							Institution
411,725	159,873	220,485	31,367	N	21,958	522,647	Yavapai C

1 -- See Footnotes   -1 -- Unavailable   -2 -- Not Applicable

ACRL LIBRARY DATA TABLES 2005

SUMMARY DATA: ELECTRONIC MATERIALS EXPENDITURES

INSTITUTIONS GRANTING ASSOCIATE OF ARTS DEGREES (Carnegie Code A)

| (Survey Question #) | Computer Files 21 | Electronic Serials 22 | Bibl. Util./Networks/Consortia | | Computer Hardware & Software 24 | Doc. Delivery ILL 25 |
			Internal Library Sources 23a	External Sources 23b		
High	81,297	285,922	97,316	1,850,200	271,616	44,948
Mean	1,881	21,118	7,871	20,044	10,893	1,043
Median	0	8,960	3,526	0	2,126	61
Low	0	0	0	0	0	0
Total	383,675	4,688,128	1,747,342	3,848,414	2,276,677	214,921
Libraries Reporting	204	222	222	192	209	206

ACRL Library Data Tables 2005

ELECTRONIC MATERIALS EXPENDITURES

INSTITUTIONS GRANTING ASSOCIATE OF ARTS DEGREES (Carnegie Code A)

Lib. No.	Institution — Survey Question #	Computer Files 21	Electronic Serials 22	Bibl. Util. / Networks / Consortia Internal Library Sources 23a	External Sources 23b	Computer Hardware & Software 24	Doc. Delivery, ILL 25
1	A Baldwin Agrl C	0	0	0	9,655	0	23
2	Adirondack CC	0	12,121	0	25,072	0	272
3	Alpena CC	671 [1]	36,000 [1]	0	0	0	307 [1]
4	Alvin CC	0	6,111	250	0	10,424	0
5	Am River C	0	44,659	8,500	0	1,400	0
6	Am Samoa CC	1,000	7,000	0	0	10,000	0
7	Andover C	0	9,104	0	0	0	416
8	Anne Arundel CC	5,000 [1]	159,685	14,381	0	0 [1]	0 [1]
9	Anoka-Ramsey CC	375	2,259	1,500	-1	0	10
10	AR ST U Beebe	77,167	41,835	14,500 [1]	2,500 [1]	32,992	0 [1]
11	Athens Tech C	1,029	375	2,466	0	12,874	10
12	AZ Western C	4,162	41,003	18,566	0 [1]	3,143	1,755
13	Bellingham Tech C	0 [1]	7,330	425	0	2,239	201
14	Belmont Tech C	2,716	0	26,779	20,877	30,750	2
15	Bergen CC	685 [1]	39,000	19,000	0	-1	-1
16	Black Hawk C	5,870	4,000	0	12,600	2,100	1,000
17	Blackhawk Tech C	0	19,444	4,552	0	0	896
18	Blue Mountain CC	0	8,167 [1]	2,850 [1]	3,985 [1]	6,945	300 [1]
19	Blue Ridge CC	0	4,634	4,324	43,592	0	3,165
20	Brazosport C	0	0	38,750	0	11,190	0
21	Bunker Hill CC	81,297	28,389	50,633 [1]	0	52,908	519
22	Butler County CC	0	38,678	700	0 [1]	3,657	0 [1]
23	C Canyons	0	0 [1]	2,903	0	0	0
24	C Edouard Montpetit	500	15,000	0	0	0	165
25	C Lake Co	0 [1]	250 [1]	1,000	0	8,741	220
26	C Merici	0	0	0	0	0	0
27	C New Caledonia	0	32,801	0	0	0	0
28	C Redwoods	0	34,454	0	2,622	0	0
29	C St Jean Richelieu	0	0	0	0	0	0
30	Camden County C	4,829	46,255	31,060	0 [1]	2,274	146
31	Cape Fear CC	0	13,956	22,376	0	271,616	218
32	Capital CC	3,320	21,816	5,000	0	5,369	594
33	Carl Sandburg C	0	0	0	6,610	0	0
34	Carroll Tech Inst	0	0	600	10,000	27,000	50
35	Carteret CC	0	0	5,333	0	2,897	1,452
36	Cedar Valley	0	0	34,253	0	7,802	0
37	CEGEP Beauce-Appalaches	1	5,650	0	0	1,770	1
38	CEGEP Trois-Rivieres	17,931	0	0	0	24,000	0
39	Central Alabama CC	0	0	2,525	0	2,126	0
40	Central Carolina Tech C	989	20,320	2,200	0	279	0 [1]

1 -- See Footnotes   -1 -- Unavailable   -2 -- Not Applicable

ACRL Library Data Tables 2005

ELECTRONIC MATERIALS EXPENDITURES

INSTITUTIONS GRANTING ASSOCIATE OF ARTS DEGREES (Carnegie Code A)

Lib. No.	Institution	Computer Files 21	Electronic Serials 22	Bibl. Util. / Networks / Consortia		Computer Hardware & Software 24	Doc. Delivery, ILL 25
	Survey Question #			Internal Library Sources 23a	External Sources 23b		
41	Central ME Tech C	0	6,544	5,600	0	0	1,036
42	Central Piedmont CC	0	39,313	0	0	0	1,078
43	Central TX C	0	0	0	0	72,196	0
44	Centralia C	0	13,500	12,470 [1]	1,431 [1]	13,800 [1]	0
45	Chabot C	0	42,740	0	2,000	0	0
46	Chattahoochee Tech	5,000	6,100	4,100	0	11,334	0
47	Chippewa V Tech C	4,511	28,933	31,628	1,850,200 [1]	43,794	31
48	Clackamas CC	0	0	0	12,446	12,440	0
49	Clark C-WA	0	33,063	33,131	0	8,472	477
50	Clinton CC	0	9,069	15,349	0	0	379
51	Cloud Co CC	2,796	5,142	2,620	0	1,323	301
52	Coastal GA CC	0	15,676	18,304	24,465	8,000	2,628
53	Colby CC	0	0	0	5,500	5,000	200
54	Columbia Junior C	0	28,026	3,000	0	24,103	850
55	Columbia ST CC	2,000	35,000	4,000	2,000	10,000	1,400
56	Columbus ST CC	0	0	0	0	0	0
57	Compton CC	0	39,787	0	0	9,923	0
58	Connors ST C	6,886	7,338	13,384	0	5,634	468
59	Corning CC	0	31,770	3,998	16,881	21,948	1,645
60	Cosumnes River C	0	46,034 [1]	0 [1]	0	0	0
61	Crowder C	0	18,832	10,878	0	420	0
62	Cuesta C	0	14,648	14,571	0	848	14
63	Cumberland Co C	0	19,690	13,510	4,548	0	0
64	CUNY Borough Manhattan CC	0	22,714	7,045	0	178,683	0
65	CUNY Bronx CC	0	63,281	0	3,281	0	0
66	CUNY Hostos CC	0	0	5,304	42,955	21,351	1,132
67	CUNY LaGuardia CC	0	16,208	9,200	15,550	15,000	0
68	CUNY Queensborough CC	0	0	12,000	110,000	0	0
69	D.S. Lancaster CC	75	520	1,223	660	0	225
70	Darton C	0	0	0	0	579	0
71	Dawson CC	607	4,140	4,000	0	0	0
72	Del Mar C	0	0	9,990	0	66,999	0 [1]
73	Delaware Co CC	0	0	0	45,267	0	3,718
74	Diablo Valley C	12,000	46,981	2,144	54,596	6,242	20
75	Dodge City CC	0	4,500	0	0	0	0
76	Dyersburg ST CC	0	28,912	0	0	9,474	0
77	East Central C	0	2,436	7,045	0	6,185	31
78	East Georgia C	0	0	12,089	13,750	1,176	240
79	East Los Angeles C	354	34,000	0	1,000	0	0
80	El Paso CC	0	0	25,000	0	7,500	0

1 -- See Footnotes   -1 -- Unavailable   -2 -- Not Applicable

ACRL Library Data Tables 2005
ELECTRONIC MATERIALS EXPENDITURES
INSTITUTIONS GRANTING ASSOCIATE OF ARTS DEGREES (Carnegie Code A)

| | | Computer Files | Electronic Serials | Bibl. Util. / Networks / Consortia | | Computer Hardware & Software | Doc. Delivery, ILL |
| | | | | Internal Library Sources | External Sources | | |
Lib. No.	Survey Question # Institution	21	22	23a	23b	24	25
81	Estrn Arizona C	0	20,600	0	0	8,140	0
82	Estrn Idaho Tech C	0	0	0	2,459	25,640	0
83	Estrn Maine Tech C	199	4,488	1,118	3,000	0	867
84	Fayetteville Tech CC	0	21,466	0	0	0	0
85	Fergus Falls CC	1,000	0	2,800	0	0	0
86	Flor Dar Tech C	0	0	0	0	0	0
87	Floyd C	2,724	4,828	4,389	23,595	5,658	1,249
88	Gadsden ST CC	0	0	17,013	0	0	0
89	Gainesville C	0	0	2,100	57,635	32,076	0
90	Gavilan C	5,972 [1]	33,314	0	5,627	2,108	0
91	GC Wallace CC	0	1,460	0	0	0	0
92	Glendale CC	0	66,934	0	500,000 [1]	0 [1]	0
93	Gogebic CC	0	0	9,108	0	0 [1]	900
94	Gordon C-GA	0	8,591	28,502	35,626	0	0
95	Grand Rapids CC	15,000	32,000	15,000	9,000	1,000 [1]	9,000
96	Harrisburg Area CC	0	285,922	12,800	0	52,313	4,886
97	Hawaii Pacific U	0	149,571	15,339	9,495	25,000	12,000
98	Hawkeye CC	0	32,251	5,239	0 [1]	10,900	4,918
99	Highland CC KS	0	722	0	0	2,930	483
100	Hillsborough CC	1,733	106,745	0	12,510	7,513	3,782
101	Hinds CC	0	9,145	0	0	58,791	14,639 [1]
102	Hiwassee C	0	1,390	6,496	0	13,760	0
103	Hocking Tech C	5,269	0	9,881	23,052	4,072	0
104	Hopkinsville CC	0	0	6,946	-2	0	0
105	Horry GTown Tech	0	58,562	6,839	17,780	0	0
106	Howard C	0	2,500	650	0	0	0
107	Hutch CC&Voc Sch	0	0	0	0	0	1,198
108	IL E CC Wabash Cntrl C	0	0	0	0	0	0
109	IL Estrn CC-Frontier	0	0	2,504	-1	0	0
110	IL Estrn CC-Lincoln Trail	0	0	1,645	0	0	0
111	IL Valley CC	0	14,991	8,682	0	876	0
112	Independence CC	0	2,395	0	0	1,149	0
113	Inst Com PR Jr C Arecibo	0	0	0	0	0	0
114	Inst Native Culture	0 [1]	0 [1]	0 [1]	0 [1]	0 [1]	0 [1]
115	Isothermal CC	100	0	100	0	3,565	564
116	J.F. Drake ST Tech C	0	3,740	0	0	0	0
117	Jacksonville C	0	0	1,365	2,000	0	0
118	Jefferson CC-NY	1,200	58,000	6,000	15,000	5,000	2,400
119	Jefferson C-MO	0	9,980	13,853	0	16,252	1,340
120	JS Reynolds CC	0	4,585	3,012	132,293	0	3,012

1 -- See Footnotes   -1 -- Unavailable   -2 -- Not Applicable

ACRL Library Data Tables 2005

ELECTRONIC MATERIALS EXPENDITURES

INSTITUTIONS GRANTING ASSOCIATE OF ARTS DEGREES (Carnegie Code A)

		Computer Files	Electronic Serials	Bibl. Util. / Networks / Consortia		Computer Hardware & Software	Doc. Delivery, ILL
				Internal Library Sources	External Sources		
	Survey Question #	21	22	23a	23b	24	25
Lib. No.	Institution						
121	Justice Inst BC	0	3,779	24,070	0	0	0
122	Kaskaskia C	-1	11,700	4,500	-1	32,250	-1
123	Kent St U E Liverpool	0	0	500	0	0	0
124	Kent St U Tuscarawas	0	1,250	0	0	0	0
125	Kilgore C	0	23,396	6,466	0	8,241	2,092
126	Kirkwood CC	0	6,452	2,355	0	2,120	2,366
127	Kirtland CC	1,849	200	0	1,275	0	25
128	Labette CC	0	29,105	0	690	2,358	84
129	Laboure C	0	9 [1]	0	0	0	0
130	Lake City CC	0	5,433	1,250	0	8,069	922
131	Lakeland CC-OH	0	0	8,884	0	0	0
132	Lane CC-OR	0	49,727	41,036	-1	73,750	-1
133	Lansdale Sch of Bus	0	2,316 [1]	37	0	0 [1]	0
134	Laramie Co CC	0	0	20,460	1,500	3,900	600
135	Lassen CC	0	30,691	3,213	0	4,905	0
136	Lexington CC	1,113 [1]	8,451 [1]	15,100 [1]	0 [1]	738	66
137	Linn ST Tech C	0	0	16,988	0	29,891	71
138	Lord Fairfax CC	0	1,227	5,966 [1]	61,098	8,184	0 [1]
139	Los Angeles Valley C	0	50,272	264	0	12,380	0
140	Luzerne County CC	0	50,000 [1]	0	0	0 [1]	21,000 [1]
141	Manatee CC	4,800	50,907	0	6,036	5,737	341
142	Maple Woods CC	0	17,319	0	8,144	0	3,225
143	Marymount C CA	0	52,000	2,000	0	1,806	1,650
144	Massasoit CC	2,871	11,352	0	10,000	0	2,500
145	McDowell Tech CC	0	2,128	0 [1]	0 [1]	0	429
146	Mesa CC	-2	28,530	0	0	0	0
147	Middlesex Co C-NJ	0	0	20,000	0	0	0
148	Midland C	5,300	9,944	250	6,105 [1]	10,853	0
149	Miles CC	0	3,735	4,901	0	0	66
150	MiraCosta C	0	23,034	9,126	26,269	0	2,331
151	Monroe CC	0	47,298	11,272	0	17,627	1,322
152	Mountain Empire CC	4,725	3,720	0	40,504	0	485
153	MS County CC	0	12,516	1,250	0	1,561	3,300
154	MS Delta CC	0	0	15,000	0	5,323	675
155	Mt Hood CC	0 [1]	34,503	19,259 [1]	0	14,225 [1]	3,980 [1]
156	N Alberta Inst	1	1	1	1	1	1
157	National Hispanic U	0	20,000	500	0	0	55
158	ND ST C Science	0	0	0	23,064	0	0
159	NE WI Tech C	0	59,653	31,461	0	0	325
160	NH CC-Berlin	0	10,394	6,894	3,500	2,443	238

1 -- See Footnotes   -1 -- Unavailable   -2 -- Not Applicable

ACRL Library Data Tables 2005

ELECTRONIC MATERIALS EXPENDITURES

INSTITUTIONS GRANTING ASSOCIATE OF ARTS DEGREES (Carnegie Code A)

		Computer Files	Electronic Serials	Bibl. Util. / Networks / Consortia		Computer Hardware & Software	Doc. Delivery, ILL
				Internal Library Sources	External Sources		
	Survey Question #	21	22	23a	23b	24	25
Lib. No.	Institution						
161	NH CC-Laconia	0	8,302	199	0	2,000	0
162	Nicolet Area Tech C	942	23,577	5,000	2,202	2,202	-296
163	NM St U-Carlsbad	386	14,237	2,075	0	11,670	710
164	Normandale CC	626	58,313	7,067	0	0	0
165	North AR C	0	0	9,987	1,200 [1]	2,418	416
166	Northeast ST Tech CC	0	25,817	6,295	0	14,951	0
167	Northeastern JC	0	5,551	974	0 [1]	19,185	0 [1]
168	Northwest C	0	13,848	3,840	0	1,245	26
169	Nwestern Business C	0	8,850	0	713	0	0
170	Nwestern CT Tech CC	0	117	16,725	0	0	0
171	OH ST U Ag Tech Inst	94	0	0	1,644	4,037 [1]	0
172	Ohlone C	482	0	2,500	35,882	13,233	0
173	Okaloosa-Walton CC	0	0	26,511	24,000	30,340	1,583
174	Orange County CC	0	20,000	17,300	0	0	300
175	Owensboro	0	9,092	0	1,922	1,782	269
176	Owensboro Jr C Bus	0	6,000	200	0	0	0
177	Oxnard C	0	35,200	0	2,353	0	0
178	Passaic County CC	0	22,000	18,000	0	40,000	0
179	Paul D. Camp CC	0	0	835	0	0	0
180	Pellissippi ST Tech CC	8,216	35,110	10,419	0	0	0
181	Pensacola Jr C	0	0	0	1,600	2,267	4,686
182	Petit Jean C	0	0	0	0	0	0
183	Piedmont Tech C	0 [1]	0	2,650 [1]	5,721	735 [1]	0
184	Pittsburgh Tech Inst	0	0	-2	2,263	-2	124
185	Portland CC	0 [1]	91,542	97,316	0	159,721	0 [1]
186	Potomac St C-WVU	0	0	4,966	0	0	0
187	Prairie ST C	0	10,883	28,990	3,214	0	0
188	Prince George CC	0	121,516	0	18,500	0 [1]	0
189	Pueblo CC	2,000	4,664	10,303	2,398 [1]	984	-1
190	Pulaski Tech C	7,910	42,434	1,958	-1	8,229	200
191	Quinebaug Vally Comm TC	0	0	4,000	0	45,126	0
192	Quinsigamond CC	0	18,979	30,268	0	3,061	0 [1]
193	Reading Area CC	1,105	33,190	0	16,000	0	0
194	Red Deer C	0	128,700	0	0	0	0
195	Redlands CC	0	3,920	1,250	0	1,457	0
196	Rend Lake C	0	14,987	4,143	80	221	0
197	Renton Tech C	3,000	14,600	2,400	0	18,000	100
198	Robeson CC	0	0	250	0	0	100
199	Rogue CC	0	8,612	0	41,788	0	1,342
200	Sacramento City C	0	57,682	0	0	0	0

1 -- See Footnotes   -1 -- Unavailable   -2 -- Not Applicable

ACRL Library Data Tables 2005

ELECTRONIC MATERIALS EXPENDITURES

INSTITUTIONS GRANTING ASSOCIATE OF ARTS DEGREES (Carnegie Code A)

		Computer Files	Electronic Serials	Bibl. Util. / Networks / Consortia		Computer Hardware & Software	Doc. Delivery, ILL
				Internal Library Sources	External Sources		
	Survey Question #	21	22	23a	23b	24	25
Lib. No.	Institution						
201	San Antonio C	0	202,300	0	28,575	0	44,948
202	San Jacinto C South	0	0	5,236	0	59,443	2,978
203	San Joaquin Delta C	37,711	75,805	6,324	0	36,364	0
204	Santa Fe CC-NM	1,000	56,604	9,403	0	23,744	2,949
205	Santa Monica C	0	58,507	4,530	0	0	0
206	Selkirk C	0	0	21,394 [1]	0	19,239	3,500 [1]
207	Seward County CC	0	0	0	0	0	0
208	South AR CC	11,720	15,749	0	6,300	19,572	125
209	South Florida CC	0	23,401	0	0	2,244	2,429
210	South Puget Sound CC	0	7,864	14,513	0	10,000	15
211	Southeast CC	0	5,990 [1]	5,056	0	3,039	531
212	Southwest VA CC	2,855	2,106	2,707	51,467	2,902	242
213	Spartanburg Tech C	1,390	14,349	17,019	0	285	67
214	Spoon River C	6,000	8,500	6,204	0	0 [1]	500
215	St Charles County CC	0	32,031	28,324	0	25,735	115
216	Sthrn U-Shreveport/Bossier	0	0	1,300	9,175	3,972	0
217	Tacoma CC	0	23,555	0	0	0	100
218	Tallahassee CC	332	58,614	9,235	2,700	0	620
219	Tech C Lowcountry	0 [1]	12,287	8,087	0	0	148
220	Temple C	0	2,757	8,304	0	13,928	741
221	Tri County Tech C	0	0	3,000	10,527	0	31
222	Trocaire C	0	0	0	0	0	25
223	Tunxis CC Tech	0	631	12,913	0	263	0
224	TX ST Tech C Waco	0	2,500	10,948	0	13,323	0
225	U Akron Wayne C	0	7,718	1,208	17,703	0	237
226	U HI-Kapiolani CC	0	32,742	0	0	5,643	36
227	U HI-Kauai CC	0	0	17,995	4,000	0	0
228	U HI-Windward CC	0	5,726	19,286	0	0	66
229	U NM Gallup Branch	93	35,200	5,505	0 [1]	0	1,250
230	VA Western CC	0	5,190	5,000	86,351	0	5,000
231	W.Rainey Harper C	272	0 [1]	24,231 [1]	10,800 [1]	0 [1]	0
232	Walsh U	1,014	50,177	58,819	20,423	0	114
233	Walters ST CC	0	64,330	0	1,415	3,202	21
234	Waycross C	0	3,066	15,085	7,983	834	356
235	Weatherford C	900	13,800	25,500	4,000	12,500	400
236	Western IA Tech CC	0	27,435	2,140	1,375	8,757	35
237	Wharton Co Jr C	-2	-2	8,800	2,500	1,676	-2
238	Whatcom CC	0	0	3,060	0	0	400
239	Wytheville CC	0	2,001	1,250	32,241	0	0
240	Yakima Valley CC	0	0	17,153	0	0	0

1 -- See Footnotes   -1 -- Unavailable   -2 -- Not Applicable

ACRL Library Data Tables 2005
ELECTRONIC MATERIALS EXPENDITURES
INSTITUTIONS GRANTING ASSOCIATE OF ARTS DEGREES (Carnegie Code A)

| Lib. No. | Institution | Computer Files 21 | Electronic Serials 22 | Bibl. Util. / Networks / Consortia | | Computer Hardware & Software 24 | Doc. Delivery, ILL 25 |
	Survey Question #			Internal Library Sources 23a	External Sources 23b		
241	Yavapai C	0	39,056	0	8,098	7,122	104 [1]

1 -- See Footnotes   -1 -- Unavailable   -2 -- Not Applicable

ACRL LIBRARY DATA TABLES 2005

SUMMARY DATA: PERSONNEL AND PUBLIC SERVICES

INSTITUTIONS GRANTING ASSOCIATE OF ARTS DEGREES (Carnegie Code A)

(Survey Question #)	Total Staff (FTE)	Professional Staff (FTE)	Support Staff (FTE)	Student Assistants (FTE)	No. of Staffed Service Points	No. of Weekly Public Service Hours
	26	26a	26b	26c	27	28
High	92	27	47	29	78	168
Mean	12	4	6	3	3.1	66.1
Median	9	3	4	2	2	65
Low	1	1	0	0	0	1
Total	3,042	1,066	1,404	672	756	16272
Libraries Reporting	247	250	247	242	244	246

ACRL LIBRARY DATA TABLES 2005

SUMMARY DATA: PERSONNEL AND PUBLIC SERVICES

INSTITUTIONS GRANTING ASSOCIATE OF ARTS DEGREES (Carnegie Code A)

Library Presentations to Groups	Participants in Group Presentations	Reference Transactions	Initial Circulation Transactions	Total Circulation Transactions	Items Loaned (ILL)	Items Borrowed (ILL)	
29	30	31	32	33	34	35	(Survey Question #)
655	16,558	154,737	142,140	146,140	5,084	4,929	High
124	2,348	7,737	14,383	16,271	548	425	Mean
91	1,669	3,961	9,000	9,600	252	217	Median
2	10	0	0	0	0	0	Low
30,489	575,245	1,779,434	2,862,127	3,709,774	130,936	101,457	Total
246	245	230	199	228	239	239	Libraries Reporting

ACRL Library Data Tables 2005
PERSONNEL AND PUBLIC SERVICES
INSTITUTIONS GRANTING ASSOCIATE OF ARTS DEGREES (Carnegie Code A)

		Total Staff (FTE)	Professional Staff (FTE)	Support Staff (FTE)	Student Assistants (FTE)	No. of Staffed Service Points	Weekly Public Service Hours
	Survey Question #	26	26a	26b	26c	27	28
Lib. No.	Institution						
1	A Baldwin Agrl C	9	2	3	4	2	76
2	Adirondack CC	13	6	4	4	2	72
3	Alpena CC	5	1 [1]	3 [1]	1 [1]	1 [1]	71
4	Alvin CC	7	2	3	2	2	65
5	Am River C	22	9	6	7	3	74
6	Am Samoa CC	10	1	5	4	48	48
7	Andover C	2	1	0	1	1	53
8	Anne Arundel CC	19	6	11	2 [1]	2	78 [1]
9	Anoka-Ramsey CC	5	2	1	2	4	62
10	AR ST U Beebe	11	2	6	3	5	75
11	Athens Tech C	9	3	2	4	3	78
12	AZ Western C	15	6	7	2	3	76
13	Bellingham Tech C	3	1	2	0 [1]	1	53
14	Belmont Tech C	10	4	5	1	4	59
15	Bergen CC	41	15	20	6	3	86
16	Black Hawk C	9	4	4	1	2	65
17	Blackhawk Tech C	5	1	3	1	3	67
18	Blue Mountain CC	5	2	2	1	1	73
19	Blue Ridge CC	6	2	3	0	2	62
20	Brazosport C	8	4	2	2	2	61
21	Bunker Hill CC	19	6	10	3	4	80
22	Butler County CC	11	3	7 [1]	1	5	69
23	C Canyons	15	4	6	5	2	65
24	C Edouard Montpetit	19	2	15	2	4	60
25	C Lake Co	35	6	27	2	2	76
26	C Merici	6	1	3	2	1	57
27	C New Caledonia	12	4	8	0	1	76
28	C Redwoods	14	2	9 [1]	3	2	38
29	C St Jean Richelieu	9	1	6	2	1	8
30	Camden County C	14	6	7	1	2	73
31	Cape Fear CC	23	7	13	3	3	68
32	Capital CC	15	5	1	9	2	58
33	Carl Sandburg C	9	2	5	2	2	64
34	Carroll Tech Inst	10	3	4	3	3	64
35	Carteret CC	6	2	4	0	2	67
36	Cedar Valley	6	4	1	0	2	64
37	CEGEP Beauce-Appalaches	5	1	4	0	1	61
38	CEGEP Trois-Rivieres	14	3	11	0	2	57
39	Central Alabama CC	6	3	1	2	2	59
40	Central Carolina Tech C	4	1	1	2	1	59

1 -- See Footnotes   -1 -- Unavailable   -2 -- Not Applicable

ACRL Library Data Tables 2005
PERSONNEL AND PUBLIC SERVICES

INSTITUTIONS GRANTING ASSOCIATE OF ARTS DEGREES (Carnegie Code A)

No. of Presentations to Groups 29	Participants in Group Presentations 30	No. of Reference Transactions 31	No. of Initial Circulations 32	Total Circulations 33	ILL Materials Provided 34	ILL Materials Received 35	Survey Question # Institution
116	2,072	8,600	8,707	9,506	477	314	A Baldwin Agrl C
155	2,490	880	9,511	9,511	743	484	Adirondack CC
40	703	4,608 [1]	10,031 [1]	11,115	217 [1]	139 [1]	Alpena CC
79	1,050	2,082	2,827	3,212	0	25	Alvin CC
242	5,069	13,392	27,112	29,586	1,634	759	Am River C
100	0	400	3,000	3,500	0	0	Am Samoa CC
66	791	0	0	3,635	599	333	Andover C
274	4,395	25,186	44,875 [1]	44,875	868	642	Anne Arundel CC
90	2,700	-1	-1	5,870	409	1,769	Anoka-Ramsey CC
53	754	2,896	9,813	12,376	186	58	AR ST U Beebe
57	1,140	3,870	5,760 [1]	5,760	254	187	Athens Tech C
166	2,490	4,570	15,751	17,107	1,538	720	AZ Western C
67	804	2,100	0	10,372	19	22	Bellingham Tech C
236	850	520	14,283	16,014	94	55	Belmont Tech C
505	10,100	19,603	32,236	41,585	2,225	381	Bergen CC
114	2,736	5,020	8,950	11,635	640	1,015	Black Hawk C
51	679	0	0 [1]	4,516	213	50	Blackhawk Tech C
27	450	0 [1]	5,131	10,223	1,106	498	Blue Mountain CC
81	1,713	2,500	17,822	20,185	547	615	Blue Ridge CC
78	1,544	194	0	12,966	0	121	Brazosport C
160	2,611	3,952	7,802	11,781	2,540	1,160	Bunker Hill CC
70	996	1,022	0 [1]	11,369	522	198	Butler County CC
106	2,089	65,122	0	29,944	23	69	C Canyons
109	3,270	8,000	0	40,536	314	165	C Edouard Montpetit
425	8,500	0 [1]	72,230	142,542	825	1,121	C Lake Co
25	20	0	0	13,161	49	58	C Merici
165	2,217	15,380	0	35,077	1,071	905	C New Caledonia
68	1,700	568	4,960	5,904	36	32	C Redwoods
25	500	0	0	19,297	25	32	C St Jean Richelieu
138	3,450	5,650	11,677	15,831	746	295	Camden County C
165	2,961	6,984	0	26,546	354	206	Cape Fear CC
97	1,983	3,312	6,951	9,641	254	175	Capital CC
550	1,115	3,752	9,510	9,823	819	495	Carl Sandburg C
7	105	856	395	395	2	10	Carroll Tech Inst
59	877	3,951	-1	11,106	246	398	Carteret CC
79	1,975	7,404	10,796	10,796	406	390	Cedar Valley
15	375	1	1	10,804	0	24	EGEP Beauce-Appalaches
101	2,500	5,364	38,232	40,644	60	49	CEGEP Trois-Rivieres
35	814	0	1,810	3,160	0	11	Central Alabama CC
88	1,597	3,360	0	5,811	67	233	Central Carolina Tech C

1 -- See Footnotes   -1 -- Unavailable   -2 -- Not Applicable

ACRL Library Data Tables 2005
PERSONNEL AND PUBLIC SERVICES
INSTITUTIONS GRANTING ASSOCIATE OF ARTS DEGREES (Carnegie Code A)

Lib. No. Institution	Total Staff (FTE) 26	Professional Staff (FTE) 26a	Support Staff (FTE) 26b	Student Assistants (FTE) 26c	No. of Staffed Service Points 27	Weekly Public Service Hours 28
41 Central ME Tech C	4	2	1	1	1	60
42 Central Piedmont CC	32	15	17	0	9	66
43 Central TX C	16	5	8	3	4	778
44 Centralia C	7	3 [1]	2 [1]	3	2	57
45 Chabot C	16	5	6	5	4	55
46 Chattahoochee Tech	10	4	5	1	3	181
47 Chippewa V Tech C	7	1	4	2	1	65
48 Clackamas CC	8	4	4	0	2	63
49 Clark C-WA	20	6	10	4	2	68
50 Clinton CC	9	5	4	1	3	52
51 Cloud Co CC	6	2	2	2	2	68
52 Coastal GA CC	14	6	5	3	2	122 [1]
53 Colby CC	6	1	3	2	2	65
54 Columbia Junior C	14	6	4	4	3	84
55 Columbia ST CC	9	4	4	1	6	66
56 Columbus ST CC	33	11	10	12	3	78
57 Compton CC	7	3	2	2	2	64
58 Connors ST C	8	2	4	2	2	63
59 Corning CC	15	7	8	1	2	51
60 Cosumnes River C	14	6	5	3	2 [1]	69 [1]
61 Crowder C	5	1	2	2	1	66
62 Cuesta C	16	7	8	2	5	60
63 Cumberland Co C	6	3	2	1	2	62
64 CUNY Borough Manhattan CC	59	13	24	22	4	80
65 CUNY Bronx CC	27	11	14	2	4	68
66 CUNY Hostos CC	28	14	6	8	4	68
67 CUNY LaGuardia CC	58	20	23	15	5	85
68 CUNY Queensborough CC	39	13	10	16	6	65
69 D.S. Lancaster CC	5	1	3 [1]	1 [1]	2	65
70 Darton C	16	3	4	9	2	69
71 Dawson CC	3	1	1	1	1	50
72 Del Mar C	40	8	22	10	4	83
73 Delaware Co CC	31	9	7	15	2	72
74 Diablo Valley C	16	5	7	4	4	61
75 Dodge City CC	4	1	2	1	1	67
76 Dyersburg ST CC	13	4	2	7	9	60
77 East Central C	5	2	3	1	2	57
78 East Georgia C	4	1	2	1	3	57
79 East Los Angeles C	14	5	6	3	4	57
80 El Paso CC	52	20	23	10	14	351

1 -- See Footnotes   -1 -- Unavailable   -2 -- Not Applicable

ACRL Library Data Tables 2005
PERSONNEL AND PUBLIC SERVICES

INSTITUTIONS GRANTING ASSOCIATE OF ARTS DEGREES (Carnegie Code A)

No. of Presentations to Groups 29	Participants in Group Presentations 30	No. of Reference Transactions 31	No. of Initial Circulations 32	Total Circulations 33	ILL Materials Provided 34	ILL Materials Received 35	Survey Question # Institution
54	864	2,773	1,773	2,598	948	811	Central ME Tech C
382	7,750	33,300	25,609	27,823	356	277	Central Piedmont CC
154	2,437	20,666	63,604 [1]	63,604	8	97	Central TX C
71	1,462	1,535	8,371	8,661	195	86	Centralia C
191	5,730	10,224	18,986	0	1	20	Chabot C
74	1,361	1,321	1	46,062	185	88	Chattahoochee Tech
153	1,889	18,491	29,230 [1]	29,230	127	62	Chippewa V Tech C
142	3,025	7,856	14,298	17,755	203	138	Clackamas CC
504	11,088	909	22,964	26,748	1,656	2,941	Clark C-WA
29	516	1,278	5,133	5,133 [1]	136	19	Clinton CC
54	962	940	2,468 [1]	2,468	265	362	Cloud Co CC
57	689	429	5,246	5,729	500	202	Coastal GA CC
45	850	425	5,408	5,408	502	411	Colby CC
75	1,262	3,315	10,064	31,081	125	81	Columbia Junior C
106	2,650	20,753	6,877	6,912	246	277	Columbia ST CC
344	7,210	16,127	20,392	122	2,876	1,640	Columbus ST CC
84	1,676	6,000	3,204	0 [1]	0	0	Compton CC
108	1,994	2,500	66,764	66,764	132	24	Connors ST C
161	3,211	2,500	10,429	11,892	400	413	Corning CC
149 [1]	4,485	23,672	20,696	23,305	2,242	1,063	Cosumnes River C
53	1,018	2,250	12,724	13,620	1,259	838	Crowder C
75	1,561	11,137	12,846	14,936	132	222	Cuesta C
79	1,412	2,282	6,915	7,431	335	59	Cumberland Co C
109	5,450	21,000	59,998	65,950	11	198	NY Borough Manhattan CC
102	2,432	18,477	12,488	12,501	293	461	CUNY Bronx CC
174	2,073	11,329	6,874	8,973	2	60	CUNY Hostos CC
673 [1]	14,133 [1]	40,611	38,040	43,398	502	1,258	CUNY LaGuardia CC
223	5,575	15,201	16,016	17,775	323	1,095	CUNY Queensborough CC
0	0	0	6,823	6,823 [1]	260	70	D.S. Lancaster CC
157	2,918	600	5,021	5,415	535	584	Darton C
30	300	0	0	1,321	116	72	Dawson CC
201	3,342	17,928	41,416	41,416 [1]	5,038	207	Del Mar C
287	5,083	8,336	-1	13,702	454	100	Delaware Co CC
136	3,803	11,298	12,053	15,506	268	185	Diablo Valley C
20	500	2,600	948	1,075	129	210	Dodge City CC
150	2,979	7,018	6,781	7,660	8	74	Dyersburg ST CC
27	483	0	13,699	15,567	1,858	978	East Central C
110	1,760	1,100	1,228	1,468	306	246	East Georgia C
140	5,600	5,000	32,712	32,712	124	269	East Los Angeles C
1,071	28,469	198,603	70,610	89,955	914	240	El Paso CC

1 -- See Footnotes   -1 -- Unavailable   -2 -- Not Applicable

47

ACRL Library Data Tables 2005

PERSONNEL AND PUBLIC SERVICES

INSTITUTIONS GRANTING ASSOCIATE OF ARTS DEGREES (Carnegie Code A)

Survey Question #	Total Staff (FTE) 26	Professional Staff (FTE) 26a	Support Staff (FTE) 26b	Student Assistants (FTE) 26c	No. of Staffed Service Points 27	Weekly Public Service Hours 28
Lib. No. Institution						
81 Estrn Arizona C	14	1	6	7	3	80
82 Estrn Idaho Tech C	3	1	1	1	1	70
83 Estrn Maine Tech C	4	2	1	1	1	66
84 Fayetteville Tech CC	10	3	6	1	2	64
85 Fergus Falls CC	4	1	1	2	1	70
86 Flor Dar Tech C	8	3	2	3	5	65
87 Floyd C	13	7	3 [1]	3	2 [1]	63
88 Gadsden ST CC	14	8	5	1	4	60
89 Gainesville C	13	5	5	3	2	72
90 Gavilan C	7	2	4	1	2	46
91 GC Wallace CC	8	2	1	5	4	60
92 Glendale CC	32	12 [1]	14 [1]	6 [1]	3	82
93 Gogebic CC	4	2	1	1	3	48
94 Gordon C-GA	8	5	2	1	2	75
95 Grand Rapids CC	19	7 [1]	7 [1]	5	3	75
96 Harrisburg Area CC	43	19	13	11	7	71
97 Hawaii Pacific U	40	15	14	11	4	77
98 Hawkeye CC	6	2	3	1	2	70
99 Highland CC KS	4	1	2	1	1	73
100 Hillsborough CC	42	12	23	7	8	60
101 Hinds CC	27	10	15	2	8	52
102 Hiwassee C	5	2	2	1	1	59
103 Hocking Tech C	8	3	2	3	3	60
104 Hopkinsville CC	5	2	2	1	2	59
105 Horry GTown Tech	12	6	5	1	4	63
106 Howard C	10	2	4	4	3	66
107 Hutch CC&Voc Sch	7	3	3	2	1	68
108 IL E CC Wabash Cntrl C	4	1	2	2	1	61
109 IL Estrn CC-Frontier	4	1	2	1	4	59
110 IL Estrn CC-Lincoln Trail	4	1	2	1	1	57
111 IL Valley CC	8	4	3	1	1	63
112 Independence CC	3	2	1	0	1	59
113 Inst Com PR Jr C Arecibo	7	1	1	5	0	64
114 Inst Native Culture	9	4	1	4	1	72
115 Isothermal CC	7	2	4	2	1	62
116 J.F. Drake ST Tech C	2	1	0	1	1	42
117 Jacksonville C	6	1	2	3	1	63
118 Jefferson CC-NY	11	4	4	3	4	61
119 Jefferson C-MO	9	3	5	1	6	68
120 JS Reynolds CC	16	8	8	0	6	59

1 -- See Footnotes   -1 -- Unavailable   -2 -- Not Applicable

ACRL Library Data Tables 2005
PERSONNEL AND PUBLIC SERVICES

INSTITUTIONS GRANTING ASSOCIATE OF ARTS DEGREES (Carnegie Code A)

No. of Presentations to Groups 29	Participants in Group Presentations 30	No. of Reference Transactions 31	No. of Initial Circulations 32	Total Circulations 33	ILL Materials Provided 34	ILL Materials Received 35	Survey Question # Institution
52	1,095	2,480	80,936	86,720	0	0	Estrn Arizona C
9	120	150	1,089	1,549	39	48	Estrn Idaho Tech C
40	538	3,071	2,456	2,777	475	596	Estrn Maine Tech C
138	2,264	5,967	31,082	32,408	551	352	Fayetteville Tech CC
68	1,670	0	2,783	2,924	95	92	Fergus Falls CC
94	1,628	0	5,375	0	141	111	Flor Dar Tech C
203	3,943	1,539	0 [1]	7,762 [1]	89	274	Floyd C
93	2,105	3,326	11,876	15,835	81	72	Gadsden ST CC
131	2,534	5,596	12,519	13,453	414	231	Gainesville C
114	1,911	8,324	0	7,089	86	90	Gavilan C
10	150	500	6,000	6,200	0	0	GC Wallace CC
116	2,088	15,272	0 [1]	42,255	0 [1]	243 [1]	Glendale CC
26	588	309	0	2,177	13	62	Gogebic CC
146	3,783	250	13,703	13,703	275	306	Gordon C-GA
384	7,038	14,787	16,489	23,355	647	470	Grand Rapids CC
491	6,679	41,377	47,049	54,412	1,980	720	Harrisburg Area CC
179	3,145	22,958	11,400	26,288	0	192	Hawaii Pacific U
182	3,640	1,640	15,510	17,729	1,283	926	Hawkeye CC
35	875	960	4,680	4,850	203	116	Highland CC KS
271	5,481	14,761	38,097	41,090	268	331	Hillsborough CC
428	10,700	160,802	0	70,941	123	873	Hinds CC
16	214	0 [1]	0	6,817	0	0	Hiwassee C
145	3	0	0	6,196	812	1,646	Hocking Tech C
41	615	-1	4,368	5,489	191	449	Hopkinsville CC
131	1,927	3,438	8,689	9,951	266	229	Horry GTown Tech
74	1,254	1,753	2,667	3,741	0	164	Howard C
110	1,866	1,519	8,600	9,059	407	231	Hutch CC&Voc Sch
34	686	259	9,862 [1]	9,896	831	286	IL E CC Wabash Cntrl C
20	315	5,100	6,662	10,776	4,095	1,398	IL Estrn CC-Frontier
38	400	333	2,840	3,070	1,292	1,067	IL Estrn CC-Lincoln Trail
88	1,772	50	7,787	9,032	1,567	929	IL Valley CC
57	792	775	5,580	6,124	267	277	Independence CC
10	259	1,114	2,949	3,001	0	0	Inst Com PR Jr C Arecibo
60	100	2,500	3,500	6,500	30	0	Inst Native Culture
66	1,627	7,200	9,250	10,112	114	179	Isothermal CC
27	296	140	1,214	0	0	0	J.F. Drake ST Tech C
4	250	819	992	1,811	0	0	Jacksonville C
230	6,660	6,629	7,138	8,208	1,521	1,657	Jefferson CC-NY
82	1,653	2,600	8,832	10,710	989	933	Jefferson C-MO
125	2,834	35,747	12,224	17,364	203	93	JS Reynolds CC

1 -- See Footnotes   -1 -- Unavailable   -2 -- Not Applicable

ACRL Library Data Tables 2005

PERSONNEL AND PUBLIC SERVICES

INSTITUTIONS GRANTING ASSOCIATE OF ARTS DEGREES (Carnegie Code A)

	Survey Question #	Total Staff (FTE) 26	Professional Staff (FTE) 26a	Support Staff (FTE) 26b	Student Assistants (FTE) 26c	No. of Staffed Service Points 27	Weekly Public Service Hours 28
Lib. No.	**Institution**						
121	Justice Inst BC	6	3	3	0	1	52
122	Kaskaskia C	3	2	2	0	1	62
123	Kent St U E Liverpool	3	1	1	1	1	58
124	Kent St U Tuscarawas	6	1	2	3	2	70
125	Kilgore C	11	4	4	3	1	62
126	Kirkwood CC	14	6	7	1	2	78
127	Kirtland CC	4	2	1	1	2	56
128	Labette CC	5	1	3	1	1	59
129	Laboure C	6	1	1	4	1	85
130	Lake City CC	7	2	4	1	5	67
131	Lakeland CC-OH	13	4	7	2	2	78
132	Lane CC-OR	14	5	9	1	2	66
133	Lansdale Sch of Bus	1	1 [1]	0	0	1	25 [1]
134	Laramie Co CC	12	4	7	1	2	74
135	Lassen CC	4	1	2	1	1	56
136	Lexington CC	17	8	5	4	3 [1]	66
137	Linn ST Tech C	9	1	2	6	9	703
138	Lord Fairfax CC	12	1	9	2	3	132
139	Los Angeles Valley C	15	6	7	2	3	65
140	Luzerne County CC	11	4	7	0	3	68
141	Manatee CC	20	7	8	5	3	70
142	Maple Woods CC	8	3	5	0	2	57
143	Marymount C CA	5	3	1	2	2	72
144	Massasoit CC	11	7	3	1	3	69
145	McDowell Tech CC	3	2	1 [1]	0	1	60
146	Mesa CC	29	10	19	0	9	103
147	Middlesex Co C-NJ	53	9	16	28	4	77
148	Midland C	10	4	5	1	4	70
149	Miles CC	4	1	2	1	1	64
150	MiraCosta C	18	6	7	5	7	68
151	Monroe CC	26	14	9	3	4	67
152	Mountain Empire CC	5	1	4	1	1	63
153	MS County CC	6	1	4	1	2	82
154	MS Delta CC	27	5	4	18	3	120
155	Mt Hood CC	16	5 [1]	9 [1]	3 [1]	1	68 [1]
156	N Alberta Inst	29	7	21	1	5	80
157	National Hispanic U	3	1	2	1	1	48
158	ND ST C Science	10	3	4	4	2	72
159	NE WI Tech C	7	2	5 [1]	0	5	75
160	NH CC-Berlin	3	1	1	1	1	71

1 -- See Footnotes   -1 -- Unavailable   -2 -- Not Applicable

ACRL Library Data Tables 2005
PERSONNEL AND PUBLIC SERVICES

INSTITUTIONS GRANTING ASSOCIATE OF ARTS DEGREES (Carnegie Code A)

No. of Presentations to Groups 29	Participants in Group Presentations 30	No. of Reference Transactions 31	No. of Initial Circulations 32	Total Circulations 33	ILL Materials Provided 34	ILL Materials Received 35	Survey Question # Institution
27	353	4,517	-1	8,729	965	193	Justice Inst BC
0	505	500	4,300	4,903	1,267	1,768	Kaskaskia C
52	1,032	13,500	3,945	6,259	1,294	873	Kent St U E Liverpool
45	1,050	8,502	6,375	12,180	125	300	Kent St U Tuscarawas
85	2,072	936	8,513	8,904	43	49	Kilgore C
128	2,396	8,704	14,104	0	576	580	Kirkwood CC
28	560	320	5,700	5,757	240	83	Kirtland CC
45	710	380	2,848	3,153	140	271	Labette CC
10	150	3,000	115	115	6	120	Laboure C
42	669	2,595	5,322	6,304	58	29	Lake City CC
302	4,270	220 [1]	0	14,276	268	330	Lakeland CC-OH
135	2,700	-1	31,105	40	342	312	Lane CC-OR
15	250	110	167	219	0	0	Lansdale Sch of Bus
137	2,342	3,640	17,445 [1]	0 [1]	735	859	Laramie Co CC
139	456	5,000	5,478	6,345	25	1,720	Lassen CC
149	3,150	3,668 [1]	22,338 [1]	30,159	775 [1]	146 [1]	Lexington CC
147	1,373	3,059	2,592	3,014	585	222	Linn ST Tech C
96	1,625	6,776	0	45,327	608	403	Lord Fairfax CC
101	1,781	45,804	18,033	21,835	205	186	Los Angeles Valley C
119	2,154	1,631	3,681	4,293	263	79	Luzerne County CC
170	4,930	12,370	29,085	30,818	628	584	Manatee CC
188	3,138	3,220	5,954	7,167	1,349	922	Maple Woods CC
150	1,441	1,243	5,564	5,732	0	77	Marymount C CA
239	3,585	1,039	4,569	4,659	3,263	1,082	Massasoit CC
84	519	5,000	7,104 [1]	7,104	183	64	McDowell Tech CC
431	7,991	21,464	21,655	25,536	649	179	Mesa CC
250	5,000	9,600	11,000	0	785	962	Middlesex Co C-NJ
179	3,597 [1]	23,000	9,852	0	0	18	Midland C
28	651	5,814	1,311	0 [1]	8	57	Miles CC
173	4,168	0 [1]	16,926	20,081	198	72	MiraCosta C
243	5,382	20,478	27,899	51,011	1,551	935	Monroe CC
30	600	5,000	9,050	11,250	47	55	Mountain Empire CC
30	500	0	4,406	4,406	112	140	MS County CC
30	623	150	600	600	0	58	MS Delta CC
138	2,914	2,880 [1]	32,371	62,234	586	1,008	Mt Hood CC
375	7,977	17,660	1	33,268 [1]	325	888	N Alberta Inst
15	12	650	1,000	1,100	0	3	National Hispanic U
28	581	1,782	0 [1]	16,005	1,453	19	ND ST C Science
93	1,292	2,723	16,415 [1]	16,415	772	171	NE WI Tech C
68	1,025	2,511	5,028	6,443	493	1,184	NH CC-Berlin

1 -- See Footnotes   -1 -- Unavailable   -2 -- Not Applicable

ACRL Library Data Tables 2005
PERSONNEL AND PUBLIC SERVICES
INSTITUTIONS GRANTING ASSOCIATE OF ARTS DEGREES (Carnegie Code A)

		Total Staff (FTE) 26	Professional Staff (FTE) 26a	Support Staff (FTE) 26b	Student Assistants (FTE) 26c	No. of Staffed Service Points 27	Weekly Public Service Hours 28
Lib. No.	**Institution**	**Survey Question #**					
161	NH CC-Laconia	3	1	1	1	1	61
162	Nicolet Area Tech C	11	5	5	1	2	64
163	NM St U-Carlsbad	7	1	3	3	4	50
164	Normandale CC	13	4	7	2	2	72
165	North AR C	8	1 [1]	5	2 [1]	2	73 [1]
166	Northeast ST Tech CC	12	6	6	0	3	69
167	Northeastern JC	5	1	4	1	3	70
168	Northwest C	6	2	2	2	1	79
169	Nwestern Business C	5	3	1	1	3	62
170	Nwestern CT Tech CC	6	2	3	1	1	62
171	OH ST U Ag Tech Inst	7	2	2	3	4	65
172	Ohlone C	10	4	5	1	4	62
173	Okaloosa-Walton CC	19	5	14	0	2	68
174	Orange County CC	16	6	9	1	2	71
175	Owensboro	9	2	6	1	3	62
176	Owensboro Jr C Bus	2	1	0	1	1	68
177	Oxnard C	5	3	2	1	2	61
178	Passaic County CC	17	6	2	9	3	76
179	Paul D. Camp CC	6	2	3	1	2	52
180	Pellissippi ST Tech CC	13	8 [1]	4	1	5	54
181	Pensacola Jr C	30	11	16	3	8	65
182	Petit Jean C	2	1	1	0	3	36
183	Piedmont Tech C	5	2	2	1	3	64
184	Pittsburgh Tech Inst	6	3	-2	5	1	53
185	Portland CC	35	9	26	0	13	205
186	Potomac St C-WVU	6	2	3	1	3	67
187	Prairie ST C	12	4	8	1	3	70
188	Prince George CC	24	10	14	0	3	79
189	Pueblo CC	7	2	4	2	3	83
190	Pulaski Tech C	5	2	3	0	3	57
191	Quinebaug Vally Comm TC	7	4	0	3	2	55
192	Quinsigamond CC	9	5	4	0	2	66 [1]
193	Reading Area CC	11	3	6	2	2	77
194	Red Deer C	21	5 [1]	16 [1]	0	3 [1]	86 [1]
195	Redlands CC	4	1	2	1	1	61
196	Rend Lake C	10	4	3	3	2	69
197	Renton Tech C	7	3	4	1	1	65
198	Robeson CC	6	2	4	0	15	63
199	Rogue CC	13	5	6	2	4	60
200	Sacramento City C	33	10	18	5	5	72

1 -- See Footnotes   -1 -- Unavailable   -2 -- Not Applicable

ACRL Library Data Tables 2005
PERSONNEL AND PUBLIC SERVICES

INSTITUTIONS GRANTING ASSOCIATE OF ARTS DEGREES (Carnegie Code A)

No. of Presentations to Groups 29	Participants in Group Presentations 30	No. of Reference Transactions 31	No. of Initial Circulations 32	Total Circulations 33	ILL Materials Provided 34	ILL Materials Received 35	Survey Question # Institution
39	853	400	1,000	1,061	230	34	NH CC-Laconia
53	795	200	36,056 [1]	36,056 [1]	3,060	456	Nicolet Area Tech C
14	353	396	1,851	2,120	42	148	NM St U-Carlsbad
143	3,135	5,009	28,702	0	1,620	1,557	Normandale CC
56 [1]	872	1,217	10,639	11,371	67	156	North AR C
130	3,250	2,799	28,302	28,302	446	191	Northeast ST Tech CC
17	292	3,171	14,774	14,774 [1]	422	174	Northeastern JC
91	1,818	11,940	9,330	10,014	593	554	Northwest C
89	1,380	2,402	4,004	4,004	116	82	Nwestern Business C
42	848	0	5,742	6,326	254	169	Nwestern CT Tech CC
68	1,225	13,676	1,823	10,424	40	2,624	OH ST U Ag Tech Inst
73	1,460	5,000	5,896	0	19	12	Ohlone C
162	3,179	19,001	18,539	20,007	551	370	Okaloosa-Walton CC
141	3,525	6,010	11,555	11,555	94	358	Orange County CC
98	2,019	7,126	6,144	6,653	434	143	Owensboro
14	145	400	400	415	0	0	Owensboro Jr C Bus
110	2,841	2,315	5,526	2,190	34	21	Oxnard C
90	1,350	12,000	7,757	7,757	1,100	0 [1]	Passaic County CC
34	465	633	1,169	1,273	0	81	Paul D. Camp CC
174	3,898	35,389	0 [1]	29,804	248	2	Pellissippi ST Tech CC
204	2,915	19,908	0	22,573	873	1,101	Pensacola Jr C
1,100	30	450 [1]	1,275	1,253	0	0	Petit Jean C
11	208	3,471	7,792	11,222	13	28	Piedmont Tech C
95	2,336	-1	6,172	7,213	33	12	Pittsburgh Tech Inst
364	6,763	484	67,093	76,628	2,007	800	Portland CC
18	317	589	0	4,530	154	101	Potomac St C-WVU
169	4,275	857	7,129	7,740	3,869	534	Prairie ST C
203	3,346	15,000	10,104	10,104	44	113	Prince George CC
60	1,388	534	26,097	28,730	133	99	Pueblo CC
167	3,490	7,375	3,179	3,307	54	74	Pulaski Tech C
88	1,769	6,000	2,900	3,053	92	158	Quinebaug Vally Comm TC
188	3,769	6,223	0 [1]	8,385	920	168	Quinsigamond CC
271	4,939	40,000	0	285,720	12,294	2,872	Reading Area CC
186 [1]	3,429 [1]	6,812 [1]	0	0	6,470 [1]	4,372 [1]	Red Deer C
25	423	3,408	1,413	1,708	24	19	Redlands CC
107	1,260	1,138	3,304	5,851	1,452	537	Rend Lake C
307	5,560	4,820	8,626	11,560	116	55	Renton Tech C
28	418	890	5,590	400	85	76	Robeson CC
137	2,436	8,926	0	17,431	13,558	8,685	Rogue CC
242	5,163	36,237	87,275	91,488	1,708	766	Sacramento City C

1 -- See Footnotes   -1 -- Unavailable   -2 -- Not Applicable

ACRL Library Data Tables 2005

PERSONNEL AND PUBLIC SERVICES

INSTITUTIONS GRANTING ASSOCIATE OF ARTS DEGREES (Carnegie Code A)

		Total Staff (FTE)	Professional Staff (FTE)	Support Staff (FTE)	Student Assistants (FTE)	No. of Staffed Service Points	Weekly Public Service Hours
	Survey Question #	26	26a	26b	26c	27	28
Lib. No.	Institution						
201	San Antonio C	95	19	32	44	6	82
202	San Jacinto C South	10	3	3	4	4	62
203	San Joaquin Delta C	20	6	11	4	2	68
204	Santa Fe CC-NM	21	7	4	10	3	84
205	Santa Monica C	17	7	6	4	2	68
206	Selkirk C	9	3	6	0	3	62
207	Seward County CC	4	1	3	0	1	80
208	South AR CC	4	1	3	0	1	62
209	South Florida CC	8	2	5	2	2	69
210	South Puget Sound CC	9	4	3	2	3	67
211	Southeast CC	12	5	5	3 [1]	5	55
212	Southwest VA CC	7	3	3	1	2	66
213	Spartanburg Tech C	8	3	4	1	2 [1]	64
214	Spoon River C	7	1	4	2	3	52
215	St Charles County CC	12	6	6	0	2	62
216	Sthrn U-Shreveport/Bossier	14	3	7	4	1	65
217	Tacoma CC	15	7	8	0	4	67
218	Tallahassee CC	23	7	11	5	3	68
219	Tech C Lowcountry	5	2	2	1	2	61
220	Temple C	6	4	1	1	1	64
221	Tri County Tech C	8	3	3	2	2	67
222	Trocaire C	4	3	0	1	4	60
223	Tunxis CC Tech	11	8	1	2	3	67
224	TX ST Tech C Waco	15	5	5	5	4	67
225	U Akron Wayne C	5	1	3	2	2	73
226	U HI-Kapiolani CC	39	8	11	20	4	54
227	U HI-Kauai CC	7	4	3	0	2	56
228	U HI-Windward CC	9	3	3	3	2	52
229	U NM Gallup Branch	9	1	5	3 [1]	1	66
230	VA Western CC	8	3	4	1	2	70
231	W.Rainey Harper C	33	8	22	3	3	78
232	Walsh U	10	3	3	4	2	80
233	Walters ST CC	8	5	4	0	3	62
234	Waycross C	7	2	3	2	2	66
235	Weatherford C	14	4	7	3	4	70
236	Western IA Tech CC	4	2	2	1	1	66
237	Wharton Co Jr C	10	3	5	2	3	63
238	Whatcom CC	10	3	6	1	3 [1]	65
239	Wytheville CC	4	2	1	1	1	57
240	Yakima Valley CC	11	3	7	1	1	69

1 -- See Footnotes   -1 -- Unavailable   -2 -- Not Applicable

ACRL Library Data Tables 2005
PERSONNEL AND PUBLIC SERVICES

INSTITUTIONS GRANTING ASSOCIATE OF ARTS DEGREES (Carnegie Code A)

No. of Presentations to Groups 29	Participants in Group Presentations 30	No. of Reference Transactions 31	No. of Initial Circulations 32	Total Circulations 33	ILL Materials Provided 34	ILL Materials Received 35	Survey Question # Institution
318	13,489	13,489	42,728	44,608	3,772	1,457	San Antonio C
117	1,955	-1 [1]	9,447	10,287	226	36	San Jacinto C South
84	1,456	23,246	60,531	18,066	264	84	San Joaquin Delta C
210	4,332	14,913	32,944	36,016	756	228	Santa Fe CC-NM
316	11,060	58,500	35,944	39,342	0	0	Santa Monica C
131 [1]	1,500 [1]	7,500 [1]	0	22,400	609	536	Selkirk C
42	1,109	75	2,053	2,053	199	91	Seward County CC
128	2,560 [1]	8,430 [1]	2,911	3,722	0	91	South AR CC
54	893	3,045	19,011	20,223	112	492	South Florida CC
212	5,300	6,136	117,429 [1]	117,429	15	11	South Puget Sound CC
62	1,577	346	8,484	10	566	751	Southeast CC
57	1,425	5,243	20,421	29,253	258	150	Southwest VA CC
242	4,554	397 [1]	11,506	12,532	156	113	Spartanburg Tech C
37	19	20,919	2,262	2,388	222	158	Spoon River C
182	3,017	7,600	26,194	29,094	358	164	St Charles County CC
41	764	471	1,352	1,824	0	0	Sthrn U-Shreveport/Bossier
252	6,300	6,404	0	9,431	139	81	Tacoma CC
367	10,925	12,802	42,062	48,146	774	323	Tallahassee CC
47	705	3,056	0 [1]	2,637	0	53	Tech C Lowcountry
65	1,367	1,935	6,340	0	1	40	Temple C
169	2,719	4,167	7,131	0	157	122	Tri County Tech C
43	713	2,456	3,904	4,292	0	57	Trocaire C
99	2,772	9,454	0	21,225	597	423	Tunxis CC Tech
31	257	7,848	8,511	8,986	5	17	TX ST Tech C Waco
128	1,298	4,230	6,461	7,477	2,856	1,575	U Akron Wayne C
165	2,326	5,964	19,531	22,393	829	397	U HI-Kapiolani CC
54	856	4,767	0	2,861	0	0	U HI-Kauai CC
58	1,287	5,702	0 [1]	5,948	333	68	U HI-Windward CC
54	1,296	2,150	7,186	7,186	48	0	U NM Gallup Branch
137	2,710	14,725	4,989	5,726	231	292	VA Western CC
324	5,612	22,053	43,317	52,327	4,713	1,677	W.Rainey Harper C
66	1,126	3,000	9,622	12,172	3,922	1,734	Walsh U
176	4,400	0	18,900	18,900	29	43	Walters ST CC
14	399	373	2,505	2,742	149	209	Waycross C
141	2,961	722	5,305	8,200	15	78	Weatherford C
30 [1]	690	6,500	6,554	7,417	145	236	Western IA Tech CC
90	2,457	5,774	3,659	4,150	121	38	Wharton Co Jr C
176	1,885	2,974	12,820	14,422	253	115	Whatcom CC
44	988	3,120	0	6,710	249	117	Wytheville CC
93	2,020	12,126	17,163	17,318	144	48	Yakima Valley CC

1 -- See Footnotes   -1 -- Unavailable   -2 -- Not Applicable

ACRL Library Data Tables 2005
PERSONNEL AND PUBLIC SERVICES
INSTITUTIONS GRANTING ASSOCIATE OF ARTS DEGREES (Carnegie Code A)

Lib. No.	Survey Question # Institution	Total Staff (FTE) 26	Professional Staff (FTE) 26a	Support Staff (FTE) 26b	Student Assistants (FTE) 26c	No. of Staffed Service Points 27	Weekly Public Service Hours 28
241	Yavapai C	18	3	10	5	2	73

1 -- See Footnotes   -1 -- Unavailable   -2 -- Not Applicable

ACRL Library Data Tables 2005
PERSONNEL AND PUBLIC SERVICES

INSTITUTIONS GRANTING ASSOCIATE OF ARTS DEGREES (Carnegie Code A)

No. of Presentations to Groups 29	Participants in Group Presentations 30	No. of Reference Transactions 31	No. of Initial Circulations 32	Total Circulations 33	ILL Materials Provided 34	ILL Materials Received 35	Survey Question #
							Institution
129	2,288	26,243	0 [1]	106,894	20,557	1,235	Yavapai C

1 -- See Footnotes   -1 -- Unavailable   -2 -- Not Applicable

Errata

The page for Summary Data for Ph.D., Faculty, and Enrollment Statistics (page 58) was mistakenly printed with Summary Data for Electronic Expenditures. The correct information appears below.

ACRL LIBRARY DATA TABLES 2005

SUMMARY DATA: PH.D., FACULTY, AND ENROLLMENT STATISTICS

INSTITUTIONS GRANTING ASSOCIATE OF ARTS DEGREES (Carnegie Code A)

| | Ph.D.s Awarded | Ph.D. Fields | Faculty | ENROLLMENT | | | |
				Total FTE Full-time*	Total Part-time*	Grad FTE Full-time	Graduate Part-time
(Survey Question #)	46	47	48	49	50	51	52
High			2,400	20,461	37,445		
Mean			129	2,930	3,522		
Median			83	2,048	2,208		
Low			0	0	0		
Total			28,844	662,183	707,908		
Libraries Reporting			224	226	201		

PH.D., FACULTY, AND ENROLLMENT STATISTICS

INSTITUTIONS GRANTING ASSOCIATE OF ARTS DEGREES (Carnegie Code A)

		Ph.D.'s Awarded	Ph.D. Fields	Full-Time Faculty	ENROLLMENT			
					Full-time, Undergrad. & Grad.	Part-time, Undergrad. & Grad.	Full-time, Grad.	Part-time, Grad.
	Survey Question #	36	37	38	39	40	41	42
Lib. No.	Institution							
1	A Baldwin Agrl C	0	0	98	2,099	1,263	0	0
2	Adirondack CC	0	0	100	2,240	960	0	0
3	Alpena CC	-2 [1]	-2 [1]	47 [1]	937	916	-2	-2
4	Alvin CC	0	0	105	1,611	2,321	0	0
5	Am River C	0	0	357	8,280	21,775	0	0
6	Am Samoa CC	0	0	60	800	400	0	0
7	Andover C	0	0	13	500	10	0	0
8	Anne Arundel CC	0	0	240	8,492	0	0	0
9	Anoka-Ramsey CC	-2	-2	85	3,361	-1	-2	-2
10	AR ST U Beebe	0	0	0	1,983	1,655	0	0
11	Athens Tech C	0	0	78	1,146 [1]	1,669 [1]	0	0
12	AZ Western C	0	0	95	1,830	4,620	0	0
13	Bellingham Tech C	0	0	48	906 [1]	1,667 [1]	0	0
14	Belmont Tech C	0	0	39	0	0	0	0
15	Bergen CC	0	0	299	7,258	7,067	0	0
16	Black Hawk C	0	0	151	2,734	2,227	0	0
17	Blackhawk Tech C	0	0	100	1,043	1,558	0	0
18	Blue Mountain CC	0	0	0	493 [1]	0	0	0
19	Blue Ridge CC	0	0	47	1,445	2,497	0	0
20	Brazosport C	0	0	87	890	2,558	0	0
21	Bunker Hill CC	0	0	118	2,581	5,240	0	0
22	Butler County CC	0	0	140	3,506	3,087 [1]	0	0
23	C Canyons	0	0	161	4,666	9,287	0	0
24	C Edouard Montpetit	0	0	375	6,300	2,600	0	0
25	C Lake Co	0	1	5	8,184 [1]	15,745 [1]	0	0
26	C Merici	0	0	0	1,100	0	0	0
27	C New Caledonia	0	0	240	2,959	0	0	0
28	C Redwoods	0	0	0	2,555	0	0	0
29	C St Jean Richelieu	0	0	2,400	0	0	0	0
30	Camden County C	0	0	140	7,384	7,732	0	0
31	Cape Fear CC	0	0	190	0	0	0	0
32	Capital CC	0	0	52	896	2,540	0	0
33	Carl Sandburg C	0	0	74	1,205	3,586	0	0
34	Carroll Tech Inst	0	0	76	1,809	2,951	0	0
35	Carteret CC	-2	-2	55 [1]	722	1,021	-2	-2
36	Cedar Valley	0	0	64	1,447	2,845	0	0
37	CEGEP Beauce-Appala	-2	-2	-2	-2	-2	-2	-2
38	CEGEP Trois-Rivieres	0	0	0	4,154	0	0	0
39	Central Alabama CC	0	0	0	1,134	818	0	0
40	Central Carolina Tech C	0	0	76	3,238 [1]	0	0	0

1 -- See Footnotes   -1 -- Unavailable   -2 -- Not Applicable

ACRL Library Data Tables 2005
PH.D., FACULTY, AND ENROLLMENT STATISTICS
INSTITUTIONS GRANTING ASSOCIATE OF ARTS DEGREES (Carnegie Code A)

| | | Ph.D.'s Awarded | Ph.D. Fields | Full-Time Faculty | ENROLLMENT | | | |
					Full-time, Undergrad. & Grad.	Part-time, Undergrad. & Grad.	Full-time, Grad.	Part-time, Grad.
	Survey Question #	36	37	38	39	40	41	42
Lib. No.	Institution							
41	Central ME Tech C	0	0	50	838	1,118	0	0
42	Central Piedmont CC	0	0	0	0 [1]	0	0 [1]	0 [1]
43	Central TX C	0 [1]	0 [1]	300	0 [1]	0 [1]	0 [1]	0 [1]
44	Centralia C	0	0	59	0	0	0	0
45	Chabot C	0	2	188	14,477	0	0	0
46	Chattahoochee Tech	0	0	60	2,076	4,004	0	0
47	Chippewa V Tech C	0	0	215	2,330	3,294	0	0
48	Clackamas CC	0	0	163	1,618	13,377	0	0
49	Clark C-WA	0	0	160	4,944	7,025	0	0
50	Clinton CC	0	0	54	1,356	862	0	0
51	Cloud Co CC	0	0	38	903	1,958	0	0
52	Coastal GA CC	0	0	63	970	1,909	0	0
53	Colby CC	0	0	69	1,000	1,000	0	0
54	Columbia Junior C	-2	-2	81	1,143	310	248	895
55	Columbia ST CC	0	0	104	2,352	2,395	0	0
56	Columbus ST CC	-2	-2	-1	12,885	-2	-2	-2
57	Compton CC	0	0	100	2,797	3,501	0	0
58	Connors ST C	0	0	51	1,379	1,008	0	0
59	Corning CC	0	0	100	4,987	0	0	0
60	Cosumnes River C	0	0	164 [1]	4,266 [1]	7,170 [1]	0	0
61	Crowder C	0	0	64	1,319	1,296	0	0
62	Cuesta C	0	0	154	4,648	6,123	0	0
63	Cumberland Co C	0	0	44	1,639	1,537	0	0
64	CUNY Borough Manhat	0	0	379	10,979	7,875	0	0
65	CUNY Bronx CC	0	0	221	4,561	2,548	0	0
66	CUNY Hostos CC	0	0	155	3,327	1,013	0	0
67	CUNY LaGuardia CC	0	0	286	7,619	5,973	0	0
68	CUNY Queensborough C	0	0	258	6,171	6,322	0	0
69	D.S. Lancaster CC	0	0	21	368	1,191	0	0
70	Darton C	0	0	84	3,088	2,541	0	0
71	Dawson CC	0	0	27	391	133	0	0
72	Del Mar C	0	0	308	3,732	7,613	0	0
73	Delaware Co CC	0	0	150	6,197	4,430	0	0
74	Diablo Valley C	0	0	241	6,972	14,003	0	0
75	Dodge City CC	0	0	51	1,192 [1]	0 [1]	0	0
76	Dyersburg ST CC	-2	-2	57	1,549	966	-2	-2
77	East Central C	0	0	56	1,525	2,208	0	0
78	East Georgia C	0	0	35	890	428	0	0
79	East Los Angeles C	0	0	560	7,005	16,018	0	0
80	El Paso CC	0	0	13	10,789	15,289	0	0

1 -- See Footnotes   -1 -- Unavailable   -2 -- Not Applicable

ACRL Library Data Tables 2005
PH.D., FACULTY, AND ENROLLMENT STATISTICS
INSTITUTIONS GRANTING ASSOCIATE OF ARTS DEGREES (Carnegie Code A)

		Ph.D.'s Awarded	Ph.D. Fields	Full-Time Faculty	Full-time, Undergrad. & Grad.	Part-time, Undergrad. & Grad.	Full-time, Grad.	Part-time, Grad.
	Survey Question #	36	37	38	39	40	41	42
Lib. No.	Institution							
81	Estrn Arizona C	0	0	69	1,464	2,268	0	0
82	Estrn Idaho Tech C	0	0	35	414	374	0	0
83	Estrn Maine Tech C	0	0	56	973	1,078	0 [1]	0 [1]
84	Fayetteville Tech CC	0	0	300	4,290	5,680	0	0
85	Fergus Falls CC	0	0	40	725	230	0	0
86	Flor Dar Tech C	0	0	0	2,224	0	0	0
87	Floyd C	0	0	98	0 [1]	0 [1]	0	0
88	Gadsden ST CC	0	0	141	3,016	2,533	0	0
89	Gainesville C	0	0	101	4,244	975	0	0
90	Gavilan C	0	0	70	2,057	0	0	0
91	GC Wallace CC	0	0	62	1,070	770	0	0
92	Glendale CC	0	0	260 [1]	6,195 [1]	14,454 [1]	0	0
93	Gogebic CC	0	0	30	517	442	0	0
94	Gordon C-GA	0	0	96	2,297	1,152	0	0
95	Grand Rapids CC	0	0	224	6,374	7,832	0	0
96	Harrisburg Area CC	0	0	260	6,413	9,696	0	0
97	Hawaii Pacific U	0	0	351	6,122	0	934	5,188
98	Hawkeye CC	0 [1]	0 [1]	114	2,751	2,521	0 [1]	0 [1]
99	Highland CC KS	0	0	35	951	2,038	0	0
100	Hillsborough CC	0 [1]	0 [1]	243	7,670	37,445	0 [1]	0 [1]
101	Hinds CC	0	0	382	7,667	2,557	0	0
102	Hiwassee C	0	0	24	279	76	0	0
103	Hocking Tech C	0	0	0	1,289 [1]	3,556 [1]	0	0
104	Hopkinsville CC	0	0	60	1,415	1,689	0	0
105	Horry GTown Tech	0	0	0	2,482	2,547	0	0
106	Howard C	0	0	127	986	1,742	0	0
107	Hutch CC&Voc Sch	0	0	110	2,100	3,327	0	0
108	IL E CC Wabash Cntrl C	-2	-2	34	411	1,085	-2	-2
109	IL Estrn CC-Frontier	0	0	0	229	1,731	0	0
110	IL Estrn CC-Lincoln Trail	0	0	25	411	1,085	0	0
111	IL Valley CC	0	0	78	1,809	2,269	0	0
112	Independence CC	0	0	31	0	0	0	0
113	Inst Com PR Jr C Arecib	0	0	28	352	113	0	0
114	Inst Native Culture	0	0	18	175	20	0	0
115	Isothermal CC	0	0	66	865	120	0	0
116	J.F. Drake ST Tech C	0	0	23	486	296	0	0
117	Jacksonville C	0	0	10	223	77	0	0
118	Jefferson CC-NY	0 [1]	0	77	2,498	1,477	0	0
119	Jefferson C-MO	0	0	89	2,277	1,859	0	0
120	JS Reynolds CC	0	0	0	2,531	4,016	0	0

1 -- See Footnotes   -1 -- Unavailable   -2 -- Not Applicable

Lib. No.	Institution	Ph.D.'s Awarded	Ph.D. Fields	Full-Time Faculty	ENROLLMENT Full-time, Undergrad. & Grad.	Part-time, Undergrad. & Grad.	Full-time, Grad.	Part-time, Grad.
Survey Question #		36	37	38	39	40	41	42
121	Justice Inst BC	-2	-2	115	1,939	-1	-1	-1
122	Kaskaskia C	-1	-1	-1	-1	-1	0	0
123	Kent St U E Liverpool	0	0	20	439	329	1	0
124	Kent St U Tuscarawas	0	0	0	1,094	841	7	5
125	Kilgore C	0	0	115	3,385	1,572	0	0
126	Kirkwood CC	0	0	260	6,701	8,661	0	0
127	Kirtland CC	0	0	32	643	1,230	0	0
128	Labette CC	0	0	30	764	235	0	0
129	Laboure C	0	0	40	84	566	0	0
130	Lake City CC	0	0	56	1,216	1,561	0	0
131	Lakeland CC-OH	0	0	118	3,153	5,452	0	0
132	Lane CC-OR	0	0	260	2,177	-1	0	0
133	Lansdale Sch of Bus	0	0	6	159	191	0	0
134	Laramie Co CC	0	0	85	2,152	1,313	0	0
135	Lassen CC	-2	-2	45	757	1,734	-2	-2
136	Lexington CC	0	0	185 [1]	5,399	3,409	0	0
137	Linn ST Tech C	0	0	0	778	90	0	0
138	Lord Fairfax CC	0	0	55	1,471	3,945	0	0
139	Los Angeles Valley C	0	0	240	3,722	13,980	0	0
140	Luzerne County CC	0	0	138	3,222	3,174	0	0
141	Manatee CC	-2	0	121	3,718	5,012	-2	-2
142	Maple Woods CC	-2	-2	49	2,092	2,488	-2	-2
143	Marymount C CA	0	0	42	729	28	0	0
144	Massasoit CC	0	0	120	4,060	0	0	0
145	McDowell Tech CC	0	0	38	584	632	0	0
146	Mesa CC	-2	-2	324	8,706	18,626	-2	-2
147	Middlesex Co C-NJ	0	0	190	5,700	6,200	0	0
148	Midland C	0	0	126	1,971	3,618	0	0
149	Miles CC	0	0	20	449	185	0	0
150	MiraCosta C	0	0	116	8,284	1,360	0	0
151	Monroe CC	0	0	311	10,213	7,081	0	0
152	Mountain Empire CC	0	0	47	1,219	1,688	0	0
153	MS County CC	0	0	72	1,117	901	0	0
154	MS Delta CC	0	0	119	2,631	640	0	0
155	Mt Hood CC	0	0	158	3,843	6,381	0	0
156	N Alberta Inst	-2	-2	970	11,219 [1]	1	-2	-2
157	National Hispanic U	0	0	12	91	373	50	109
158	ND ST C Science	0	0	129	2,129	0	0	0
159	NE WI Tech C	0	0	300 [1]	2,854	8,011	0	0
160	NH CC-Berlin	0	0	33	259	522	0	0

1 -- See Footnotes   -1 -- Unavailable   -2 -- Not Applicable

ACRL Library Data Tables 2005

PH.D., FACULTY, AND ENROLLMENT STATISTICS

INSTITUTIONS GRANTING ASSOCIATE OF ARTS DEGREES (Carnegie Code A)

		Ph.D.'s Awarded	Ph.D. Fields	Full-Time Faculty	ENROLLMENT			
					Full-time, Undergrad. & Grad.	Part-time, Undergrad. & Grad.	Full-time, Grad.	Part-time, Grad.
	Survey Question #	36	37	38	39	40	41	42
Lib. No.	Institution							
161	NH CC-Laconia	0	0	34	503	322	0	0
162	Nicolet Area Tech C	0	0	61	655	682	0	0
163	NM St U-Carlsbad	0	0	30	622	614	0	0
164	Normandale CC	0	0	204	4,200	4,362	0	0
165	North AR C	0 [1]	0	86	1,356	1,178	0	0
166	Northeast ST Tech CC	0	0	97	2,797	2,288	0	0
167	Northeastern JC	0	0	51	869	2,043	0	0
168	Northwest C	0	0	78	1,536	236	0	0
169	Nwestern Business C	0	0	0	0	0	0	0
170	Nwestern CT Tech CC	0	0	28	513	1,003	0	0
171	OH ST U Ag Tech Inst	0	0	39	682	109	0	0
172	Ohlone C	0	0	144	2,705	8,864	0	0
173	Okaloosa-Walton CC	0	0	83	2,050	6,678	0	0
174	Orange County CC	0	0	117	1,243	551	0	0
175	Owensboro	0	0	93	2,588 [1]	0	0	0
176	Owensboro Jr C Bus	0	0	7	243	82	0	0
177	Oxnard C	0	0	100	2,189	4,405	0	0
178	Passaic County CC	0	0	0	2,127	4,957	0	0
179	Paul D. Camp CC	0	0	23	367	1,155	0	0
180	Pellissippi ST Tech CC	0	0	460 [1]	3,978	3,584	0	0
181	Pensacola Jr C	0	0	204	14,967	3,705	0	0
182	Petit Jean C	0	46	46	1,092	419	0	0
183	Piedmont Tech C	0	0	98	1,887	2,705	0	0
184	Pittsburgh Tech Inst	-2	-2	76	1,889	-2	-2	-2
185	Portland CC	0	0	410	1,271	4,506	0	0
186	Potomac St C-WVU	0	0	32	858	446	0	0
187	Prairie ST C	0	0	85	5,679 [1]	0	0	0
188	Prince George CC	0 [1]	0	255	3,317	9,142	0	0
189	Pueblo CC	-1	-1	76	2,270	3,320	-1	-1
190	Pulaski Tech C	-2	-2	100	3,590	3,632	-2	-2
191	Quinebaug Vally Comm T	0	0	26	901 [1]	0	0	0
192	Quinsigamond CC	0	0	104	2,779	3,322	0	0
193	Reading Area CC	0	0	65	1,660	2,630	0	0
194	Red Deer C	0	0	297	3,731 [1]	915 [1]	0	0
195	Redlands CC	0	0	35	0	0	0	0
196	Rend Lake C	0	0	60	2,283	2,186	0	0
197	Renton Tech C	0	0	93	3,957	11,694	0	0
198	Robeson CC	0	0	0	0	0	0	0
199	Rogue CC	0	0	0	0	0	0	0
200	Sacramento City C	0	0	296	6,861	14,848	0	0

1 -- See Footnotes   -1 -- Unavailable   -2 -- Not Applicable

ACRL Library Data Tables 2005
PH.D., FACULTY, AND ENROLLMENT STATISTICS
INSTITUTIONS GRANTING ASSOCIATE OF ARTS DEGREES (Carnegie Code A)

| | | Ph.D.'s Awarded | Ph.D. Fields | Full-Time Faculty | ENROLLMENT | | | |
					Full-time, Undergrad. & Grad.	Part-time, Undergrad. & Grad.	Full-time, Grad.	Part-time, Grad.
	Survey Question #	36	37	38	39	40	41	42
Lib. No.	Institution							
201	San Antonio C	0	0	454	8,338	13,803	0	0
202	San Jacinto C South	-2	-2	158	2,804	5,171	-2	-2
203	San Joaquin Delta C	0	0	265	6,885	10,228	0	0
204	Santa Fe CC-NM	0	0	266	7,633	8,108	0	0
205	Santa Monica C	0	0	321	0	0	0	0
206	Selkirk C	0	0	187	2,200 [1]	0	0	0
207	Seward County CC	0	0	47	1,996	1,354	0	0
208	South AR CC	0	0	53	558	837	0	0
209	South Florida CC	0	0	61	1,087	1,464	0	0
210	South Puget Sound CC	0	0	102	3,444	2,288	0	0
211	Southeast CC	0	0	107	1,896	2,631	0	0
212	Southwest VA CC	0	0	72	1,611	2,224	0	0
213	Spartanburg Tech C	0	0	0	2,827	4,095	0	0
214	Spoon River C	0	0	41	1,037	1,346	0	0
215	St Charles County CC	0	0	78	3,339	3,433	0	0
216	Sthrn U-Shreveport/Bossi	0	0	80	1,660	557	0	0
217	Tacoma CC	0	0	4 [1]	5,092	3,692	0	0
218	Tallahassee CC	0	0	170	10,259	8,454	0	0
219	Tech C Lowcountry	0	0	47	654	1,032	0	0
220	Temple C	0	0	83	1,533	2,535	0	0
221	Tri County Tech C	0	0	0	4,548	0	0	0
222	Trocaire C	0	0	52	658	351	0	0
223	Tunxis CC Tech	0	0	59	1,437	2,505	0	0
224	TX ST Tech C Waco	0	0	257	0	592	0	0
225	U Akron Wayne C	0	0	31	962	775	0	0
226	U HI-Kapiolani CC	0	0	0	7,174 [1]	0	0	0
227	U HI-Kauai CC	0	0	72	0	0	0	0
228	U HI-Windward CC	0	0	77	669	372	0	0
229	U NM Gallup Branch	0	0	73	1,108 [1]	2,134	0 [1]	0
230	VA Western CC	0	0	87	2,046	6,315	0	0
231	W.Rainey Harper C	0	0	215	20,461 [1]	0 [1]	0	0
232	Walsh U	0	0	80	1,343	608	82	175
233	Walters ST CC	0	0	129	3,063	2,842	0	0
234	Waycross C	0	0	21	375	630	0	0
235	Weatherford C	0	0	95	2,287	2,265	0	0
236	Western IA Tech CC	0	0	89	2,148	3,222	0 [1]	0
237	Wharton Co Jr C	-2	-2	125	2,805	3,295	-2	-2
238	Whatcom CC	0	0	3	2,088	1,092	0	0
239	Wytheville CC	0	0	34	923	1,777	0	0
240	Yakima Valley CC	0	0	152	5,418	5,075	0	0

1 -- See Footnotes   -1 -- Unavailable   -2 -- Not Applicable

ACRL Library Data Tables 2005

PH.D., FACULTY, AND ENROLLMENT STATISTICS

INSTITUTIONS GRANTING ASSOCIATE OF ARTS DEGREES (Carnegie Code A)

		Ph.D.'s Awarded	Ph.D. Fields	Full-Time Faculty	ENROLLMENT Full-time, Undergrad. & Grad.	Part-time, Undergrad. & Grad.	Full-time, Grad.	Part-time, Grad.
	Survey Question #	36	37	38	39	40	41	42
Lib. No.	Institution							
241	Yavapai C	0 [1]	0 [1]	192 [1]	1,369	6,010	0 [1]	0 [1]

ACRL LIBRARY DATA TABLES 2005

ANALYSIS OF SELECTED VARIABLES

INSTITUTIONS GRANTING ASSOCIATE OF ARTS DEGREES (CARNEGIE CODE A)

Category	High	Mean	Median	Low	Libraries Reporting
1. Professional staff as percent of Total Staff	100.00	35.42	33.33	7.14	242
2. Support Staff as percent of Total Staff	80.00	43.34	44.95	0.00	240
3. Student Assistant Staff as percent of Total Staff	83.33	22.28	21.39	0.00	236
4. Ratio of Professional to Support Staff (excluding student Assistant Staff)	8.00	0.99	0.77	0.11	234
5. Ratio of Items Loaned to Items Borrowed	124.00	2.66	1.35	0.00	222
6. Serial Expenditures as percent of Total Library Materials Expenditures	100.00	32.28	30.56	2.06	236
7. Total Library Material Expenditures as percent of Total Library Expenditures	96.54	21.66	19.87	2.00	239
8. Contract Binding as percent of Total Library Expenditures	3.70	0.16	0.00	0.00	218
9. Salary and Wages Expenditures as percent of Total Library Expenditures	100.00	70.51	71.90	3.46	238
10. Other Operating Expenditures as percent of Total Library Expenditures	53.23	8.92	6.55	0.00	225
11. Unit cost of monographs (per volume)	240.00	41.21	34.32	1.07	202

ACRL LIBRARY DATA TABLES 2005

SUMMARY DATA: ELECTRONIC RESOURCES

INSTITUTIONS GRANTING ASSOCIATE OF ARTS DEGREES (Carnegie Code A)

(Survey Question #)	Electronic journals purchased 1	Electronic full-text journals purchased 2	Electronic journals not purchased 3	Electronic reference sources 4	Electronic books 5
High	82,490	31,350	63,045	157,736	103,772
Mean	5,871	2,755	1,456	1,730	10,409
Median	3	0	0	17	1,984
Low	0	0	0	0	0
Total	1,103,664	498,637	257,772	349,378	2,154,632
Libraries Reporting	188	181	177	202	207

ACRL LIBRARY DATA TABLES 2005

SUMMARY DATA: NETWORKED RESOURCES AND SERVICES

INSTITUTIONS GRANTING ASSOCIATE OF ARTS DEGREES (Carnegie Code A)

	EXPENDITURES				
	Electronic journals purchased	Electronic full-text journals	Electronic reference sources	Electronic books	Virtual reference transactions
(Survey Question #)	7	8	9	10	11
High	234,300	150,314	165,679	20,744	2,202
Mean	15,022	7,029	14,379	1,495	83
Median	899	0	4,787	0	12
Low	0	0	0	0	0
Total	2,734,020	1,159,745	2,732,044	276,496	14,006
Libraries Reporting	182	165	190	185	168

68

ACRL LIBRARY DATA TABLES 2005

SUMMARY DATA: NETWORKED RESOURCES AND SERVICES

INSTITUTIONS GRANTING ASSOCIATE OF ARTS DEGREES (Carnegie Code A)

Logins to electronic databases	No. of databases reported	Queries in electronic databases	No. of databases reported	Items requested in electronic databases	No. of databases reported	Virtual visits to website	Virtual visits to catalog	
13	13a	14	14a	15	15a	16a	16b	(Survey Question #)
245,715	361	4,315,812	273,067	394,234	42,803	2,276,140	1,164,432	High
25,602	30	125,812	1,805	31,355	324	104,044	35,426	Mean
10,593	9	43,081	10	6,694	5	999	0	Median
0	0	0	0	0	0	0	0	Low
3,661,151	4,338	19,752,412	277,956	4,421,011	46,958	11,756,943	3,542,641	Total
143	146	157	154	141	145	113	100	Libraries Reporting

69

ACRL LIBRARY DATA TABLES 2005

SUMMARY DATA: DIGITIZATION ACTIVITIES

INSTITUTIONS GRANTING ASSOCIATE OF ARTS DEGREES (Carnegie Code A)

	DIGITAL COLLECTIONS			USAGE		DIRECT COSTS		
	No. of collections	Size (MB)	Items	No. of times accessed	No. of queries	Personnel	Equipment, software, or contract services	Volumes Held Collectively
(Survey Question #)	17a	17b	17c	18a	18b	19a	19b	20
High	35	2,000	35,000	1,997	2	7,000	27,614	200
Mean	0	31	306	24	0	104	378	2
Median	0	0	0	0	0	0	0	0
Low	0	0	0	0	0	0	0	0
Total	65	4,038	40,132	2,944	4	13,004	47,618	204
Libraries Reporting	151	129	131	125	122	125	126	125

ACRL Library Data Tables 2005
ELECTRONIC RESOURCES
INSTITUTIONS GRANTING ASSOCIATE OF ARTS DEGREES (Carnegie Code A)

Lib. No.	Survey Question # Institution	Electronic journals purchased 1	Electronic full-text journals purchased 2	Electronic journals not purchased 3	Electronic Reference Sources 4	Electronic books 5
1	A Baldwin Agrl C	240	0	0	2	27,150
2	Adirondack CC	23,854	0	0	68	72
3	Alpena CC	21,002	1,000	-1	4	21,084
4	Alvin CC	0	0	0	0	0
5	Am River C	7,952	0	0	11	1,110
6	Am Samoa CC	1,000	3,000	0	300	100
7	Andover C	0	0	0	2	0
8	Anne Arundel CC	6,000	4,000	0	7	7
9	Anoka-Ramsey CC	250	-1	-1	-1	0
10	AR ST U Beebe	66	55	0	18	33,223
11	Athens Tech C	85	0	0	259	4
12	AZ Western C	69,180	0	5,073	13	29,367
13	Bellingham Tech C	11,507	0	0	10	2,878
14	Belmont Tech C	0	0	0	0	0
15	Bergen CC	15,362	745	4,463	70	4,814
16	Black Hawk C	0	0	0	72	13,200
17	Blackhawk Tech C	0	0	0	38	23,000
18	Blue Mountain CC	0	0	0	8	0
19	Blue Ridge CC	7,076	3	1,187	55	2
20	Brazosport C	0	0	0	35	34,718
21	Bunker Hill CC	18,000	2	0	15	3,400
22	Butler County CC	0	0	0	12	1,297
23	C Canyons	0	0	0	14	0
24	C Edouard Montpetit	0	0	0	0	0
25	C Lake Co	3	0	0	0	0
26	C Merici	0	0	0	8	0
27	C New Caledonia	0	4,500	0	0	4,450
28	C Redwoods	0	0	0	0	0
29	C St Jean Richelieu	2	2	0	5	0
30	Camden County C	7,313	3,836	6,988	27	37
31	Cape Fear CC	0	0	0	103	24,130
32	Capital CC	0	0	0	40	0
33	Carl Sandburg C	0	0	0	0	200
34	Carroll Tech Inst	0	0	0	0	0
35	Carteret CC	0	0	-1	-1	-1
36	Cedar Valley	0	0	0	116	24,850
37	CEGEP Beauce-Appalaches	-2	-2	-2	-2	-2
38	CEGEP Trois-Rivieres	0	0	0	3	0
39	Central Alabama CC	0	0	0	0	0
40	Central Carolina Tech C	1	1	0	54	43,200

-1 -- Unavailable   -2 -- Not Applicable

Lib. No.	Survey Question # Institution	Electronic journals purchased 1	Electronic full-text journals purchased 2	Electronic journals not purchased 3	Electronic Reference Sources 4	Electronic books 5
41	Central ME Tech C	0	0	0	0	0
42	Central Piedmont CC	671	671	0	0	24,775
43	Central TX C	0	0	0	0	0
44	Centralia C	0	7	0	0	0
45	Chabot C	14,821	9,195	5,626	8	2
46	Chattahoochee Tech	0	0	1	1	43,796
47	Chippewa V Tech C	0	0	7,030	11	8,639
48	Clackamas CC	0	8,000	0	63	5,000
49	Clark C-WA	0	0	0	0	0
50	Clinton CC	0	12,954	0	0	9,727
51	Cloud Co CC	19,293	0	0	43	9,193
52	Coastal GA CC	0	0	0	190	27,499
53	Colby CC	3	3	0	5	3,000
54	Columbia Junior C	331	331	16,790	50	0
55	Columbia ST CC	0	1,500	14,000	450	46,500
56	Columbus ST CC	0	0	0	0	0
57	Compton CC	0	0	0	10	0
58	Connors ST C	0	0	0	0	0
59	Corning CC	18,471	1,825	7,752	68	1,176
60	Cosumnes River C	7,953	1	0	11	1,110
61	Crowder C	0	0	0	0	19,700
62	Cuesta C	0	0	171	0	7,830
63	Cumberland Co C	0	0	0	39	3,210
64	CUNY Borough Manhattan CC	22,714	0	0	88	5,550
65	CUNY Bronx CC	19,471	19,471	0	2,610	4,506
66	CUNY Hostos CC	0	0	0	6	0
67	CUNY LaGuardia CC	2,956	779	23,552	84	1,787
68	CUNY Queensborough CC	4	0	2	0	0
69	D.S. Lancaster CC	7,076	1	0	55	0
70	Darton C	28,610	22,830	187	96	27,441
71	Dawson CC	0	0	0	0	0
72	Del Mar C	0	31,350	0	25	28,300
73	Delaware Co CC	5,100	0	0	9	25
74	Diablo Valley C	8,312	0	5	18	5,486
75	Dodge City CC	0	0	0	1	0
76	Dyersburg ST CC	0	0	5,556	28	47,760
77	East Central C	13,300	10,300	0	26	9,338
78	East Georgia C	-1	-1	-1	65	27,501
79	East Los Angeles C	0	0	0	31	5,000
80	El Paso CC	87	87	0	9	103,772

-1 -- Unavailable   -2 -- Not Applicable

ACRL Library Data Tables 2005
ELECTRONIC RESOURCES

INSTITUTIONS GRANTING ASSOCIATE OF ARTS DEGREES (Carnegie Code A)

Lib. No.	Survey Question # Institution	Electronic journals purchased 1	Electronic full-text journals purchased 2	Electronic journals not purchased 3	Electronic Reference Sources 4	Electronic books 5
81	Estrn Arizona C	3,769	1,201	2,739	7	24
82	Estrn Idaho Tech C	0	0	0	46	1,270
83	Estrn Maine Tech C	0	0	0	0	0
84	Fayetteville Tech CC	0	0	0	9	22,000
85	Fergus Falls CC	0	0	0	0	2,750
86	Flor Dar Tech C	0	0	56	0	46,280
87	Floyd C	28,692	22,830	187	96	27,441
88	Gadsden ST CC	0	0	0	0	30,000
89	Gainesville C	0	0	0	181	27,441
90	Gavilan C	2,534	0	0	21	11,246
91	GC Wallace CC	1	1	1	3	96
92	Glendale CC	0	0	0	0	0
93	Gogebic CC	0	0	0	6	4,600
94	Gordon C-GA	0	3,666	0	0	27,417
95	Grand Rapids CC	15,000	9,600	2,000	500	22,000
96	Harrisburg Area CC	16,000	8,000	0	82	1,973
97	Hawaii Pacific U	28,058	0	3,027	0	5,000
98	Hawkeye CC	9,384	0	2,313	47	11,489
99	Highland CC KS	0	0	0	31	12,000
100	Hillsborough CC	0	0	0	86	3,379
101	Hinds CC	0	7	76	6	11,179
102	Hiwassee C	3	3	0	28	0
103	Hocking Tech C	0	0	0	95	19,775
104	Hopkinsville CC	-1	-1	0	-1	18,832
105	Horry GTown Tech	0	0	0	11	46,184
106	Howard C	19,708	19,708	0	2,031	28,281
107	Hutch CC&Voc Sch	0	0	0	3	12,000
108	IL E CC Wabash Cntrl C	0	0	0	0	0
109	IL Estrn CC-Frontier	1	1	0	157,736	0
110	IL Estrn CC-Lincoln Trail	1	1	0	157,736	0
111	IL Valley CC	6,600	0	5,718	8	7,956
112	Independence CC	0	0	22,934	0	0
113	Inst Com PR Jr C Arecibo	0	0	0	0	0
114	Inst Native Culture	0	0	0	0	0
115	Isothermal CC	0	0	0	19	24,000
116	J.F. Drake ST Tech C	0	0	0	0	0
117	Jacksonville C	1	1	0	0	0
118	Jefferson CC-NY	0	17,000	0	65	11,600
119	Jefferson C-MO	5,870	0	8,736	29	9,340
120	JS Reynolds CC	7,076	1,087	0	61	196

-1 -- Unavailable   -2 -- Not Applicable

ACRL Library Data Tables 2005
ELECTRONIC RESOURCES

INSTITUTIONS GRANTING ASSOCIATE OF ARTS DEGREES (Carnegie Code A)

Lib. No.	Survey Question # Institution	Electronic journals purchased 1	Electronic full-text journals purchased 2	Electronic journals not purchased 3	Electronic Reference Sources 4	Electronic books 5
121	Justice Inst BC	7,731	0	0	30	803
122	Kaskaskia C	-1	-1	0	0	0
123	Kent St U E Liverpool	0	0	0	0	0
124	Kent St U Tuscarawas	0	0	0	2	0
125	Kilgore C	17,073	17,073	0	17	27,545
126	Kirkwood CC	0	0	26	0	0
127	Kirtland CC	0	0	0	3	19,800
128	Labette CC	0	0	0	2	0
129	Laboure C	7	7	8	0	0
130	Lake City CC	5,626	5,626	0	110	27,000
131	Lakeland CC-OH	0	0	0	0	0
132	Lane CC-OR	14,868	0	-1	54	385
133	Lansdale Sch of Bus	2,130	2,130	0	1	0
134	Laramie Co CC	10,326	296	15,151	42	0
135	Lassen CC	0	0	0	0	0
136	Lexington CC	12,181	12	0	37	0
137	Linn ST Tech C	0	0	0	10	1,929
138	Lord Fairfax CC	7,077	1,188	0	55	30,685
139	Los Angeles Valley C	0	0	0	20	8,450
140	Luzerne County CC	64	0	0	16	0
141	Manatee CC	-1	-1	0	69	487
142	Maple Woods CC	0	0	0	63	6,296
143	Marymount C CA	13,000	8,000	0	0	0
144	Massasoit CC	0	0	0	38	0
145	McDowell Tech CC	0	0	0	3	0
146	Mesa CC	58,405	441	63,045	53	24,798
147	Middlesex Co C-NJ	0	0	0	25	0
148	Midland C	18,876	18,876	0	98	27,660
149	Miles CC	0	0	0	27	0
150	MiraCosta C	6,350	348	0	20	8,958
151	Monroe CC	0	0	0	0	0
152	Mountain Empire CC	0	0	0	0	0
153	MS County CC	0	0	0	3	0
154	MS Delta CC	0	0	0	0	0
155	Mt Hood CC	123	123	48	53	1,984
156	N Alberta Inst	13	6,145	1	1	4,010
157	National Hispanic U	25	20	1	12	18,000
158	ND ST C Science	0	0	0	0	12,000
159	NE WI Tech C	6,250	0	1,455	11	13,130
160	NH CC-Berlin	0	0	0	382	5,356

-1 -- Unavailable   -2 -- Not Applicable

ACRL Library Data Tables 2005
ELECTRONIC RESOURCES

INSTITUTIONS GRANTING ASSOCIATE OF ARTS DEGREES (Carnegie Code A)

Lib. No.	Survey Question # Institution	Electronic journals purchased 1	Electronic full-text journals purchased 2	Electronic journals not purchased 3	Electronic Reference Sources 4	Electronic books 5
161	NH CC-Laconia	0	0	0	5	230
162	Nicolet Area Tech C	6,186	5,741	13,534	10	0
163	NM St U-Carlsbad	0	0	0	0	90
164	Normandale CC	41,267	0	0	77	0
165	North AR C	0	0	0	16	0
166	Northeast ST Tech CC	0	0	0	45	47
167	Northeastern JC	4,461	0	0	3	4,314
168	Northwest C	13	0	0	15	0
169	Nwestern Business C	6,000	0	0	5	0
170	Nwestern CT Tech CC	9,687	1	0	19	0
171	OH ST U Ag Tech Inst	0	0	0	0	0
172	Ohlone C	0	0	0	0	0
173	Okaloosa-Walton CC	71	61	0	1	3,000
174	Orange County CC	0	0	0	32	2
175	Owensboro	0	0	5	41	46,173
176	Owensboro Jr C Bus	0	0	0	0	0
177	Oxnard C	8,000	7,500	0	6	0
178	Passaic County CC	10,000	6,000	5,000	20,000	0
179	Paul D. Camp CC	0	0	0	0	36,000
180	Pellissippi ST Tech CC	50	2	5	213	55,077
181	Pensacola Jr C	0	0	0	11	28
182	Petit Jean C	0	3	2	2	0
183	Piedmont Tech C	0	0	0	41	23,202
184	Pittsburgh Tech Inst	-1	-1	-1	10	-2
185	Portland CC	50	0	0	0	7,195
186	Potomac St C-WVU	600	0	0	6	900
187	Prairie ST C	0	0	0	17	0
188	Prince George CC	7,023	0	0	27	21
189	Pueblo CC	23,764	17,401	13	36	12,305
190	Pulaski Tech C	-1	1	-1	20	11,349
191	Quinebaug Vally Comm TC	0	0	0	0	5,800
192	Quinsigamond CC	0	0	0	13	0
193	Reading Area CC	0	19,125	0	150	13,000
194	Red Deer C	0	0	0	4	750
195	Redlands CC	0	0	0	0	0
196	Rend Lake C	20	10	0	16	1,900
197	Renton Tech C	3,800	0	2,320	10	6
198	Robeson CC	0	0	0	0	0
199	Rogue CC	0	0	0	0	0
200	Sacramento City C	0	0	56	12	1,313

-1 -- Unavailable   -2 -- Not Applicable

ACRL Library Data Tables 2005
ELECTRONIC RESOURCES

INSTITUTIONS GRANTING ASSOCIATE OF ARTS DEGREES (Carnegie Code A)

Lib. No.	Survey Question # Institution	Electronic journals purchased 1	Electronic full-text journals purchased 2	Electronic journals not purchased 3	Electronic Reference Sources 4	Electronic books 5
201	San Antonio C	1	30,000	0	35	28,274
202	San Jacinto C South	0	0	0	0	0
203	San Joaquin Delta C	0	6,000	0	19	10,049
204	Santa Fe CC-NM	0	7,171	0	77	1,300
205	Santa Monica C	18,000	0	0	0	8,858
206	Selkirk C	5,733	0	0	31	800
207	Seward County CC	0	0	0	0	0
208	South AR CC	0	0	0	23	0
209	South Florida CC	0	0	0	0	1,238
210	South Puget Sound CC	2	2	0	9	1
211	Southeast CC	0	0	0	6	18,832
212	Southwest VA CC	7,076	1,187	0	55	46,172
213	Spartanburg Tech C	0	0	0	0	42,880
214	Spoon River C	11,680	11,680	3	3	0
215	St Charles County CC	17,017	0	5	136	25,032
216	Sthrn U-Shreveport/Bossier	22,244	22,244	0	118	11,079
217	Tacoma CC	0	0	0	0	0
218	Tallahassee CC	82,490	18,671	450	90	1,446
219	Tech C Lowcountry	0	0	0	0	0
220	Temple C	16,554	0	18	28	41,389
221	Tri County Tech C	0	0	0	0	200
222	Trocaire C	0	0	0	2	0
223	Tunxis CC Tech	0	0	0	33	0
224	TX ST Tech C Waco	3	3	3	3	3
225	U Akron Wayne C	0	0	0	3	0
226	U HI-Kapiolani CC	38,948	17,348	2	1,017	21,588
227	U HI-Kauai CC	5	4	0	0	0
228	U HI-Windward CC	1	1	0	3	0
229	U NM Gallup Branch	0	0	0	0	0
230	VA Western CC	7,076	1,087	0	55	0
231	W.Rainey Harper C	0	8,194	0	0	6,221
232	Walsh U	25,212	6,121	7,253	594	60,053
233	Walters ST CC	2	2	0	51	53,542
234	Waycross C	28,692	22,830	187	96	27,441
235	Weatherford C	0	0	0	28	28,274
236	Western IA Tech CC	0	0	6	206	12,441
237	Wharton Co Jr C	-2	-2	-2	31	27,000
238	Whatcom CC	0	0	0	5	2,876
239	Wytheville CC	7,076	1,187	0	55	0
240	Yakima Valley CC	0	0	0	0	0

-1 -- Unavailable   -2 -- Not Applicable

ACRL Library Data Tables 2005
ELECTRONIC RESOURCES

INSTITUTIONS GRANTING ASSOCIATE OF ARTS DEGREES (Carnegie Code A)

Lib. No.	Survey Question # Institution	Electronic journals purchased 1	Electronic full-text journals purchased 2	Electronic journals not purchased 3	Electronic Reference Sources 4	Electronic books 5
241	Yavapai C	13,971	9,220	3,005	34	0

-1 -- Unavailable   -2 -- Not Applicable

ACRL Library Data Tables 2005
NETWORKED ELECTRONIC RESOURCES AND SERVICES
INSTITUTIONS GRANTING ASSOCIATE OF ARTS DEGREES (Carnegie Code A)

Lib. No.	Survey Question # Institution	Reported in Canadian $ 6	EXPENDITURES				Virtual reference transactions 11	Federated searching across networked electronic resources? 12
			Electronic journals purchased 7	Electronic full-text journals 8	Electronic reference sources 9	Electronic books 10		
1	A Baldwin Agrl C	N	9,700	0	2,200	0	0	N
2	Adirondack CC	N	12,121	0	11,053	0	0	N
3	Alpena CC	N	15,480	15,480	279	671	-1	Y
4	Alvin CC	N	0	0	0	0	2	N
5	Am River C	N	0	0	46,972	1,305	75	Y
6	Am Samoa CC	N	3,000	2,000	1,000	1,000	0	N
7	Andover C	N	0	0	5,082	0	0	N
8	Anne Arundel CC	N	159,684	0	5,000	0	150	N
9	Anoka-Ramsey CC	N	2,490	-1	0	0	-1	Y
10	AR ST U Beebe	N	0	0	0	9,290	0	N
11	Athens Tech C	N	375	0	4,745	0	0	N
12	AZ Western C	N	37,168	0	4,162	100	204	N
13	Bellingham Tech C	N	8,362	0	8,362	0	25	N
14	Belmont Tech C	N	0	0	0	0	0	
15	Bergen CC	N	49,600	12,544	86,300	685	81	N
16	Black Hawk C	N	0	0	38,200	2,800	40	N
17	Blackhawk Tech C	N	0	0	14,959	2,625	0	N
18	Blue Mountain CC	N	0	0	8,167	0	0	
19	Blue Ridge CC	N	0	4,634	0	2,950	195	N
20	Brazosport C	N	0	0	37,750	2,500	0	N
21	Bunker Hill CC	N	26,889	3,241	28,389	1,500	0	N
22	Butler County CC	N	0	0	38,678	55	0	N
23	C Canyons	N	0	0	42,000	0	0	N
24	C Edouard Montpetit	Y	0	0	0	0	0	N
25	C Lake Co	N	200	0	0	3,000	50	N
26	C Merici	Y	0	0	8,060	0	0	N
27	C New Caledonia	Y	0	32,801	0	0	0	N
28	C Redwoods	N	34,454	0	0	0	0	N
29	C St Jean Richelieu	Y	8,000	0	0	0	0	N
30	Camden County C	N	18,322	8,819	4,829	0	20	N
31	Cape Fear CC	N	0	0	0	0	0	N
32	Capital CC	N	0	0	21,816	0	0	N
33	Carl Sandburg C	N	0	0	0	5,000	0	N
34	Carroll Tech Inst	N	0	0	0	0	0	N
35	Carteret CC	N	0	0	0	0	60	Y
36	Cedar Valley	N	0	0	0	0	0	Y
37	CEGEP Beauce-Appalaches	N	-2	-2	5,650	-2	-2	N
38	CEGEP Trois-Rivieres	Y	0	0	0	0	0	N
39	Central Alabama CC	N	0	0	0	0	0	Y
40	Central Carolina Tech C	N	750	750	18,820	989	0	N

-1 -- Unavailable   -2 -- Not Applicable   NA - Not Answered

ACRL Library Data Tables 2005
NETWORKED RESOURCES AND SERVICES

INSTITUTIONS GRANTING ASSOCIATE OF ARTS DEGREES (Carnegie Code A)

Logins to electronic databases 13	No. of databases reported 13a	Queries (searches) in electronic databases 14	No. of databases reported 14a	No. of full-text article requests 15	No. of databases reported 15a	Virtual visits to website 16a	Virtual visits to catalog 16b	Excl. visits fr. inside library 16c	Survey Question # Institution
0	0	0	0	0	0	0	0		A Baldwin Agrl C
0	0	0	0	0	0	0	0	N	Adirondack CC
-1	-1	38,782	-1	-1	-1	185,619	-1	N	Alpena CC
7,455	26	24,892	26	18,202	26	2	2	N	Alvin CC
104,152	3	313,139	3	217,761	3	0	0		Am River C
0	0	0	0	0	0	0	0	N	Am Samoa CC
0	0	0	0	0	0	0	0		Andover C
0	0	0	0	173,665	20	0	0	N	Anne Arundel CC
-1	-2	-1	-2	-1	-2	-1	-1	N	Anoka-Ramsey CC
0	0	0	0	0	0	0	0		AR ST U Beebe
0	0	0	0	0	0	0	0		Athens Tech C
16,582	53	40,857	53	19,583	34	0	0	N	AZ Western C
0	0	23,440	8	0	0	0	0		Bellingham Tech C
0	0	0	0	0	0	0	0		Belmont Tech C
130,880	36	327,826	38	176,700	33	-1	-1		Bergen CC
0	0	0	0	0	0	0	0	Y	Black Hawk C
1,785	4	26,669	9	4,130	4	0	0	N	Blackhawk Tech C
4,630	0	17,085	8	0	0	0	0		Blue Mountain CC
0	0	0	0	33,385	0	98,023	0	N	Blue Ridge CC
0	0	0	0	0	0	0	0		Brazosport C
0	0	112,941	8	600	1	106,444	0	N	Bunker Hill CC
179,275	12	179,275	12	0	12	0	0	N	Butler County CC
0	0	173,070	4	148,551	1	443,234	80,000	N	C Canyons
0	0	0	0	0	0	0	0	N	C Edouard Montpetit
0	0	0	0	0	0	0	0		C Lake Co
0	0	0	0	0	0	0	0		C Merici
0	0	0	0	0	0	0	0	N	C New Caledonia
0	0	0	0	0	0	0	0	Y	C Redwoods
0	0	0	0	0	0	0	0		C St Jean Richelieu
0	0	0	0	0	0	0	0	N	Camden County C
0	0	0	0	0	0	0	0		Cape Fear CC
0	0	0	0	0	0	0	0	N	Capital CC
0	0	0	0	0	0	0	0	N	Carl Sandburg C
0	0	0	0	0	0	0	0		Carroll Tech Inst
-1	-1	-1	-1	-1	-1	-1	-1	N	Carteret CC
0	0	0	0	0	0	0	0	Y	Cedar Valley
-2	0	-2	-2	-2	-2	1	1	Y	EGEP Beauce-Appalaches
0	0	0	0	0	0	0	0		CEGEP Trois-Rivieres
11,027	1	21,236	13	1,695	4	0	0	Y	Central Alabama CC
0	0	46,061	25	0	0	0	0		Central Carolina Tech C

-1 -- Unavailable   -2 -- Not Applicable

ACRL Library Data Tables 2005
NETWORKED ELECTRONIC RESOURCES AND SERVICES
INSTITUTIONS GRANTING ASSOCIATE OF ARTS DEGREES (Carnegie Code A)

			EXPENDITURES					
Lib. No.	Survey Question # Institution	Reported in Canadian $ 6	Electronic journals purchased 7	Electronic full-text journals 8	Electronic reference sources 9	Electronic books 10	Virtual reference transactions 11	Federated searching across networked electronic resources? 12
41	Central ME Tech C	N	0	0	0	0	0	N
42	Central Piedmont CC	N	0	0	0	0	0	N
43	Central TX C	N	0	0	0	0	0	N
44	Centralia C	NA	0	0	0	0	0	
45	Chabot C	N	33,142	0	9,598	50	24	N
46	Chattahoochee Tech	N	0	0	0	5,000	1	N
47	Chippewa V Tech C	N	18,800	18,800	10,133	1,132	196	N
48	Clackamas CC	N	0	15,000	0	2,500	0	N
49	Clark C-WA	N	0	0	0	0	0	Y
50	Clinton CC	N	0	7,529	0	1,162	0	N
51	Cloud Co CC	N	1,250	0	3,091	3,690	15	N
52	Coastal GA CC	N	0	0	0	0	21	N
53	Colby CC	N	300	300	9,000	0	0	N
54	Columbia Junior C	N	8,676	8,676	34,324	0	0	N
55	Columbia ST CC	N	38,000	16,000	11,000	4,500	125	Y
56	Columbus ST CC	NA	0	0	0	0	0	
57	Compton CC	N	0	0	42,075	0	0	N
58	Connors ST C	N	0	0	0	0	5	N
59	Corning CC	N	26,692	0	0	0	0	N
60	Cosumnes River C	N	0	310	43,354	1,305	0	N
61	Crowder C	N	0	0	0	0	300	N
62	Cuesta C	N	6,012	4,113	4,840	0	0	N
63	Cumberland Co C	N	0	0	19,690	0	20	Y
64	CUNY Borough Manhattan C	N	4,773	0	20,046	1,900	140	N
65	CUNY Bronx CC	N	62,413	62,413	0	0	0	N
66	CUNY Hostos CC	N	0	0	19,735	0	70	Y
67	CUNY LaGuardia CC	N	16,208	16,208	43,909	10,844	264	Y
68	CUNY Queensborough CC	N	0	0	0	0	240	N
69	D.S. Lancaster CC	N	568	87	4	0	0	N
70	Darton C	N	53,850	0	2,011	0	1	N
71	Dawson CC	NA	0	0	0	0	0	N
72	Del Mar C	N	0	0	38,509	0	20	N
73	Delaware Co CC	N	43,182	0	-1	735	522	N
74	Diablo Valley C	N	0	0	42,241	13,100	0	N
75	Dodge City CC	N	0	0	4,500	0	0	N
76	Dyersburg ST CC	N	0	0	25,036	3,876	0	N
77	East Central C	N	3,186	2,850	7,851	1,300	28	N
78	East Georgia C	N	13,750	-1	-1	-1	19	N
79	East Los Angeles C	N	34,000	0	9,800	0	0	N
80	El Paso CC	N	122,724	122,724	0	0	0	N

-1 -- Unavailable   -2 -- Not Applicable   NA - Not Answered

ACRL Library Data Tables 2005
NETWORKED RESOURCES AND SERVICES

INSTITUTIONS GRANTING ASSOCIATE OF ARTS DEGREES (Carnegie Code A)

Logins to electronic databases 13	No. of databases reported 13a	Queries (searches) in electronic databases 14	No. of databases reported 14a	No. of full-text article requests 15	No. of databases reported 15a	Virtual visits to website 16a	Virtual visits to catalog 16b	Excl. visits fr. inside library 16c	Survey Question # Institution
0	0	0	0	0	0	0	0	Y	Central ME Tech C
0	0	0	0	0	0	0	0	Y	Central Piedmont CC
0	0	0	0	0	0	0	0	Y	Central TX C
0	0	0	0	0	0	0	0		Centralia C
26,536	7	153,172	7	60,376	7	300,000	0	N	Chabot C
1	1	1	1	1	1	1	1	N	Chattahoochee Tech
15,251	2	127,477	4	44,925	4	0	0	N	Chippewa V Tech C
9,600	7	48,000	7	73,200	7	0	0	N	Clackamas CC
0	0	0	0	0	0	0	0		Clark C-WA
0	0	0	0	0	0	0	0	Y	Clinton CC
2,250	6	17,700	8	4,436	6	1,926	0	Y	Cloud Co CC
70,881	190	31,864	190	22,391	190	42,168	14,100	N	Coastal GA CC
0	0	0	0	0	0	0	0	N	Colby CC
41,846	16	137,189	16	79,707	16	-1	-1	Y	Columbia Junior C
17,504	47	55,722	47	0	47	0	0	N	Columbia ST CC
0	0	0	0	0	0	0	0		Columbus ST CC
0	0	0	0	0	0	0	0		Compton CC
19,113	10	57,340	10	38,226	10	0	0	N	Connors ST C
8,396	9	158,044	20	95,908	13	0	32,573	N	Corning CC
32,783	18	92,117	18	52,902	18	0	0	Y	Cosumnes River C
10,724	5	43,081	6	31,319	4	0	0	Y	Crowder C
30,881	9	151,859	9	0	0	0	0		Cuesta C
15,920	19	101,199	19	0	0	22,301	200	N	Cumberland Co C
145,646	48	240,111	87	79,976	44	9,807	0	Y	Borough Manhattan CC
0	0	0	0	0	0	0	0		CUNY Bronx CC
2,533	6	10,089	6	4,880	6	41,958	0	Y	CUNY Hostos CC
0	0	0	0	0	0	560,000	0	N	CUNY LaGuardia CC
0	0	0	0	0	0	750,000	0	N	CUNY Queensborough CC
0	55	0	0	0	0	0	0	N	D.S. Lancaster CC
15,167	193	29,893	8	15,033	8	0	0	Y	Darton C
0	0	0	0	0	0	0	0		Dawson CC
111,571	12	378,946	12	0	0	305,294	0	N	Del Mar C
-1	10	323,651	10	171,410	7	-2	-2	N	Delaware Co CC
0	0	210,008	18	101,482	25	0	0		Diablo Valley C
0	0	0	0	0	0	0	0		Dodge City CC
-1	-1	79,489	28	-1	-1	56,463	-1	N	Dyersburg ST CC
10,593	18	29,748	18	14,931	18	0	0	Y	East Central C
15,786	189	33,895	189	4,960	189	-1	-1		East Georgia C
35,138	9	133,549	9	89,216	9	-1	-1	N	East Los Angeles C
245,715	87	833,578	87	394,234	87	0	0	N	El Paso CC

-1 -- Unavailable   -2 -- Not Applicable

ACRL Library Data Tables 2005
NETWORKED ELECTRONIC RESOURCES AND SERVICES
INSTITUTIONS GRANTING ASSOCIATE OF ARTS DEGREES (Carnegie Code A)

Lib. No.	Survey Question # Institution	Reported in Canadian $ 6	EXPENDITURES				Virtual reference transactions 11	Federated searching across networked electronic resources? 12
			Electronic journals purchased 7	Electronic full-text journals 8	Electronic reference sources 9	Electronic books 10		
81	Estrn Arizona C	N	20,600	11,100	20,600	3,000	5	Y
82	Estrn Idaho Tech C	N	0	0	15,000	1,000	0	Y
83	Estrn Maine Tech C	N	0	0	0	0	0	N
84	Fayetteville Tech CC	N	0	0	29,057	0	20	N
85	Fergus Falls CC	N	0	0	0	1,000	0	Y
86	Flor Dar Tech C	N	0	0	0	0	213	N
87	Floyd C	NA	12,172	0	0	0	0	N
88	Gadsden ST CC	N	0	0	0	0	0	N
89	Gainesville C	N	57,635	0	0	0	4	N
90	Gavilan C	N	234,300	0	9,884	5,972	0	N
91	GC Wallace CC	N	1,460	1,460	0	4,000	0	Y
92	Glendale CC	NA	0	0	0	0	0	
93	Gogebic CC	N	0	0	8,799	300	0	N
94	Gordon C-GA	N	44,217	0	0	0	0	N
95	Grand Rapids CC	NA	0	0	0	0	52	N
96	Harrisburg Area CC	N	97,835	0	165,679	0	0	N
97	Hawaii Pacific U	N	0	0	0	8,000	0	N
98	Hawkeye CC	N	30,810	0	7,416	0	8	N
99	Highland CC KS	N	0	0	722	0	8	N
100	Hillsborough CC	N	0	0	107,845	0	103	Y
101	Hinds CC	N	0	135	7,184	0	0	N
102	Hiwassee C	N	1,140	1,140	914	0	6	N
103	Hocking Tech C	N	0	0	0	0	0	Y
104	Hopkinsville CC	N	-1	-1	-1	1,147	-1	Y
105	Horry GTown Tech	N	0	0	58,961	1,465	16	N
106	Howard C	N	2,500	2,500	2,500	2,500	12	Y
107	Hutch CC&Voc Sch	N	0	0	26,001	2,550	112	N
108	IL E CC Wabash Cntrl C	NA	0	0	0	0	0	
109	IL Estrn CC-Frontier	N	-1	-1	-1	-1	-1	N
110	IL Estrn CC-Lincoln Trail	N	0	0	0	0	0	N
111	IL Valley CC	N	14,991	0	4,623	1,147	0	N
112	Independence CC	N	0	0	0	0	0	N
113	Inst Com PR Jr C Arecibo	N	0	0	0	0	0	N
114	Inst Native Culture	NA	0	0	0	0	0	
115	Isothermal CC	N	0	0	90	90	25	Y
116	J.F. Drake ST Tech C	N	0	0	0	0	0	N
117	Jacksonville C	N	500	500	0	0	0	N
118	Jefferson CC-NY	N	0	50	56,000	1,500	10	N
119	Jefferson C-MO	N	9,035	945	15,168	0	0	N
120	JS Reynolds CC	N	126,108	19,372	980	6,550	32	N

-1 -- Unavailable   -2 -- Not Applicable   NA - Not Answered

ACRL Library Data Tables 2005
NETWORKED RESOURCES AND SERVICES

INSTITUTIONS GRANTING ASSOCIATE OF ARTS DEGREES (Carnegie Code A)

Logins to electronic databases 13	No. of databases reported 13a	Queries (searches) in electronic databases 14	No. of databases reported 14a	No. of full-text article requests 15	No. of databases reported 15a	Virtual visits to website 16a	Virtual visits to catalog 16b	Excl. visits fr. inside library 16c	Survey Question # Institution
5,432	4	26,497	6	20,684	6	8,000	3,000	Y	Estrn Arizona C
1,600	35	5,800	35	2,400	35	0	0	N	Estrn Idaho Tech C
0	0	0	0	0	0	0	0	Y	Estrn Maine Tech C
50	9	20	9	551	1	200	200	Y	Fayetteville Tech CC
0	0	0	0	0	0	0	0	N	Fergus Falls CC
0	0	0	0	0	0	0	0		Flor Dar Tech C
0	0	0	0	0	0	0	0	N	Floyd C
0	0	0	0	0	0	0	0		Gadsden ST CC
176,818	182	0	182	0	182	6,000	5,022	N	Gainesville C
0	0	0	0	0	0	0	0		Gavilan C
502	3	455	3	600	3	1,500	653	N	GC Wallace CC
0	0	0	0	0	0	0	0		Glendale CC
0	0	0	0	0	0	0	0	N	Gogebic CC
0	0	0	0	0	0	0	0		Gordon C-GA
53,000	43	198,000	43	95,000	43	0	0		Grand Rapids CC
0	0	0	0	0	0	0	0	N	Harrisburg Area CC
0	0	0	0	0	0	0	0	N	Hawaii Pacific U
55,079	47	243,239	47	105,725	42	0	0	N	Hawkeye CC
2,534	31	10,672	31	1,937	31	0	0	Y	Highland CC KS
43,541	86	4,315,812	86	4,375	7	2,625	115,265	N	Hillsborough CC
20,122	6	0	0	0	0	0	0		Hinds CC
0	0	0	0	0	0	0	0	Y	Hiwassee C
0	0	0	0	0	0	0	0	N	Hocking Tech C
9,004	9	59,613	10	-1	-2	-1	-1	N	Hopkinsville CC
0	0	142,795	14	0	0	0	0		Horry GTown Tech
20,965	0	20,965	0	0	0	5,889	0	Y	Howard C
0	0	110,096	36	0	0	0	0		Hutch CC&Voc Sch
0	0	0	0	0	0	0	0		IL E CC Wabash Cntrl C
-1	-1	-1	-1	-1	-1	-1	-1		IL Estrn CC-Frontier
0	0	0	0	0	0	0	0		IL Estrn CC-Lincoln Trail
21,620	3	73,117	4	37,333	4	0	0		IL Valley CC
1,550	6	3,678	6	3,678	6	0	0	Y	Independence CC
0	0	0	0	0	0	0	0	N	Inst Com PR Jr C Arecibo
0	0	0	0	0	0	0	0		Inst Native Culture
0	0	0	0	0	0	0	0	N	Isothermal CC
0	0	0	0	0	0	0	0	Y	J.F. Drake ST Tech C
2,704	3	12,069	3	4,648	3	0	0	Y	Jacksonville C
0	65	0	65	0	65	2,276,140	0	N	Jefferson CC-NY
20,570	24	66,230	26	44,395	26	0	0	N	Jefferson C-MO
42,713	61	273,067	273,067	42,803	42,803	0	0	N	JS Reynolds CC

-1 -- Unavailable   -2 -- Not Applicable

ACRL Library Data Tables 2005
NETWORKED ELECTRONIC RESOURCES AND SERVICES
INSTITUTIONS GRANTING ASSOCIATE OF ARTS DEGREES (Carnegie Code A)

Lib. No.	Survey Question # Institution	Reported in Canadian $ 6	EXPENDITURES				Virtual reference transactions 11	Federated searching across networked electronic resources? 12
			Electronic journals purchased 7	Electronic full-text journals 8	Electronic reference sources 9	Electronic books 10		
121	Justice Inst BC	Y	27,849	0	27,849	0	0	N
122	Kaskaskia C	N	11,700	-1	-1	0	0	N
123	Kent St U E Liverpool	N	0	0	0	0	0	N
124	Kent St U Tuscarawas	N	0	0	3,500	0	0	N
125	Kilgore C	N	10,419	7,919	32,873	6,102	40	N
126	Kirkwood CC	N	0	0	3,144	0	0	N
127	Kirtland CC	N	0	0	2,500	500	0	N
128	Labette CC	N	0	0	570	0	74	N
129	Laboure C	N	0	1,000	0	0	0	Y
130	Lake City CC	N	5,433	5,433	1,275	0	52	Y
131	Lakeland CC-OH	N	0	0	0	0	0	Y
132	Lane CC-OR	N	0	0	49,727	0	0	Y
133	Lansdale Sch of Bus	N	0	1,897	116	0	27	N
134	Laramie Co CC	N	4,000	13,260	3,200	0	191	N
135	Lassen CC	NA	0	0	0	0	0	
136	Lexington CC	N	3,424	0	3,424	0	63	N
137	Linn ST Tech C	N	0	0	2,876	1,000	0	N
138	Lord Fairfax CC	N	1,227	1,227	2,167	0	19	N
139	Los Angeles Valley C	N	0	0	50,272	9,000	0	N
140	Luzerne County CC	N	27,000	0	50,000	0	25	N
141	Manatee CC	N	-1	-1	50,907	4,800	436	Y
142	Maple Woods CC	N	0	0	17,319	0	-2	N
143	Marymount C CA	N	15,000	35,000	0	0	0	N
144	Massasoit CC	N	0	0	11,352	0	0	N
145	McDowell Tech CC	N	0	0	2,128	0	0	Y
146	Mesa CC	N	16,900	-1	7,747	0	221	Y
147	Middlesex Co C-NJ	N	0	0	60,000	0	0	N
148	Midland C	N	7,949	7,949	1,995	5,300	0	N
149	Miles CC	N	0	0	0	0	0	N
150	MiraCosta C	N	24,444	2,920	17,523	4,000	144	N
151	Monroe CC	NA	0	0	0	0	0	
152	Mountain Empire CC	N	0	0	0	0	0	Y
153	MS County CC	N	0	0	12,516	0	0	Y
154	MS Delta CC	N	0	0	0	0	0	N
155	Mt Hood CC	N	2,977	2,977	35,000	831	1,080	N
156	N Alberta Inst	Y	837	114,720	1	1	1	N
157	National Hispanic U	N	20,000	19,000	2,000	500	4	N
158	ND ST C Science	N	0	0	0	0	0	N
159	NE WI Tech C	N	30,719	0	17,197	8,871	65	N
160	NH CC-Berlin	N	0	0	10,394	0	48	Y

-1 -- Unavailable   -2 -- Not Applicable   NA - Not Answered

ACRL Library Data Tables 2005
NETWORKED RESOURCES AND SERVICES

INSTITUTIONS GRANTING ASSOCIATE OF ARTS DEGREES (Carnegie Code A)

Logins to electronic databases 13	No. of databases reported 13a	Queries (searches) in electronic databases 14	No. of databases reported 14a	No. of full-text article requests 15	No. of databases reported 15a	Virtual visits to website 16a	Virtual visits to catalog 16b	Excl. visits fr. inside library 16c	Survey Question # Institution
8,572	30	11,920	30	-1	-1	67,224	-1	N	Justice Inst BC
-1	-1	55,538	-1	-1	-1	-1	-1	N	Kaskaskia C
0	0	0	0	0	0	0	0	Y	Kent St U E Liverpool
6,273	30	14,898	30	13,715	30	0	0	Y	Kent St U Tuscarawas
29,181	84	91,191	84	0	84	14,230	3,730	N	Kilgore C
0	0	0	0	0	0	0	0	N	Kirkwood CC
3,662	4	13,228	4	7,089	4	7,000	3,500	N	Kirtland CC
36,131	9	43,738	9	24,258	9	0	0	N	Labette CC
0	0	0	8	0	0	0	0		Laboure C
7,074	40	35,764	40	0	0	0	13,303	N	Lake City CC
0	0	0	0	0	0	0	0		Lakeland CC-OH
-1	54	99,660	54	56,449	54	-2	-2		Lane CC-OR
0	0	0	0	0	0	0	0	Y	Lansdale Sch of Bus
0	8	89,586	8	64,407	8	3,524	19,475	N	Laramie Co CC
0	0	0	0	0	0	0	0		Lassen CC
0	0	0	0	0	0	0	0	N	Lexington CC
1,332	1	3,815	2	2,656	1	0	0	N	Linn ST Tech C
11,076	55	0	0	18,330	0	202,706	0	N	Lord Fairfax CC
0	0	0	0	0	0	0	0	Y	Los Angeles Valley C
107,039	16	113,524	16	52,429	16	0	0		Luzerne County CC
40,235	69	857,993	-1	-1	-1	152,402	62,781	N	Manatee CC
-1	-1	-1	-1	-1	-1	73,048	-1	N	Maple Woods CC
13,787	32	27,500	32	18,146	16	0	0	N	Marymount C CA
0	0	0	0	0	0	0	0		Massasoit CC
2,341	0	0	0	0	0	0	0	Y	McDowell Tech CC
-1	-2	624,769	53	-1	53	0	-2	N	Mesa CC
0	25	0	25	0	0	0	0	N	Middlesex Co C-NJ
0	0	0	0	0	0	12,000	4,000	N	Midland C
4,254	27	7,793	27	5,371	27	29,528	15,164	N	Miles CC
89,547	11	237,986	16	180,641	16	0	0	Y	MiraCosta C
0	0	0	0	0	0	0	0		Monroe CC
0	0	0	0	0	0	0	0		Mountain Empire CC
0	0	0	0	0	0	0	0		MS County CC
0	0	0	0	0	0	0	0	Y	MS Delta CC
33,545	33	90,300	40	50,538	33	0	179,628		Mt Hood CC
1	1	55,021	26	1	1	1	1		N Alberta Inst
6,000	12	10,000	12	0	0	0	0		National Hispanic U
0	0	0	0	0	0	0	0	Y	ND ST C Science
11,483	4	27,288	5	25,263	5	73,919	364,349	N	NE WI Tech C
6,328	25	25,686	26	8,244	26	0	0		NH CC-Berlin

-1 -- Unavailable   -2 -- Not Applicable

ACRL Library Data Tables 2005
NETWORKED ELECTRONIC RESOURCES AND SERVICES
INSTITUTIONS GRANTING ASSOCIATE OF ARTS DEGREES (Carnegie Code A)

Lib. No.	Survey Question # Institution	Reported in Canadian $ 6	EXPENDITURES				Virtual reference transactions 11	Federated searching across networked electronic resources? 12
			Electronic journals purchased 7	Electronic full-text journals 8	Electronic reference sources 9	Electronic books 10		
161	NH CC-Laconia	N	0	0	10,450	1,450	0	N
162	Nicolet Area Tech C	N	1,883	1,883	715	0	0	N
163	NM St U-Carlsbad	N	0	0	0	3,880	0	Y
164	Normandale CC	N	0	58,313	8,903	0	0	N
165	North AR C	N	0	0	12,276	0	1	N
166	Northeast ST Tech CC	N	0	0	26	6	0	Y
167	Northeastern JC	N	5,550	0	5,550	0	0	N
168	Northwest C	N	9,900	0	5,388	0	0	N
169	Nwestern Business C	N	0	0	0	0	0	N
170	Nwestern CT Tech CC	N	10,066	117	9,201	0	0	Y
171	OH ST U Ag Tech Inst	N	0	0	0	0	0	N
172	Ohlone C	N	0	0	0	0	20	N
173	Okaloosa-Walton CC	N	54,000	0	761	1,700	460	Y
174	Orange County CC	N	0	0	20,000	0	35	Y
175	Owensboro	N	0	9,092	0	550	4	N
176	Owensboro Jr C Bus	N	0	0	0	0	0	N
177	Oxnard C	N	32,000	32,000	0	0	800	Y
178	Passaic County CC	N	22,000	0	0	0	0	
179	Paul D. Camp CC	N	0	0	966	20,744	0	N
180	Pellissippi ST Tech CC	N	70,100	900	6,140	18,592	101	Y
181	Pensacola Jr C	N	0	0	33,969	11,284	2,202	Y
182	Petit Jean C	N	0	7,711	1,200	0	0	
183	Piedmont Tech C	N	0	0	0	0	0	N
184	Pittsburgh Tech Inst	N	-1	-1	21,447	-2	-2	N
185	Portland CC	N	70,656	0	0	0	0	N
186	Potomac St C-WVU	N	1,098	0	5,249	0	16	N
187	Prairie ST C	N	0	0	30,000	0	0	N
188	Prince George CC	N	127,457	0	127,457	5,200	392	N
189	Pueblo CC	N	4,344	4,344	5,828	2,000	0	N
190	Pulaski Tech C	N	-1	1,250	39,684	8,300	103	N
191	Quinebaug Vally Comm TC	NA	0	0	0	1,000	35	N
192	Quinsigamond CC	N	18,979	0	18,979	0	0	N
193	Reading Area CC	N	0	20,330	21,675	0	0	N
194	Red Deer C	Y	0	0	0	0	866	N
195	Redlands CC	N	3,920	0	0	0	20	N
196	Rend Lake C	N	6,193	3,268	14,986	0	69	N
197	Renton Tech C	N	10,000	0	6,000	600	12	N
198	Robeson CC	N	0	0	0	0	0	Y
199	Rogue CC	N	0	0	0	0	0	Y
200	Sacramento City C	N	0	0	0	2,077	0	Y

-1 -- Unavailable   -2 -- Not Applicable   NA - Not Answered

ACRL Library Data Tables 2005
NETWORKED RESOURCES AND SERVICES

INSTITUTIONS GRANTING ASSOCIATE OF ARTS DEGREES (Carnegie Code A)

Logins to electronic databases 13	No. of databases reported 13a	Queries (searches) in electronic databases 14	No. of databases reported 14a	No. of full-text article requests 15	No. of databases reported 15a	Virtual visits to website 16a	Virtual visits to catalog 16b	Excl. visits fr. inside library 16c	Survey Question # Institution
0	0	43,216	5	0	0	0	0	Y	NH CC-Laconia
5,731	1	23,177	2	16,325	2	0	0		Nicolet Area Tech C
9,623	68	9,623	68	4,719	68	0	0		NM St U-Carlsbad
0	44	126,354	44	0	44	0	893,880	N	Normandale CC
5,276	3	16,367	3	4,955	1	999	999	N	North AR C
0	0	0	0	0	0	137,724	0	N	Northeast ST Tech CC
12,000	3	9,848	3	0	0	0	0	N	Northeastern JC
0	0	36,448	13	0	0	0	0	N	Northwest C
962	1	3,274	1	1,764	1	0	0		Nwestern Business C
9,841	13	25,746	13	9,370	13	0	0	N	Nwestern CT Tech CC
0	0	0	0	0	0	0	0	N	OH ST U Ag Tech Inst
35,689	8	129,886	9	100,815	10	0	0	N	Ohlone C
68,775	42	842,091	42	24,996	42	165,961	72,190	N	Okaloosa-Walton CC
0	0	0	0	0	0	0	0		Orange County CC
26,882	4	115,416	4	33,140	4	0	0	Y	Owensboro
0	0	0	0	0	0	0	0	N	Owensboro Jr C Bus
94,600	6	94,600	6	94,600	6	130,000	100,000	N	Oxnard C
0	0	0	0	0	0	0	0	Y	Passaic County CC
4,289	60	6,211	60	0	60	0	0	Y	Paul D. Camp CC
95,739	68	347,209	70	0	0	2,079,956	27,658	N	Pellissippi ST Tech CC
28,629	71	28,629	71	0	0	213,662	0	N	Pensacola Jr C
0	0	0	0	0	0	0	0	Y	Petit Jean C
2,486	41	6,090	41	6,694	17	12,595	33,412	N	Piedmont Tech C
-1	-2	51,072	7	-1	-2	-1	-1		Pittsburgh Tech Inst
0	50	636,414	50	220,118	17	0	1,164,432	N	Portland CC
7,927	1	23,618	1	26,654	1	0	0	N	Potomac St C-WVU
0	0	0	0	0	0	0	0	N	Prairie ST C
0	0	369,579	27	0	0	0	0	N	Prince George CC
16,835	9	60,923	9	-1	0	14,438	0	N	Pueblo CC
-1	18	112,081	18	85,261	18	-1	-1		Pulaski Tech C
0	0	0	0	0	0	0	0	N	uinebaug Vally Comm TC
25,537	323	99,315	323	50,908	484	0	0	N	Quinsigamond CC
37,610	1	246,109	1	118,959	1	0	0	N	Reading Area CC
0	0	288,591	42	0	0	0	0		Red Deer C
5,268	0	30,009	0	11,607	0	0	0	N	Redlands CC
19,700	13	76,953	15	34,649	14	0	0	N	Rend Lake C
0	0	23,786	7	0	0	100,000	0	N	Renton Tech C
4,000	0	4,500	0	0	0	4,600	4,900	N	Robeson CC
0	0	0	0	0	0	0	0	N	Rogue CC
36,270	1	98,210	1	59,710	1	0	0		Sacramento City C

-1 -- Unavailable   -2 -- Not Applicable

ACRL Library Data Tables 2005
NETWORKED ELECTRONIC RESOURCES AND SERVICES
INSTITUTIONS GRANTING ASSOCIATE OF ARTS DEGREES (Carnegie Code A)

Lib. No.	Survey Question # Institution	Reported in Canadian $ 6	EXPENDITURES				Virtual reference transactions 11	Federated searching across networked electronic resources? 12
			Electronic journals purchased 7	Electronic full-text journals 8	Electronic reference sources 9	Electronic books 10		
201	San Antonio C	N	2,750	110,026	115,934	0	177	N
202	San Jacinto C South	N	0	0	0	0	-2	Y
203	San Joaquin Delta C	N	75,805	0	0	6,000	0	N
204	Santa Fe CC-NM	N	0	0	56,604	0	237	Y
205	Santa Monica C	N	0	0	0	0	0	N
206	Selkirk C	Y	21,394	0	0	0	0	N
207	Seward County CC	N	0	0	0	0	0	N
208	South AR CC	N	0	0	11,720	0	32	N
209	South Florida CC	N	0	0	0	0	18	Y
210	South Puget Sound CC	N	6,898	6,898	7,864	1,000	20	N
211	Southeast CC	N	5,990	0	500	930	0	N
212	Southwest VA CC	N	46,129	7,086	359	0	42	N
213	Spartanburg Tech C	N	0	0	0	1,390	424	
214	Spoon River C	N	20,500	20,500	3,000	0	773	Y
215	St Charles County CC	N	32,032	0	0	4,098	47	N
216	Sthrn U-Shreveport/Bossier	N	9,175	9,175	0	0	0	N
217	Tacoma CC	NA	0	0	0	0	0	
218	Tallahassee CC	N	87,145	39,498	90,213	6,551	254	Y
219	Tech C Lowcountry	N	0	0	0	0	0	
220	Temple C	N	3,749	0	9,789	2,800	35	N
221	Tri County Tech C	N	0	0	0	0	0	Y
222	Trocaire C	N	0	0	2,478	0	15	N
223	Tunxis CC Tech	N	0	0	25,196	0	130	Y
224	TX ST Tech C Waco	N	300	500	0	0	30	N
225	U Akron Wayne C	N	0	0	3,475	0	0	N
226	U HI-Kapiolani CC	N	41,147	23,300	2,727	0	106	N
227	U HI-Kauai CC	N	0	3,359	0	0	0	N
228	U HI-Windward CC	N	338	338	5,388	0	0	N
229	U NM Gallup Branch	NA	0	0	0	0	0	N
230	VA Western CC	N	78,820	12,108	613	0	60	N
231	W.Rainey Harper C	N	0	150,314	0	0	0	N
232	Walsh U	N	33,304	25,943	11,404	3,192	35	Y
233	Walters ST CC	N	961	961	61,641	2,362	68	Y
234	Waycross C	N	12,172	0	0	0	1	N
235	Weatherford C	N	0	0	26,770	1,600	212	N
236	Western IA Tech CC	N	0	0	0	0	17	Y
237	Wharton Co Jr C	N	-2	-2	14,063	2,500	40	Y
238	Whatcom CC	N	0	0	15,001	0	18	N
239	Wytheville CC	N	30,908	4,748	240	0	50	N
240	Yakima Valley CC	NA	0	0	0	0	0	

-1 -- Unavailable   -2 -- Not Applicable   NA - Not Answered

ACRL Library Data Tables 2005
NETWORKED RESOURCES AND SERVICES

INSTITUTIONS GRANTING ASSOCIATE OF ARTS DEGREES (Carnegie Code A)

Logins to electronic databases 13	No. of databases reported 13a	Queries (searches) in electronic databases 14	No. of databases reported 14a	No. of full-text article requests 15	No. of databases reported 15a	Virtual visits to website 16a	Virtual visits to catalog 16b	Excl. visits fr. inside library 16c	Survey Question # Institution
171,523	135	0	0	0	0	0	0		San Antonio C
-2	1	-2	1	-2	1	-2	1	N	San Jacinto C South
0	19	203,291	18	0	0	0	0	N	San Joaquin Delta C
41,400	77	629,162	77	0	77	387,696	121,890	N	Santa Fe CC-NM
0	0	0	0	0	0	0	0		Santa Monica C
11,857	4	0	0	26,157	4	0	0		Selkirk C
0	0	0	0	0	0	0	0	N	Seward County CC
22,932	9	50,652	9	16,212	7	0	19,501	Y	South AR CC
0	0	0	0	0	0	0	0		South Florida CC
0	0	0	0	0	0	129,168	0	N	South Puget Sound CC
16,133	7	92,756	7	0	0	0	0	N	Southeast CC
17,125	55	109,483	1,187	6,308	1,187	18,050	14,065	N	Southwest VA CC
0	0	0	0	0	0	1,110,575	0	N	Spartanburg Tech C
4,502	6	772	4	500	0	3,000	500	Y	Spoon River C
33,159	22	150,184	24	87,381	23	188,607	620	N	St Charles County CC
1,818	29	3,941	29	0	0	0	0		thrn U-Shreveport/Bossier
0	0	0	0	0	0	0	0		Tacoma CC
59,033	93	0	0	0	0	199,157	125,289	Y	Tallahassee CC
0	0	0	0	0	0	0	0		Tech C Lowcountry
22,804	28	72,312	28	46,677	28	0	0	N	Temple C
0	0	0	0	0	0	0	0	Y	Tri County Tech C
3,654	2	48,035	2	8,336	2	20,769	0	N	Trocaire C
29,130	32	94,121	37	49,419	31	217,008	0	N	Tunxis CC Tech
9,001	4	20,002	4	18,000	4	40,000	12,000	N	TX ST Tech C Waco
0	0	0	0	0	0	0	0	Y	U Akron Wayne C
28,080	361	125,858	51	60,168	50	144,956	21,320	N	U HI-Kapiolani CC
3,961	0	11,718	0	0	0	0	0		U HI-Kauai CC
5,720	2	24,834	3	10,716	3	0	0		U HI-Windward CC
0	0	0	0	0	0	92,000	0	N	U NM Gallup Branch
21,126	55	135,059	55	34,009	55	0	0	N	VA Western CC
147,241	13	468,492	14	0	0	306,754	0	N	W.Rainey Harper C
11,741	41	75,904	56	43,615	51	0	0		Walsh U
44,024	51	0	0	0	0	0	0	Y	Walters ST CC
2,698	2	11,787	2	6,793	2	93,443	871	Y	Waycross C
37,640	20	0	0	18	9	42,952	0	N	Weatherford C
11,460	6	44,091	6	21,363	6	0	0	Y	Western IA Tech CC
72,480	31	50,970	31	7,591	31	18,096	12,165	N	Wharton Co Jr C
0	0	133,705	5	0	0	25,600	0	Y	Whatcom CC
10,784	55	68,944	55	7,053	55	0	0		Wytheville CC
0	0	0	0	0	0	0	0		Yakima Valley CC

-1 -- Unavailable   -2 -- Not Applicable

ACRL Library Data Tables 2005

NETWORKED ELECTRONIC RESOURCES AND SERVICES

INSTITUTIONS GRANTING ASSOCIATE OF ARTS DEGREES (Carnegie Code A)

| Lib. No. | Survey Question # Institution | Reported in Canadian $ 6 | EXPENDITURES | | | | Virtual reference transactions 11 | Federated searching across networked electronic resources? 12 |
			Electronic journals purchased 7	Electronic full-text journals 8	Electronic reference sources 9	Electronic books 10		
241	Yavapai C	N	39,055	0	0	0	0	N

-1 -- Unavailable   -2 -- Not Applicable   NA - Not Answered

ACRL Library Data Tables 2005
NETWORKED RESOURCES AND SERVICES

INSTITUTIONS GRANTING ASSOCIATE OF ARTS DEGREES (Carnegie Code A)

Logins to electronic databases 13	No. of databases reported 13a	Queries (searches) in electronic databases 14	No. of databases reported 14a	No. of full-text article requests 15	No. of databases reported 15a	Virtual visits to website 16a	Virtual visits to catalog 16b	Excl. visits fr. inside library 16c	Survey Question # Institution
31,170	34	218,676	34	0	34	0	0	N	Yavapai C

-1 -- Unavailable   -2 -- Not Applicable

ACRL Library Data Tables 2005
DIGITIZATION ACTIVITIES

INSTITUTIONS GRANTING ASSOCIATE OF ARTS DEGREES (Carnegie Code A)

Lib. No.	Institution	DIGITAL COLLECTIONS			USAGE		DIRECT COSTS		
		No. of collections	Size (MB)	Items	No. of times accessed	No. of queries	Personnel	Equipment, software, or contract services	Volumes Held Collectively
	Survey Question #	17a	17b	17c	18a	18b	19a	19b	20
1	A Baldwin Agrl C	0	0	0	0	0	0	0	0
2	Adirondack CC	0	0	0	0	0	0	0	0
3	Alpena CC	0	0	0	0	0	0	0	0 [1]
4	Alvin CC	2	2	2	2	2	2	2	2
5	Am River C	0	0	0	0	0	0	0	0 [1]
6	Am Samoa CC	0	0	0	0	0	0	0	0
7	Andover C	0	0	0	0	0	0	0	0
8	Anne Arundel CC	0	0	0	0	0	0	0	0 [1]
9	Anoka-Ramsey CC	-1	-2	-2	-1	-1	-1	-1	-1
10	AR ST U Beebe	0	0	0	0	0	0	0	0
11	Athens Tech C	0	0	0	0	0	0	0	0
12	AZ Western C	0	0	0	0	0	0	0	0
13	Bellingham Tech C	0	0	0	0	0	0	0	0
14	Belmont Tech C	0	0	0	0	0	0	0	0
15	Bergen CC	-1	-1	-1	-1	-1	-1	-1	-1
16	Black Hawk C	0	0	0	0	0	0	0	0
17	Blackhawk Tech C	0	0	0	0	0	0	0	0
18	Blue Mountain CC	0	0	0	0	0	0	0	0
19	Blue Ridge CC	0	0	0	0	0	0	0	0
20	Brazosport C	0	0	0	0	0	0	0	0
21	Bunker Hill CC	5	2,000	0	943	0	0	27,614	0 [1]
22	Butler County CC	0	0	0	0	0	0	0	0 [1]
23	C Canyons	0	0	0	0	0	0	0	0
24	C Edouard Montpetit	0	0	0	0	0	0	0	0
25	C Lake Co	0	0	0	0	0	0	0	0
26	C Merici	0	0	0	0	0	0	0	0
27	C New Caledonia	0	0	0	0	0	0	0	0
28	C Redwoods	0	0	0	0	0	0	0	0
29	C St Jean Richelieu	0	0	0	0	0	0	0	0
30	Camden County C	0	0	0	0	0	0	0	0 [1]
31	Cape Fear CC	0	0	0	0	0	0	0	0
32	Capital CC	0	0	0	0	0	0	0	0
33	Carl Sandburg C	0	0	0	0	0	0	0	200
34	Carroll Tech Inst	0	0	0	0	0	0	0	0
35	Carteret CC	0	0	0	0	0	-2	-2	0
36	Cedar Valley	0	0	0	0	0	0	0	0 [1]
37	CEGEP Beauce-Appalaches	-2	-2	-2	-2	-2	-2	-2	-2
38	CEGEP Trois-Rivieres	0	0	0	0	0	0	0	0
39	Central Alabama CC	0	0	0	0	0	0	0	0
40	Central Carolina Tech C	0	0	0	0	0	0	0	0

-1 -- Unavailable   -2 -- Not Applicable

92

ACRL Library Data Tables 2005
DIGITIZATION ACTIVITIES

INSTITUTIONS GRANTING ASSOCIATE OF ARTS DEGREES (Carnegie Code A)

		DIGITAL COLLECTIONS			USAGE		DIRECT COSTS		
		No. of collections	Size (MB)	Items	No. of times accessed	No. of queries	Personnel	Equipment, software, or contract services	Volumes Held Collectively
Lib. No.	Survey Question # Institution	17a	17b	17c	18a	18b	19a	19b	20
41	Central ME Tech C	0	0	0	0	0	0	0	0
42	Central Piedmont CC	0	0	0	0	0	0	0	0 [1]
43	Central TX C	0	0	0	0	0	0	0	0
44	Centralia C	0	0	0	0	0	0	0	0
45	Chabot C	0	0	0	0	0	0	0	0
46	Chattahoochee Tech	0	2	2	2	2	2	2	2
47	Chippewa V Tech C	0	0	0	0	0	0	0	0
48	Clackamas CC	0	0	0	0	0	0	0	0
49	Clark C-WA	0	0	0	0	0	0	0	0
50	Clinton CC	0	0	0	0	0	0	0	0 [1]
51	Cloud Co CC	0	0	0	0	0	0	0	0
52	Coastal GA CC	0	0	0	0	0	0	0	0
53	Colby CC	0	0	0	0	0	0	0	0
54	Columbia Junior C	0	0	0	0	0	0	0	0
55	Columbia ST CC	0	0	0	0	0	0	0	0
56	Columbus ST CC	0	0	0	0	0	0	0	0
57	Compton CC	0	0	0	0	0	0	0	0
58	Connors ST C	0	0	0	0	0	0	0	0
59	Corning CC	0	0	0	0	0	0	0	0
60	Cosumnes River C	0	0	0	0	0	0	0	0
61	Crowder C	0	0	0	0	0	0	0	0
62	Cuesta C	0	0	0	0	0	0	0	0
63	Cumberland Co C	0	0	0	0	0	0	0	0 [1]
64	CUNY Borough Manhattan C	0	0	0	0	0	0	0	0
65	CUNY Bronx CC	0	0	0	0	0	0	0	0
66	CUNY Hostos CC	0	0	0	0	0	0	0	0
67	CUNY LaGuardia CC	0	0	0	0	0	0	0	0
68	CUNY Queensborough CC	1	771	481	0	0	7,000	15,000	0
69	D.S. Lancaster CC	0	0	0	0	0	0	0	0
70	Darton C	0	0	0	0	0	0	0	0
71	Dawson CC	0	0	0	0	0	0	0	0
72	Del Mar C	0	0	0	0	0	0	0	0 [1]
73	Delaware Co CC	0	-2	-2	-2	-2	-2	-2	-2
74	Diablo Valley C	0	0	0	0	0	0	0	0 [1]
75	Dodge City CC	0	0	0	0	0	0	0	0 [1]
76	Dyersburg ST CC	-2	-2	-2	-2	-2	-2	-2	-2
77	East Central C	0	0	0	0	0	0	0	0
78	East Georgia C	0	0	0	0	0	0	0	0
79	East Los Angeles C	0	0	0	0	0	0	0	0
80	El Paso CC	0	0	0	0	0	0	0	0

-1 -- Unavailable   -2 -- Not Applicable

ACRL Library Data Tables 2005
DIGITIZATION ACTIVITIES

INSTITUTIONS GRANTING ASSOCIATE OF ARTS DEGREES (Carnegie Code A)

		DIGITAL COLLECTIONS			USAGE		DIRECT COSTS		
		No. of collections	Size (MB)	Items	No. of times accessed	No. of queries	Personnel	Equipment, software, or contract services	Volumes Held Collectively
Lib. No.	Survey Question # Institution	17a	17b	17c	18a	18b	19a	19b	20
81	Estrn Arizona C	0	0	0	0	0	0	0	0 [1]
82	Estrn Idaho Tech C	1	0	500	0	0	0	0	0
83	Estrn Maine Tech C	0	0	0	0	0	0	0	0
84	Fayetteville Tech CC	0	0	0	0	0	0	0	0
85	Fergus Falls CC	0	0	0	0	0	0	0	0
86	Flor Dar Tech C	0	0	0	0	0	0	0	0
87	Floyd C	0	0	0	0	0	0	0	0 [1]
88	Gadsden ST CC	0	0	0	0	0	0	0	0
89	Gainesville C	1	31	60	1,997	0	6,000	5,000	0
90	Gavilan C	0	0	0	0	0	0	0	0
91	GC Wallace CC	0	0	0	0	0	0	0	0 [1]
92	Glendale CC	0	0	0	0	0	0	0	0
93	Gogebic CC	0	0	0	0	0	0	0	0 [1]
94	Gordon C-GA	0	0	0	0	0	0	0	0
95	Grand Rapids CC	0	0	0	0	0	0	0	0
96	Harrisburg Area CC	0	0	0	0	0	0	0	0
97	Hawaii Pacific U	0	0	0	0	0	0	0	0
98	Hawkeye CC	0	0	0	0	0	0	0	0 [1]
99	Highland CC KS	0	0	0	0	0	0	0	0
100	Hillsborough CC	0	0	0	0	0	0	0	0
101	Hinds CC	11	808	186	0	0	0	0	0
102	Hiwassee C	0	0	0	0	0	0	0	0 [1]
103	Hocking Tech C	0	0	0	0	0	0	0	0
104	Hopkinsville CC	0	0	0	0	0	0	0	0
105	Horry GTown Tech	0	0	0	0	0	0	0	0 [1]
106	Howard C	0	0	0	0	0	0	0	0
107	Hutch CC&Voc Sch	0	0	0	0	0	0	0	0 [1]
108	IL E CC Wabash Cntrl C	0	0	0	0	0	0	0	0
109	IL Estrn CC-Frontier	0	0	0	0	0	0	0	0 [1]
110	IL Estrn CC-Lincoln Trail	0	0	0	0	0	0	0	0
111	IL Valley CC	0	0	0	0	0	0	0	0
112	Independence CC	0	0	0	0	0	0	0	0
113	Inst Com PR Jr C Arecibo	0	0	0	0	0	0	0	0
114	Inst Native Culture	0	0	0	0	0	0	0	0
115	Isothermal CC	0	0	0	0	0	0	0	0
116	J.F. Drake ST Tech C	0	0	0	0	0	0	0	0
117	Jacksonville C	0	0	0	0	0	0	0	0
118	Jefferson CC-NY	0	0	0	0	0	0	0	0
119	Jefferson C-MO	0	0	0	0	0	0	0	0
120	JS Reynolds CC	0	0	0	0	0	0	0	0

-1 -- Unavailable   -2 -- Not Applicable

ACRL Library Data Tables 2005
DIGITIZATION ACTIVITIES

INSTITUTIONS GRANTING ASSOCIATE OF ARTS DEGREES (Carnegie Code A)

		DIGITAL COLLECTIONS			USAGE		DIRECT COSTS		
		No. of collections	Size (MB)	Items	No. of times accessed	No. of queries	Personnel	Equipment, software, or contract services	Volumes Held Collectively
Lib. No.	Survey Question # Institution	17a	17b	17c	18a	18b	19a	19b	20
121	Justice Inst BC	-2	-2	-2	-2	-2	-2	-2	-2
122	Kaskaskia C	-1	-1	-1	-1	-1	-1	-1	-1
123	Kent St U E Liverpool	0	0	0	0	0	0	0	0 [1]
124	Kent St U Tuscarawas	0	0	0	0	0	0	0	0
125	Kilgore C	0	0	0	0	0	0	0	0
126	Kirkwood CC	0	0	0	0	0	0	0	0 [1]
127	Kirtland CC	0	0	0	0	0	0	0	0 [1]
128	Labette CC	0	0	0	0	0	0	0	0
129	Laboure C	0	0	0	0	0	0	0	0 [1]
130	Lake City CC	0	0	0	0	0	0	0	0 [1]
131	Lakeland CC-OH	0	0	0	0	0	0	0	0
132	Lane CC-OR	-2	-2	-2	-2	-2	-2	-2	-2
133	Lansdale Sch of Bus	0	0	0	0	0	0	0	0 [1]
134	Laramie Co CC	0	0	0	0	0	0	0	0
135	Lassen CC	0	0	0	0	0	0	0	0
136	Lexington CC	0	0	0	0	0	0	0	0 [1]
137	Linn ST Tech C	0	0	0	0	0	0	0	0
138	Lord Fairfax CC	0	0	0	0	0	0	0	0
139	Los Angeles Valley C	0	0	0	0	0	0	0	0
140	Luzerne County CC	0	0	0	0	0	0	0	0 [1]
141	Manatee CC	0	-2	-2	-2	-2	-2	-2	-2
142	Maple Woods CC	-2	-2	-2	-2	-2	-2	-2	-2
143	Marymount C CA	0	0	0	0	0	0	0	0
144	Massasoit CC	0	0	0	0	0	0	0	0
145	McDowell Tech CC	0	0	0	0	0	0	0	0 [1]
146	Mesa CC	-2	-2	-2	-2	-2	-2	-2	-2
147	Middlesex Co C-NJ	0	0	0	0	0	0	0	0
148	Midland C	0	0	0	0	0	0	0	0
149	Miles CC	0	0	0	0	0	0	0	0 [1]
150	MiraCosta C	0	0	0	0	0	0	0	0
151	Monroe CC	0	0	0	0	0	0	0	0
152	Mountain Empire CC	0	0	0	0	0	0	0	0
153	MS County CC	0	0	0	0	0	0	0	0
154	MS Delta CC	0	0	0	0	0	0	0	0
155	Mt Hood CC	0	0	0	0	0	0	0	0
156	N Alberta Inst	0	0	0	0	0	0	0	0
157	National Hispanic U	0	0	0	0	0	0	0	0 [1]
158	ND ST C Science	0	0	0	0	0	0	0	0
159	NE WI Tech C	0	0	0	0	0	0	0	0
160	NH CC-Berlin	0	0	0	0	0	0	0	0 [1]

-1 -- Unavailable   -2 -- Not Applicable

ACRL Library Data Tables 2005
DIGITIZATION ACTIVITIES

INSTITUTIONS GRANTING ASSOCIATE OF ARTS DEGREES (Carnegie Code A)

Lib. No.	Survey Question # / Institution	DIGITAL COLLECTIONS No. of collections 17a	Size (MB) 17b	Items 17c	USAGE No. of times accessed 18a	No. of queries 18b	DIRECT COSTS Personnel 19a	Equipment, software, or contract services 19b	Volumes Held Collectively 20
161	NH CC-Laconia	0	0	0	0	0	0	0	0
162	Nicolet Area Tech C	0	0	0	0	0	0	0	0 [1]
163	NM St U-Carlsbad	0	0	0	0	0	0	0	0
164	Normandale CC	0	0	0	0	0	0	0	0 [1]
165	North AR C	0	0	0	0	0	0	0	0
166	Northeast ST Tech CC	0	0	0	0	0	0	0	0
167	Northeastern JC	0	0	0	0	0	0	0	0 [1]
168	Northwest C	1	0	222	0	0	0	0	0
169	Nwestern Business C	0	0	0	0	0	0	0	0
170	Nwestern CT Tech CC	0	0	0	0	0	0	0	0
171	OH ST U Ag Tech Inst	0	0	0	0	0	0	0	0
172	Ohlone C	0	0	0	0	0	0	0	0
173	Okaloosa-Walton CC	0	0	0	0	0	0	0	0
174	Orange County CC	0	0	0	0	0	0	0	0
175	Owensboro	0	0	0	0	0	0	0	0
176	Owensboro Jr C Bus	0	0	0	0	0	0	0	0
177	Oxnard C	0	0	0	0	0	0	0	0 [1]
178	Passaic County CC	0	0	0	0	0	0	0	0
179	Paul D. Camp CC	0	0	0	0	0	0	0	0
180	Pellissippi ST Tech CC	0	0	0	0	0	0	0	0
181	Pensacola Jr C	0	0	0	0	0	0	0	0
182	Petit Jean C	0	0	0	0	0	0	0	0
183	Piedmont Tech C	0	0	0	0	0	0	0	0
184	Pittsburgh Tech Inst	-2	-2	-2	-2	-2	-2	-2	-2
185	Portland CC	0	0	0	0	0	0	0	0
186	Potomac St C-WVU	0	0	0	0	0	0	0	0
187	Prairie ST C	0	0	0	0	0	0	0	0
188	Prince George CC	0	0	0	0	0	0	0	0
189	Pueblo CC	0	0	0	0	0	0	0	0 [1]
190	Pulaski Tech C	0	-2	-2	-2	-2	-2	-2	-2
191	Quinebaug Vally Comm TC	0	0	0	0	0	0	0	0
192	Quinsigamond CC	0	0	0	0	0	0	0	0 [1]
193	Reading Area CC	0	0	0	0	0	0	0	0
194	Red Deer C	0	0	0	0	0	0	0	0
195	Redlands CC	0	0	0	0	0	0	0	0
196	Rend Lake C	0	0	0	0	0	0	0	0
197	Renton Tech C	0	0	0	0	0	0	0	0
198	Robeson CC	0	0	0	0	0	0	0	0
199	Rogue CC	0	0	0	0	0	0	0	0
200	Sacramento City C	0	0	0	0	0	0	0	0 [1]

-1 -- Unavailable   -2 -- Not Applicable

ACRL Library Data Tables 2005
DIGITIZATION ACTIVITIES

INSTITUTIONS GRANTING ASSOCIATE OF ARTS DEGREES (Carnegie Code A)

Lib. No.	Survey Question # Institution	DIGITAL COLLECTIONS			USAGE		DIRECT COSTS		
		No. of collections 17a	Size (MB) 17b	Items 17c	No. of times accessed 18a	No. of queries 18b	Personnel 19a	Equipment, software, or contract services 19b	Volumes Held Collectively 20
201	San Antonio C	0	0	0	0	0	0	0	0
202	San Jacinto C South	0	-2	-2	-2	-2	-2	-2	-2
203	San Joaquin Delta C	0	0	0	0	0	0	0	0
204	Santa Fe CC-NM	0	0	0	0	0	0	0	0
205	Santa Monica C	0	0	0	0	0	0	0	0
206	Selkirk C	0	0	0	0	0	0	0	0 [1]
207	Seward County CC	0	0	0	0	0	0	0	0
208	South AR CC	0	0	0	0	0	0	0	0
209	South Florida CC	0	0	0	0	0	0	0	0
210	South Puget Sound CC	35	0	35,000	0	0	0	0	0
211	Southeast CC	0	0	0	0	0	0	0	0 [1]
212	Southwest VA CC	0	0	0	0	0	0	0	0
213	Spartanburg Tech C	0	0	0	0	0	0	0	0
214	Spoon River C	0	0	0	0	0	0	0	0
215	St Charles County CC	0	0	0	0	0	0	0	0
216	Sthrn U-Shreveport/Bossier	0	0	0	0	0	0	0	0
217	Tacoma CC	0	0	0	0	0	0	0	0
218	Tallahassee CC	0	0	0	0	0	0	0	0
219	Tech C Lowcountry	0	0	0	0	0	0	0	0 [1]
220	Temple C	0	0	0	0	0	0	0	0
221	Tri County Tech C	0	0	0	0	0	0	0	0
222	Trocaire C	0	0	0	0	0	0	0	0 [1]
223	Tunxis CC Tech	0	0	0	0	0	0	0	0
224	TX ST Tech C Waco	0	0	0	0	0	0	0	0
225	U Akron Wayne C	0	0	0	0	0	0	0	0
226	U HI-Kapiolani CC	8	424	3,679	0	0	0	0	0
227	U HI-Kauai CC	0	0	0	0	0	0	0	0
228	U HI-Windward CC	0	0	0	0	0	0	0	0
229	U NM Gallup Branch	0	0	0	0	0	0	0	0 [1]
230	VA Western CC	0	0	0	0	0	0	0	0
231	W.Rainey Harper C	0	0	0	0	0	0	0	0 [1]
232	Walsh U	0	0	0	0	0	0	0	0
233	Walters ST CC	0	0	0	0	0	0	0	0
234	Waycross C	0	0	0	0	0	0	0	0 [1]
235	Weatherford C	0	0	0	0	0	0	0	0
236	Western IA Tech CC	0	0	0	0	0	0	0	0
237	Wharton Co Jr C	-2	-2	-2	-2	-2	-2	-2	-2
238	Whatcom CC	0	0	0	0	0	0	0	0
239	Wytheville CC	0	0	0	0	0	0	0	0
240	Yakima Valley CC	0	0	0	0	0	0	0	0

-1 -- Unavailable   -2 -- Not Applicable

INSTITUTIONS GRANTING ASSOCIATE OF ARTS DEGREES (Carnegie Code A)

		DIGITAL COLLECTIONS			USAGE		DIRECT COSTS		
		No. of collections	Size (MB)	Items	No. of times accessed	No. of queries	Personnel	Equipment, software, or contract services	Volumes Held Collectively
Lib. No.	Survey Question # Institution	17a	17b	17c	18a	18b	19a	19b	20
241	Yavapai C	0	0	0	0	0	0	0	0 [1]

-1 -- Unavailable   -2 -- Not Applicable

2005
FOOTNOTES TO THE ACRL STATISTICS

Footnotes are listed for any institution included in this volume that provided a text footnote to one or more questions in the survey. The notes are arranged alphabetically by the abbreviated institution name and then ordered by question number. For a listing of abbreviated names and full institution names, including schools not listed in this volume, see the "Key to Participating Institutions" that follows this section.

Stray clicks on the footnote indicator button during the survey may have left a few footnote indicators in the data where no actual note exists. The footnotes have been formatted and some were edited for publication.

Institution	Q. No	Note
Alpena CC	17a	Included in Item 17b,FY budget not separated
	17b	Includes Professional and Staff
	17c	Line item fund only and does not include federal work study students
	19	Includes other (12890)plus fringes (78904)
	21	e-books
	22	On line databases and services
	25	300 OCLC fee and one out of state at 6.68
	26a	Associate Dean
	26b	2 library tech's, 1 AV tech. & a part-time 10hrs a wk Lib.Tech
	26c	Est. AV and Lib Work Study students (each working 6.5 hrs a week)
	27	Circulation Desk
	31	128 per wk (2 samplings,1 in fall & 1 in Spring),X 4 weeks,X 9 months
	32	Books only, does not include on line data base usage, book renewals or reserve usage
	34	Primarily books
	35	On line data base has reduced our ILL of Periiodicals dramatically
	36	NA
	37	NA
	38	Actual full time instructional faculty not FTE instructional faculty
	46a	-2
	46b	-2
Am River C	1a	Total adjusted to agree with 2005 figures.
	6	We do not count the physical units. We have 166 titles on microforms.
	20_supp	Question 4 figure includes two ebook databases. Figures in Questions 13,14,15 include access through proxy server for several libraries. Figures for American River College cannot be extracted. Resources in 13a, 14a, 15a are full-text journal and pe
Andover C	2	estimate
	15d	bibliographic utility ($92)& delivery service ($416)
	46b	Andover College - Lewiston campus
Anne Arundel CC	4	This is an estimate.
	4a	This is an estimate.
	4b	Do not track this.
	6	This is an estimate.
	7	Government documents are counted with the appropriate format.
	17c	Student worker salaries are charged to the Financial Aid Office budget and this information is not available.
	21	This is an estimate.
	24	Computer hardware and software appear in the Information Services budget.
	25	Do not track these charges.
	26c	This is an average of the number of student worker FTE positions over the year.
	28	The library is open shorter hours when classes are not in session.
	32	This number includes reserves circulation. We do not track reserves circulation separately from other circulatin.
	20_supp	We do not track number of sessions and number of searches in electronic resources. We do not count visits to the library's web site or catalog.
Anoka-Ramsey CC	15d	1037 = Supplies 200 = Membership 4144 = Electronic expenditures below
AR ST U Beebe	23a	OCLC
	23b	Net Lib. Shared Resource
	25	We don't charge.
	46b	ASU-Searcy, ASU-Heber Springs
Athens Tech C		Not able to obtain volumes purchased. Used volumes added instead.
	47	All stats apply to both the main and Elbert County campuses. The enrollment on the Elbert County campus is less than 200, so the library is very small, and their stats are small also, so are included in main campus stats. Not counted are 11,847 NetLi
AZ Western C	7	formula used for estimating government documents in question #7

Institution	Q. No	Note
AZ Western C	23b	figure not available
Bellingham Tech C	15a	Includes all formats such as a/v
	17c	not available
	21	included in 15a
	26c	not available
	39	All full-time students whether degree seeking or not
	40	All part-time students whether degree seeking or not
Bergen CC	21	NetLibrary E-books
Black Hawk C	46b	Kewanee II campus
Blackhawk Tech C	4b	estimated
	15a	includes audio, cannot separate from books in records
	19	travel
	32	cannot separate renewal from initial
	46a	Monroe CTS (Center for Transportation Studies) Airport
Blue Mountain CC	4b	deposits
	15d	archives/electronic subscriptions
	17c	1125hrs. x $7.90
	20	does not include benefits
	22	reported in 15d
	23a	OCLC
	23b	Sage/ORBIS
	25	courier fees
	31	no reference staff, no longer keep track
	39	lower division collegiate & professional technical
Bunker Hill CC	9	Processed only
	15d	Includes operating expenditures and expeses for digital preservation
	23a	Not including Inter-Library Loan
	20_supp	Line 1 - An appoximation from November 2004 Line 13 - Not all services collect these statistics Line 15 - Not all services collect these statistics Line 16b - Not collected by our library consortium
Butler County CC	19	includes software, $500 within 24 below
	23b	Unknown. State Library of Kansas and Kan-ed pay for.
	25	Institution covers postage costs, State covers access costs
	26b	Includes staff we pay for at joint-use facility.
	32	Unknown
	46a	Andover and Rose Hill are included. They are shared, joint-use High School/college libraries in contractual relationship.
	48	* I did not include electronic resources within my 'total library expenditures' as indicated above, just in questions 21-25. Add them in if you will, I certainly consider it part of my costs! * Phone was not answered 3.23.06 when I tried to find out
	20_supp	I thought I could enter N/A, but the survey is not letting me! #11. Shared with State of Kansas. We put in 2 hrs per week on total. No record of how many we alone have answered, or how many our students have asked. #13. I have only recorded # of
C Canyons	22	Under Other Operating Expenditures
	46a	-2
	46b	-2
	47	-2
	48	-2
C Lake Co	6	We don't keep this stat.
	7	We don't keep a record of these types of items.
	16	We do not bind.
	21	Computer software is purchased by another department within the college. Computer software within the collection for circulation is not broken out of the AV budget.
	22	This is an estimate since we don't break this number from our regular serials budget.

Institution	Q. No	Note
C Lake Co	31	We don't keep this figure.
	39	This is our fte. I don't have any other number available.
	40	This is our total headcount.
C Redwoods	17a	Includes support staff and two branch campuses
	26b	Includes Learning Assistance/Tutorial Services
	46a	Del Norte Campus Mendocino Campus
Camden County C	1	includes 7290 bound periodical volumes, physically counted
	2	I tried to enter NA/UA, but it would not accept this.
	4a	includes print, m-film, ScienceDirect, individual e-jrnls.
	23b	Once again, the survey would not accept NA/UA. I do not know the monetary value of the resources that are underwritten by the NJ State Library.
	46b	Rohrer Center, Cherry Hill
	20_supp	The figures for questions 13-16 are clearly not 0, but not available; the survey would not accept NA.
Cape Fear CC	46a	North Campus
Carl Sandburg C	46a	Carthage Branch Campus of Carl Sandburg College
Carroll Tech Inst	46a	Douglas County Campus Carroll County Campus
Carteret CC	38	Last year I mistakenly reported 155, which was the number of full-time employees, instead of instructional faculty.
Cedar Valley	20_supp	Electronic reference sources are shared resources amoung DCCCD Libraries with the cost sharing charge-back amount included in the materials expeditures. Electronic books are a part of netLibrary. Number of logins to networked electronic resources are co
CEGEP Beauce-Appalaches	46a	-2
	46b	-2
Central Carolina Tech C	17	This does not include student assistants
	25	Data not available
	39	I do not have a breakdown of full time and part time
Central Piedmont CC	39	Numbers are kept as FTE for the NCCCS (North Carolina Community College System)
	41	2year institution
	42	2year institution
	20_supp	Plans to move toward federated searching but budget constraints have blocked current efforts.
Central TX C	17	Budget report does not divide total salaries into categories
	32	we do not count initial circulations and renewals separately
	36	We are a community college - we don't award Ph.Ds
	37	We are a community college - we don't award Ph.Ds
	39	information not available
	41	We are a community college - we have no graduate students
	42	We have no graduate students
	40	information not available
Centralia C	1a	General circulating nf, fiction, reference, ebook, paperback, archive, cd-non music
	1bi	Approximate, we do not count volumes added, but do run a bibliographic record by create date report.
	4a	107 paper from Ebsco 5 paper direct from pub 6 mf
	9	Items, not linear foot
	12	Books on tape and CD, Music CDs
	13	VHS + DVD
	15	Reflects $10,000 cut that was paid for out of dropped microfilm.
	15a	Includes all items in paper format: general circulating collection & reference
	15b	Includes only paper periodicals budgeted amount. Actual expenditure $9,739.
	15c	Includes microfilm and all media
	15d	$600 memberships $100 purchased services $13,500 electronic databases
	17	Amount does not include $4649 substitute budget that may be used for either support or professional staff.
	17c	$12,657 from library budget $634 from sub budget $9746 from federal workstudy budget

Institution	Q. No	Note
Centralia C	19	$4649 substitutes $4500 supplies $3100 copier/machine maint $200 printing $170 insurance $4500 OCLC $1000 travel $7970 ILS (Endeavor) $13800 equipment
	23a	$4500 OCLC $7970 ORCA Consortium for Endeavor
	23b	50% WSL subsidy of statewide Proquest contract
	24	Computer maintenance annual $3750. Total equipment budget $13,800 -- cannot separate out just computers and software.
	26a	1 FT Associate Dean 1 FT Librarian 1 60% Librarian 1 50% Librarian
	26b	1 FT Parapro 4 1 80% Parapro 4
Chattahoochee Tech	13	Includes audio count
	46a	Paulding, Mountain View, South Cobb
Chippewa V Tech C	1b	This is a negative number.
	23b	BadgerLink state project--funded by state of Wisconsin
	32	This number does not exclude reserves and renewals
Clinton CC	33	Do not have stats on renewals.
	20_supp	Do not have stats on traffic to our library web site and have not compiled stats on visits by our users to databases.
Cloud Co CC	15c	audiovisual, $1699; consortial subscriptions, $5320
	15d	consortial staff salary, $93; memberships for publications, $145
	17c	This is completely paid by institutional Work/Study program funds.
	32	Our automated system does not count renewals separately.
	46b	Geary County Campus, Junction City, KS
Coastal GA CC	6	Number based on a physical count completed in September, 2005
	28	Hours are combined for 2 locations - 71 hours per week in Brunswick; 51 hours per week in Kingsland
	46a	Camden Center - Kingsland, GA
Columbia ST CC	46a	Williamson, Lawrenceburg, Clifton, Lewisburg
Compton CC	15d	Online databases = $39,787 Annual automation maint. = $9,272 - Supplies = $2974 - Equipment = $9,923 - Security = $1,850
	33	figure unknown
Corning CC	17c	Estimated from College-wide budget.
Cosumnes River C	1a	Figure represents classified print volumes + unclassified bound periodical volumes.
	1bi	Print volumes, e-books added, and bound periodical vols.
	19	Supplies
	22	Includes all electronic serials/database services, including Choicereviews and Ingram's IPage.
	23a	Deposits to OCLC were made in the year preceding and following this fiscal year.
	27	Reference Desk and Circulation Desk
	28	M-TH 0730-2100; F0730-1630; SA 1000-1600
	29	Our for credit Library course is all online
	38	Per Instruction Office 3/3/06
	39	Per Research Office 3/3/06
	46a	None
	48	In completing Information Services and Use: Metrics, for 2. Number of electronic 'full-text' journals purchased, we reported 1 for Choicereviews.org subscription. In 9. Expenditures for electronic reference sources, we entered expenditures, rather than
Cuesta C	15c	Audiovisual inluded in 15a
	46a	San Luis Obispo Campus and Paso Robles North County Campus
Cumberland Co C	20_supp	16b. We belong to a consortium for our library automation system; and the individual Library metrics on virtual access to the catalog are not available. When I responded 'UA', I received the message about needing to use a number. The number 200 is a r
CUNY LaGuardia CC	4a	Increase in e-journals collection
	4b	Includes gov docs, database subscriptions and gifts
	29	Number of total hours of instruction, including credit classes
D.S. Lancaster CC	26	total FTE is 4.22

Institution	Q. No	Note
D.S. Lancaster CC	26b	actual FTE is 2.75
	26c	actual FTE is .47
	33	automated circulation system does not distinguish initial circs from renewals
Darton C	47	Final expenditures not available due to last years institutional reporting system. ACRLI Supplemental: Q 4 (includes GALILEO sources and CQ Researcher);Q8 expenditures included in Q7; 14a (includes CQ Researcher, International Humanities Index and 5 Proq
Del Mar C	25	This is minimal and charged as a supply item in our budget.
	33	Library does not separate out types of circulations.
	46a	Technical Branch
	20_supp	Library does not count visits to library catalog or measure number of successful full-text article requests.
Diablo Valley C	46a	San Ramon Valley Campus
	20_supp	14a: ARTStor; Business & Company Resource Center (Gale); College Source; Congressional Digest Pro and Con Full Service; Country Watch; CQ Researcher; Encyclopedia Britannica; ERIC: Education Resources Information Center; Ethnic NewsWatch; Health Referenc
Dodge City CC	7	We did a massive weeding during this year and do not have an accurate number. We are in the processing of counting items now.
	15a	Includes audiovisuals
	15b	includes one microfilm title
	15c	Included in 15a
	15d	Includes online periodical indexes
	39	This is our FTE, I do not have head count numbers
	20_supp	For the year reporting we received most of our electronic resources through a state project which provided online reference and periodical sources, some in full text, to the citizens of the state. We only purchased one periodical index in full text.
	40	Have listed our FTE in 39
Dyersburg ST CC	46a	Jimmy Naifeh Tipton County Center Gibson County Center
East Los Angeles C	46a	South Gate Educational Center Library
El Paso CC	1a	Our fiscal year runs from September-August.
	19	We have a standing contract with Amigos that provides OCLC and other bibliographic resources.
	46a	Valle Verde, Transmountain, Rio Grande, Mission Del Paso, Northwest
	46b	-2
Estrn Arizona C	20_supp	(4) - E-books database included here. (16) - No counter available; this is estimate based partly on (13). Sorry.
Estrn Maine Tech C	6	Included in #7
	41	Associate degree is highest credential awarded
	42	Associate degree is highest credential awarded
Fayetteville Tech CC	2	Titles
	46b	Spring Lake Branch campus
	47	The Spring Lake Branch campus is supported by the adjacent public library branch. We have supplied that library with a librarian and materials.
	48	see above comment
Floyd C	15c	Purchases were made for microforms from a gift.
	26b	includes one contract laborer.
	27	includes one branch library
	32	we no longer break our statistice into initial and renewal categories
	33	includes all circulation statistics
	39	at time survey due, we are only able to provide a traditional FTE count of 3817
	46a	Georgia Highlands College at North Metro Technical College
	20_supp	For questions 11-20 the Library has not kept statistics in these areas and, although now aware that this information may be requested in the future, cannot furnish the information at this time.
	40	see footnote for question 39
Gadsden ST CC	1a	as of Sept. 30, 2004
	46a	McClellan & Ayers

Institution	Q. No	Note
Gainesville C	46a	Oconee
Gavilan C	21	e-books
GC Wallace CC	46b	Clanton Campus, Clanton, Alabama
Glendale CC	4a	Total reflects Print Subscriptions (269)and Project MUSE titles (328)
	15b	Print $30,853 Project MUSE $1,350
	15c	Microforms $7071 A/V $16,275 McNaughton Lease Collection $7,464 Electronic Databases (-Project MUSE) $65,584 Ebrary $8,165
	17b	Library Personnel $244,845 Media Personnel $243,091
	17c	Library SA's $30,226 Media SA's $28,169 (Includes Budget and College Work Study)
	19	Library Operational Supplies,etc. $21,277 Media Operational Supplies, etc. $29,489
	23b	Purchased with District funds. Line 22 purchased with internal College funds
	24	Unavailable. All computer operations supported through College IT Department.
	26a	11.6 Full-time plus day and evening adjuncts
	26b	Library Personnel 7.5 Media Personnel 6.25
	26c	Library SA's 3.14 Media SA's 3
	32	Unavailable
	34	Transitioned to new ILS. Unable to loan for part of the year.
	35	Transitioned to new ILS. Estimate--accurate data not available.
	38	Does not include adjunct FTE
	39	Not based on IPEDS data. From GCC College Research Services Fall '04.
	47	Figures listed above include total Library Media Center operations. When possible, information has been provided in the footnotes to delineate budget for Library Operations/Staff and Media Operations/Staff.
	48	Will not be completing the Supplementary Statistics Worksheet.
	40	Not based on IPEDS data. From GCC College Research Services Fall '04.
Gordon C-GA	4a	114 - print purchased and 3,666 electronic in purchased databases
	48	This is a very difficult form to follow with the directions given. No NA would go in.
Grand Rapids CC	4a	Journals only - does not include continuing orders nor does it include apporx. 9600 full-text electronic journals for which we pay
	4b	includes ejournals through a consortium or paid for by the state
	15d	Includes $31766 for electronic resources (books and serials, too difficult to separate funds for each, contracted services (i.e. ILS maintenance fee, printing,equipment repairs, etc.
	17a	6 librarians and lib director
	24	Our computer folks handle all hardware and most software purchases
	26a	6 librarians and 1 lib. director
	26b	6 secretaries and 1 computer technician
Harrisburg Area CC	46a	Gettysburg, Lancaster, Lebanon
Hawaii Pacific U	46a	Hawaii Loa campus
Hawkeye CC	23b	UA
	36	NA
	37	NA
	41	NA
	42	NA
	20_supp	5. Adjusted count for e-books. None added this year. 13a. EBSCOhost, Newsbank, OCLC WorldCat & WorldAlamanac,ProQuest,3 online encyclopedias, CQ Researcher,LexisNexis Academic,netLibrary,Patron Books in Print,Books in Print, ReferenceUSA, Serials Solutio
Hillsborough CC	7	DVD
	11	Mostly slides
	12	audio books, audio tapes, music CDs
	13	VHS, video, film strips
	36	N/A
	37	N/A
	41	N/A

Institution	Q. No	Note
Hillsborough CC	42	N/A
	46a	Brandon, Dale Mabry, Plant City, Ybor City
Hinds CC	25	There has been a dramatic increase over last year due to the fact that we are now OCLC suppliers. The load has been tremendous.
	46a	Jackson ATC, Vicksburg, Nursing Allied Health, Rankin, and Utica
Hiwassee C	31	We no longer keep statistics for reference transactions
	48	The correct response to #7, #31, #32, is NA/UA, but survey would not accept that response, so I entered 0.
	20_supp	The correct response to #3, #5, #13, #13a, #14, #14a, #15, #15a, #16a, #16b is NA/UA, but survey would not accept that response, so I entered 0.
Hocking Tech C	2	364
	39	This figure is based on the formula provided by the Ohio Board of Regents--FTE's are based on the # of hours taken by students
	40	This figure is based on the students who are not part of the FTE count
Horry GTown Tech	1	includes netLibrary collection of 46,184
	1a	includes netLibrary e-book collection of 38,633 titles
	1bi	includes 7,659 ebook titles added and 4,305 Law Library titles cataloged but not purchased this year
	46a	Elizabeth Mattocks Chapin Memorial Library on the Grand Strand Campus Georgetown Campus Library
	20_supp	We will be implementing federated searching during the 0506 fiscal year. We also have access to approximately 20 additional databases provided through our statewide consortia of academic libraries.
Howard C	46a	Howard College - San Angelo Southwest Collegiate Institute for the Deaf
Hutch CC&Voc Sch	15d	$800 MARS service $1000 CatExpress $610 ALA/ACRL
	20_supp	Circulation statistics are increasing, but ebook and online database resources are seeing dramatic increases in use. Remote access is absolutely essential. Books still matter, but they need to be complemented effectively by ebooks and online databases.
IL E CC Wabash Cntrl C	32	In 2004, closed May, June, July, and August.
IL Estrn CC-Frontier	20_supp	Some of the vendors don't offer circulation stats and some won't tell us the cost of the database due to consortial pricing.
IL Valley CC	48	Questions 39 & 40: The line and column references in the instructions do not correspond with our IPEDS reports.
Inst Native Culture	21	inc. in other operating exp
	22	inc. in other operating exp
	23a	inc. in other operating exp.
	23b	n/a
	24	inc. in other operating exp.
	25	n/a
	47	none
	48	none
J.F. Drake ST Tech C	17a	Includes fringe benefits
Jefferson CC-NY	1a	adjusted figure
	1b	we withdrew more than we added
	4a	non-electronic
	6	no longer active
	7	we don't have gov docs
	15a	This amount does not include a $6.000.00 NY State Collection Development grant
	15b	both print and electronic
	15c	media; we do not purchase anything in microform anymore
	15d	Security device
	36	this college does not offer Ph.D programs
	47	Our budget year goes from Sept 1 to August 30
JS Reynolds CC	46a	Downtown Campus Parham Campus Western Campus
Kent St U E Liverpool	1b	We are currently in a major weeding project

Institution	Q. No	Note
Kent St U E Liverpool	20_supp	Budgeting, cost, and # of electronic resources are paid through the Regional Campus office of the University and do not appear on our local financial statement
Kirkwood CC	46b	Iowa City Campus - not included
	20_supp	Questions 11-15a should be answered NA/UA but would not submit so changed answers to 0.
Kirtland CC	20_supp	for 13a, 14a, 15a we counted aggregating services, not individual databases within the services.
Laboure C	22	N/A
	20_supp	The Library continues to develop web access to digital collections
Lake City CC	20_supp	Interlibrary loan is down dramatically this year, but we anticipate it going up next year when the Ex Libris Aleph ILL module comes online for Florida's 28 community colleges. We anticipate spending more money next year on print periodicals (because of I
Lakeland CC-OH	31	IN TYPICAL WEEK
Lansdale Sch of Bus	2	Purchased 52 titles. 25 titles were gifts.
	15d	EBSCOhost subscription; LOIS LAW subscription
	22	EBSCOhost subscription; LOIS LAW subscription
	24	No purchases or upgrades - computers not included in library budget
	26a	Part-time = 25-30 hours/week
	28	unstaffed 12 additional hours
	20_supp	We do not have a count available for access to EBSCOhost
Laramie Co CC	1bi	Includes gifts, number of vol. unknown
	1b	Includes gifts, number of gift vol. unknown
	15d	Bibliographic utilities, dues, software
	19	Equipment, supplies, professional development
	32	Includes reserves
	33	Data not available
	46a	Albany County Campus
Lassen CC	7	CD-ROMs received as accompanying material to monographs
Lexington CC	2	titles, not volumes
	4	Does not include ejournals
	4a	Does not include ejournals
	4b	Does not include ejournals
	6	304 fiche; 1979 rolls
	7	titles
	11	Set titles, not pieces
	12	Titles, not pieces
	13	Titles, not pieces
	15b	Print journals, 12 with matching ejournal access.
	15c	Microforms $5552; balance A/V & computer files.
	15d	SOLINET, Newsbank, and state consortium. Costs for ejournals accessed through aggregators are bundled with courier services in state consortium costs.
	17a	7 librarians; 1 media supervisor
	21	ARTstor; computer files on disc.
	23b	Cost of funding by state by FTE not available.
	27	Leestown Campus branch library opened April 2005.
	31	Includes 63 'virtual' transactions.
	32	Circulation closed during one-week system migration, May 2005.
	34	ILL shut down 9/4/04-10/10/04.
	35	ILL shut down 9/4/04-10/10/04.
	38	Lexington Community College only.
	46a	Leestown campus included (this is the only branch library); service began there April 2005.
	20_supp	Counts not available for usage of electronic resources or visits to library Web pages.
Linn ST Tech C	46b	Linn State Technical College Library, PTA Collection-Jefferson City campus Advanced Technology Center, Mexico, MO
Lord Fairfax CC	23a	Includes all SOLINET charges for cataloging and ILL

Institution	Q. No	Note
Lord Fairfax CC	25	ILL Solinet charges included in #23a
	46a	Bob G. Sowder Library - Lord Fairfax Community College, Fauquier Campus
Luzerne County CC	9	Not sure. We do have an archives room.
	13	we also have sound slide sets and trnsparencies. Don't know which line item to put in.
	22	we actually has one line item in our budget covers periodicals and electronic databases. I divided them accordingly here in the survery.
	24	Our college has another dept. purchase any hardware and software.
	25	it is part of our library budget to pay consonsortia fee--not from concortia. But I do not know where to put this $ in your survey.
	20_supp	We donot have information on virtual visit nor digital collections.
Manatee CC	46a	Venice Campus
Massasoit CC	46a	One branch in Canton, Massachusetts
McDowell Tech CC	23a	Part of state-wide consortium - NC LIVE - paid by state - amt unknown
	23b	Part of state-wide consortium - NC LIVE -paid by state - amt unknown
	26	Actual number is 3.3
	26b	actual number is 1.3
	32	Includes renewals; cannot break renewals out of total count.
	20_supp	Response to Questions 13a - 16b: -1 means answer unavailable.
Mesa CC	46a	Red Mountain Campus
Midland C	1	includes 9,980 e-books
	1a	FY 2004-05 ended 08-31-05 includes 9,980 e-books
	2	includes 4,505 e-books
	23b	Pre-payment for 3-year access and maintenance to bibliographic cataloging database
	30	Many are exact counts, but others are estimated
	46a	Williams Regional Technical Training Center in Ft. Stockton, Texas
Miles CC	15d	$4500 supplies, $149 copies, $3600 travel $75 contracted services, $66 ILL,
	17b	for two staff members
	17c	work study
	33	included above. we do not have access to that information for this time period. we were not automated throughout this time period, so these statistics were not kept.
	20_supp	During the 2005-2006 academic year we have begun to add state government documents. Will these be considered 'government documents' next time?
Mt Hood CC	15a	107,310 books 22,469
	15c	Audio
	17a	87,212 Management 52,512 Supervisor 114,142 Librarians
	17b	46,802 Coordinator 159,518 Clerks 42,455 Specialist 927 overtime pt time 39,141
	17c	79 student aid 51,625 CWS
	19	Fringe benefits 240,851 Other 24,834
	21	not separated within budget
	23a	2,500 Portals 16,759 OCLC
	24	equipment repair 4453 small equipment 7661 maintenance 2111
	25	611 iLL 3369 postage
	26a	1.5 FTE for pt. time
	26b	1 FTE for pt. time
	26c	6,223 hours
	27	public service; reference desk; media desk
	28	M-Th 7:30-9 Fri 7:30-5 saturday 11-3
	31	72 questions for 40 weeks
N Alberta Inst	1a	NAIT and Fairview College merged July 1, 2005. The adjusted figure for June 30, 2004 includes the collections previously held by Fairview College Library. Not included in the volume count are 4010 e-books that are part of subscriptions such as Safari.
	4a	Unique titles. Includes 13 e-journals.

Institution	Q. No	Note
N Alberta Inst	13	Includes all audio visual media held.
	15d	Licensed databases $114720 E-book subscriptions $9625 Special funding $8986
	33	Includes reserves
	39	Includes part-time
	46a	Fairview Campus, Peace River Campus, High Level Campus
	48	You have sent a request for statistics to Fairview College rk:783TBJD is the coding on the letter. Fairview College and NAIT merged on July 1, 2004 and therefore Fairview College will not report any statistics in the future. Thanks.
National Hispanic U	20_supp	We have no accurate statistics for most of 2004-05.The numbers are guesses.
ND ST C Science	2	Information not available due to new ILS
	6	information not available due to new ILS
	9	Information not available due to new ILS
	12	information not available due to new ILS
	13	information not available due to new ILS
	15	PeopleSoft does not break this down for me.
	17a	all staff paid from one fund
	17b	all staff paid from one fund
	17c	student assistants are paid from Work Study funds not controlled by the library
	26	FTE is by contract, but not all contracts are for 12 months.
	32	not kept separately
NE WI Tech C	1bi	includes new netlibrary e-books
	2	approximate
	26b	Only 3 are full-time. The part-time staff equates to around 2 full-time positions.
	32	Not sure if renewals are added into this number or not.
	38	Approximate
	46a	Marinette and Sturgeon Bay
NH CC-Berlin	20_supp	16. We do not have data for these questions.
	20_supp	16. We do not have data for these questions.
Nicolet Area Tech C	1bi	1
	32	Unable to distinguish between initial circulations and renewals
	33	Unable to distinguish between initial circulations and renewals
	46a	Lakeland Center in Minocqua
	20_supp	Question 1. Unique titles Question 2. Not unique titles Questions 16a & 16b. The answer is not zero but the program would not accept NA/UA as an answer. We have no statistics for these logins.
Normandale CC	11	Individual items (i.e. individual slides) versus collective (title level) total
	15d	rentals - $15.00 ; maintenance contracts - $1,555 ; Purchased services - $11,440.62 ; Copyrights - $1,500 ; Memberships - $49,462.90 ; Databases - $58,313,35
	20_supp	Number of journals listed in 1 (41,267 include journals access via more than one database service). The library subscribes to 20,085 unique online journals.
North AR C	1b	See (ii) above
	15b	We are reducing our owned hard-copy serials subscriptions as more are available in full-text through database services like EBSCOhost and ProQuest.
	15c	We are reducing microform holdings are online resources become more available.
	17	Significant staff shortages due to director's retirement and and subsequent turn-over reduced payroll.
	17a	Director retired 30 Jun 04 new director hired 1 Jan 05. Old director's retirement bonus charged to current FY budget.
	17b	Several positions turned over after the appointment of the new director, leaving temporary vacancies
	17c	Student Assistant hours are not paid from library budget.
	19	Benefits only, no facilties assessment is made by the college for the library.
	23b	estimate
	26a	Two positions authorized, only one filled.

Institution	Q. No	Note
North AR C	26c	Fall and spring semesters only, no student assistants during the summer.
	28	During fall and spring semesters. No evening hours during summer or breaks.
	29	Includes classroom and in-library presentations for both on-campus and off-campus users.
	36	We are a two-year college
	46a	Main campus (South) and Technical programs campus (North)
Northeastern JC	4b	Figure not available...survey wouldn't allow UA as answer.
	6	143 is the # of units added for this fiscal year, the total # of units is not available and survey would not allow me to indicate UA as a valid response.
	17c	Figure unavailable, survey wouldn't allow that as a response.
	23b	Figure unavailable, survey wouldn't allow that response.
	25	Figure unavailable, survey wouldn't allow that response.
	33	System doesn't tell us # of renewals so a different figure cannot be provided.
	20_supp	If UA and NA are allowable response according to the written directions, the online form should allow one to input that value. Instead, I had to put zeros as the online survey rejected anything but a numerical value.
Nwestern Business C	46a	Bridgeview (South) Naperville (West)
Nwestern CT Tech CC	15d	supplies, memberships
	19	bibliographic utilities, on-line databases, networks
OH ST U Ag Tech Inst	2	Does not include donation count
	15d	organizational memberships
	24	hardware - $3555 software - $482
	47	ATI Library Reserves Circulation: Check Outs - 2594 Total Check Ins - 2442 Total Renewals - 61 Total Holds - 3 Total All numerical values reflect 1-year of reserve circulation activity
Okaloosa-Walton CC	46b	Our branch campuses and centers are administered by different public entities (a university, two air force base libraries and two public libraries). We have only one campus with a library owned and administered by OWC.
Passaic County CC	17c	Part-time temporary help.
	35	Statistics not kept.
Paul D. Camp CC	46a	Suffolk-Hobbs Campus
Pellissippi ST Tech CC	1a	Number of ebooks not included; ebook statistics not kept previous to 2004-2005.
	1bi	Includes all ebooks available on June 30, 2005. Includes the following ebook products and number of titles: Access Science - 1 ACLS History e-Book Project - 1,000 Encyclopedia Americana - 1 Grove Music Online - 3 Knovel Science & Technology eBooks
	1b	Includes all ebooks available on June 30, 2005.
	2	Does not include ebooks.
	13	Inventory of av materials responsibility of another department, which did not supply numbers
	17a	All MLS degreed
	26a	All MLS degreed
	32	System not able to differentiate between initial circulations and renewals.
	46a	Blount County Campus Division Street Campus Magnolia Avenue Campus
	46b	All branch campuses included in statistics.
Pensacola Jr C	7	Not Available
	46a	Milton and Warrington
Petit Jean C	15d	software maintance
	31	app. 5 per day
Piedmont Tech C	2	This amount was figured by subtracting the total donated volumes (256) from the gross volumes added (1734).
	6	Government documents are not included.
	7	Almost all computer files were packaged with a book volume.
	7	The few government documents owned are included in the volumes total.
	10	Total owned as of June 30, 2005.
	11	Total owned as of June 30, 2005.
	12	Total owned as of June 30, 2005.

Institution	Q. No	Note
Piedmont Tech C	13	Total owned as of June 30, 2005.
	15c	Includes maps and various audiovisual materials.
	15d	Includes office supplies ($8217), photocopy supplies ($1036), educational supplies ($176), postage ($781), and food supplies ($20)
	17c	Student workers are provided through the Federal Work Study program and are paid $6 per hour. In FY 2004-5, the library received 326 hours of service.
	19	Includes printing and advertising ($1463), telephone ($431), telecommunication services ($2580), photocopier rental ($1234), dues and membership ($1015), other fixed charges ($44), travel and meals ($599), and conference registrations ($565)
	20	Excludes fringe benefits and building/maintenance expenses
	21	Almost all computer software arrived packaged with book volumes.
	23a	Annual SOLINET membership ($600), OCLC searches ($1016), Online copyright tutorial ($350), PASCAL Consortial dues ($350)
	24	Annual technical support for library system.
Pittsburgh Tech Inst	1bi	Does not include donations.
	15a	Includes audiovisual materials.
Portland CC	21	NOT AVAILABLE
	25	Not Available
	46a	Sylvania Cascade Rock Creek
Prairie ST C	39	FTE Actual body count 10,648
Prince George CC	17c	Even though the staff in these positions are PGCC students, the job slots are regular part time employee slots, not student assistant positions or dollars.
	24	Computer hardware and software are purchased from another college budget, not the library.
	36	PGCC is a community college.
Pueblo CC	4	28 subscriptions were transferred to PCC when the Arkansas Valley Regional Library Service System closed
	15d	Cataloging/ILL $1219; Postage $120; Online databases $13553; Digital books $2000; Circ/Pac/Maint 10304; EDRS credit -$285; Materials for departments $210.
	17c	Funded through College Financial Aid Budget.
	23b	Perkins Vocational Funding
	46a	Fremont Campus
	20_supp	The digitized history of the college, available on the college web page, was not created by the library and is not maintained by the library.
Pulaski Tech C	2	4576 e-books
Quinebaug Vally Comm TC	15b	Answer contained in 15A
	15c	Answer contained in 15A
	39	901 is FTE equivalent.
	46a	Willimantic Center
Quinsigamond CC	25	Included in lines 19 and 23
	28	During fall and spring semesters
	32	Not available
	20_supp	Because of the way our vendors report statistics, we cannot give a figure for questions #1. We get E books for free from our consortium and we get whatever is available(question #5). Our Website does not count visits (question # 16)
Red Deer C	1a	as reported in AACL survey 2004/05
	10	in workflows, format = maps
	12	in workflows, 'sound recording' in title
	13	in workflows, 'videorecording' in title
	15	as in 15a
	15a	as reported on AACL survey 2004/05
	15b	as in 15a
	15c	as in 15a
	17	from breakdowns used to calculate TAL membership fees for 2006 (based on 2004/05)
	19	as in 17

Institution	Q. No	Note
Red Deer C	20	as in 17
	26a	from AACL survey 2004/05
	26b	as in 26a
	27	includes reference, circulation, ILL
	28	as in 26a
	29	as in 26a
	30	as in 26a
	31	basic and complex questions only, does not include AAQ
	34	as in 26a
	35	as in 26a
	39	head count, from RDC factbook
	40	as in 39
Rogue CC	12	estimated
	13	estimated
	46a	Riverside Campus
Sacramento City C	20_supp	#4 - includes e-book footnote. #12 WebBridge #16 Counters were not installed until Fall of 2005.
San Jacinto C South	1	Reporting date is August 31, 2005.
	1a	Reporting date is August 31, 2004.
	31	We don't keep this statistic.
Selkirk C	2	Estimated
	4b	Estimated
	6	Estimated
	7	Estimated
	7	Estimated
	9	Estimated
	10	Estimated
	11	Estimated
	23a	Access to online databases via B.C. Electronic Library Network.
	25	Estimated
	29	Estimated
	30	Estimated
	31	Estimated
	39	Full-time equivalent
	46a	Silver King (Nelson) Tenth Street (Nelson)
	20_supp	Library's fiscal year ends March 31. #1 - total includes #2-3 #7 - total includes #8-10
South AR CC	30	Actual count
	31	Actual count
South Florida CC	46a	DeSoto Campus, Hardee Campus, Lake Placid Center
South Puget Sound CC	13	All audiovisual units are counted together in one catagory.
	32	All circulation has been combined into one number.
Southeast CC	15	Includes amounts from regular budget, endowments and donations, fines and fees.
	17c	Paid from various non-library funds. Information not readily available.
	19	not paid from library budget
	22	Infotrac and KYVL databases not included--paid by the system before library budget was issued
	26c	Pineville-0.5; Harlan-0.75; Middlesboro-1.0; Whitesburg-0.5
	46a	Harlan, Pineville, Whitesburg, Middlesboro
	20_supp	Items not filled in are ones for which we do not have exact data. There is no NA/UA to check, as directed by the instructions. So they are left blank, because it will not let me type in and save NA/UA; it gives me an error saying I have to have a numeri
Spartanburg Tech C	27	Reference Desk and Circulation Desk
	31	Transactions in a typical week

Institution	Q. No	Note
Spoon River C	24	Not part of library budget.
	46b	We have only 1 Main library (Canton) and a library service center (Macomb) that has only a small Reserve collection and a computer lab. The Macomb library service center does not meet the Branch library definition of ACRL. I included only the 1 FTE staff
Tacoma CC	38	126 campus wide
Tech C Lowcountry	2	reporting figures of ebook titles from netlibrary.
	4a	Not counted separately from total for 4.
	4b	Not counted separately from total for 4.
	7	Not counted separately from volumes held count.
	10	Not counted separately from volumes held count.
	11	Not counted separately from volumes held and film and video count.
	12	Not counted separately from film and video count.
	21	Not separated from volumes count.
	32	Not separated from total circulation count.
	46b	Our branch campus does not have a library
	20_supp	Not completing this section at this time. May do for next report
Tri County Tech C	1	Used actual figure from Bibliographic source.
	13	Figure includes Audio due.
Trocaire C	15c	audiovisual
	20_supp	Items 13,14,15 Reporting for EBSCOhost and INFOTRAC
Tunxis CC Tech	11	Framed posters
TX ST Tech C Waco	1a	Our fiscal year ends August 31, 05
	9	True answer.
U Akron Wayne C	2	Title count only
U HI-Kapiolani CC	39	cannot determine breakdown between p/t and f/t students
U HI-Windward CC	32	Figure not available
U NM Gallup Branch	7	estimate durig migration did not transfer records
	15a	Regular budget only 16,475.27 all other special funding or grants
	23b	NA
	26c	rounded up
	39	Statistic from Com. service dept-- not sure IPEDS?
	44	small medical nursing and diabetes collection at site
	20_supp	The library's digital collection varies greatly from month to month. Within one database. We have have several varying databases. Infotrac is supplied by the State library free, but we add health and wellness. During this period we had a grant that p
W.Rainey Harper C	1a	Statistics maintained by academic year beginning June 1, 2004.
	15b	Includes full-text serial aggregators services.
	15d	Materials for new academic programs (print & AV).
	17	Does not include division dean.
	17a	Includes overload and adjunct amounts. Less one full time employee on FMLA leave.
	22	Included in 15b.
	23a	Included in 19.
	23b	Illinois Library Computer Systems Organization consortium assessment paid by IT.
	24	All covered by IT.
	39	Annual FTE total for summer, fall, and spring semesters.
	20_supp	Sorry... this information is not available.
	40	Not available
Waycross C	4b	Consortium (Galileo) serials excluded
	20	Travel excluded
	20_supp	1., 2., 3. Galileo Resources; 4. Galileo Resources and Opposing Viewpoints as one; 8. Included in #7; 9. Included in #7;
Weatherford C	46a	Mineral Wells Center/Decatur Education Center

Institution	Q. No	Note
Weatherford C	48	Please note that our method of dividing monographs and other library materials was changed this year providing a more realistic accounting for actual monographic expenditures.
Western IA Tech CC	1a	excluded ebooks from consortium and video, etc.
	29	We also have presentations on CD for students to view.
	46a	Denison and Cherokee
Wharton Co Jr C	46a	Sugar Land and Fort Bend Technical Center
Whatcom CC	1	Volume count will not batch because of other db errors edited or db change factors not formally tallied or tracked.
	17c	Estimated based on 36 hours/week, 33 weeks @ $9.82
	27	Circulation, Reference, Technical Services
	46a	not applicable
	46b	not applicable
Yavapai C	1b	negative number
	15	Total does not include Tech Services supplies
	25	does not include postage
	32	UA
	36	NA
	37	NA
	38	Fall 2004: 92 Spring 2005: 100
	41	NA
	42	NA
	46b	Yavapai College Library Verde Valley Campus
	20_supp	Many of the statistics requested were either unavailable or not applicable

KEY TO PARTICIPATING INSTITUTIONS

Institution	Full Name of Institution	Location	Carnegie Class
A Baldwin Agrl C	Abraham Baldwin College	Tifton, GA	A
AB C Art & Design	Alberta College of Art & Design	Calgary, AB	B
Abilene Christian U	Abilene Christian University	Abilene, TX	M
Adams State C	Adams State College	Alamosa, CO	M
Adirondack CC	Adirondack Community College	Queensbury, NY	A
Adrian C	Adrian College	Adrian, MI	B
Agnes Scott C	Agnes Scott College	Atlanta/Decatur, GA	M
Aiken Tech C	Aiken Technical College	Aiken, SC	A
Alabama ST U	Alabama State University	Montgomery, AL	M
Albany C Pharmacy	Albany College of Pharmacy	Albany, NY	D
Albany Medical C	Albany Medical College	Albany, NY	D
Albany ST U	Albany State University	Albany, GA	M
Albion C	Albion College	Albion, MI	B
Alcorn ST U	Alcorn State University	Lorman, MS	M
Alfred U-Herrick	Alfred University	Alfred, NY	D
Algoma UC	Algoma University College	Sault Ste, ON	B
Allen C-IA	Allen College	Waterloo, IA	M
Alliant Intl U	Alliant International University-Los Angeles	Alhambra, CA	D
Alliant Intl U-San Diego	Alliant International University-San Diego	San Diego, CA	D
Alpena CC	Alpena Community College	Alpena, MI	A
Alvernia C	Alvernia College	Reading, PA	M
Alverno C	Alverno College	Milwaukee, WI	M
Alvin CC	Alvin Community College	Alvin, TX	A
Am River C	American River College	Sacramento, CA	A
Am Samoa CC	American Samoa Community College	Pago Pago, AS	A
Am School Prof Psych/HI	Argosy University/Honolulu	Honolulu, HI	D
Amer Intl C	American International College	Springfield, MA	M
Amer U Puerto Rico	American University of Puerto Rico	Bayamon, PR	M
Amherst C	Amherst College	Amherst, MA	B
Anderson C	Anderson College	Anderson, SC	B
Anderson U	Anderson University	Anderson, IN	M
Andover C	Andover College	Portland, ME	A
Angelo ST U	Angelo State University	San Angelo, TX	M
Anne Arundel CC	Anne Arundel Community College	Arnold, MD	A
Anoka-Ramsey CC	Anoka-Ramsey Community College	Coon Rapids, MN	A
Aquinas C MI	Aquinas College	Grand Rapids, MI	M
Aquinas C TN	Aquinas College	Nashville, TN	B
AR ST U Beebe	Arkansas State University Beebe	Beebe, AR	A
Arizona St U-Main	Arizona State University-Main campus	Tempe, AZ	D
Ark Tech U	Arkansas Tech University	Russellville, AR	M
Armstrong Atlantic ST U	Armstrong Atlantic State University	Savannah, GA	M

A=Associates   B=Bachelors   M=Masters   D=Doctorate

115

KEY TO PARTICIPATING INSTITUTIONS

Institution	Full Name of Institution	Location	Carnegie Class
Art Center C Design	Art Center College of Design	Pasadena, CA	M
Asbury C	Asbury College	Wilmore, KY	M
Ashland U	Ashland University	Ashland, OH	D
Assemblies God Theo Sem	Assemblies of God Theological Seminary	Springfield, MO	M
Assumption C	Assumption College	Worcester, MA	M
Athenaeum of Ohio	Athenaeum of Ohio	Cincinnati, OH	M
Athens ST U	Athens State University	Athens, AL	B
Athens Tech C	Athens Technical College	Athens, GA	A
Atlanta C Art	Atlanta College of Art	Atlanta, GA	B
Auburn U	Auburn University	Auburn University, AL	D
Auburn U Montgomery	Auburn University at Montgomery	Montgomery, AL	M
Augusta ST U	Augusta State University	Augusta, GA	M
Augustana C RI	Augustana College	Rock Island, IL	B
Augustana C SF	Augustana College	Sioux Falls, SD	M
Aurora U	Aurora University	Aurora, IL	D
Austin C	Austin College	Sherman, TX	M
Austin Presb Theo Sem	Austin Presbyterian Theological Seminary	Austin, TX	M
Averett C	Averett University	Danville, VA	M
AZ Western C	Arizona Western College	Yuma, AZ	A
Azusa Pacific U	Azusa Pacific University	Azusa, CA	D
Babson C	Babson College	Babson Park, MA	M
Bainbridge C	Bainbridge College	Bainbridge, GA	A
Baker C System	Baker College System	Flint, MI	M
Baker U	Baker University	Baldwin City, KS	M
Bank Street C Education	Bank Street College of Education	New York, NY	M
Baptist Bible C	Baptist Bible College	Springfield, MO	M
Bates C	Bates College	Lewiston, ME	B
Bellevue CC	Bellevue Community College	Bellevue, WA	M
Bellevue U	Bellevue University	Bellevue, NE	M
Bellingham Tech C	Bellingham Technical College	Bellingham, WA	A
Belmont Tech C	Belmont Technical College	Saint Clairsville, OH	A
Belmont U	Belmont University	Nashville, TN	M
Benedict C	Benedict College	Columbia, SC	B
Benedictine U	Benedictine University	Lisle, IL	D
Bergen CC	Bergen Community College	Paramus, NJ	A
Berry C	Berry College	Mount Berry, GA	B
Bethany C Bethany	Bethany College	Bethany, WV	B
Bethany C Lindsborg	Bethany College	Lindsborg, KS	B
Bethel C IN	Bethel College	Mishawaka, IN	M
Bethel C KS	Bethel College	North Newton, KS	B
Bethel Theo Sem	Bethel Theological Seminary	Saint Paul, MN	D

A=Associates   B=Bachelors   M=Masters   D=Doctorate

KEY TO PARTICIPATING INSTITUTIONS

Institution	Full Name of Institution	Location	Carnegie Class
Biola U	Biola University	La Mirada, CA	D
Bishop's U	Bishop's University	Lennoxville, QC	B
Black Hawk C	Black Hawk College	Moline, IL	A
Blackhawk Tech C	Blackhawk Technical College	Janesville, WI	A
Bloomfield C	Bloomfield College	Bloomfield, NJ	B
Blue Mountain CC	Blue Mountain Community College	Pendleton, OR	A
Blue Ridge CC	Blue Ridge Community College	Weyers Cave, VA	A
Bluefield C	Bluefield College	Bluefield, VA	B
Bluefield ST C	Bluefield State College	Bluefield, WV	B
Bluffton C	Bluffton College	Bluffton, OH	M
Boise ST U	Boise State University	Boise, ID	D
Boston C	Boston College	Chestnut Hill, MA	D
Boston U	Boston University	Boston, MA	D
Bowdoin C	Bowdoin College	Brunswick, ME	B
BowlGrn SU Fireld	Bowling Green State University Firelands College	Huron, OH	M
Bradley U	Bradley University	Peoria, IL	M
Brandeis U	Brandeis University	Waltham, MA	D
Brazosport C	Brazosport College	Lake Jackson, TX	A
Brenau U	Brenau University	Gainesville, GA	M
Brescia U	Brescia University	Owensboro, KY	M
British Columbia Inst	British Columbia Institute of Technology	Burnaby, BC	B
Brookdale CC	Brookdale Community College	Lincroft, NJ	A
Brooklyn Law School	Brooklyn Law School	Brooklyn, NY	D
Bryan C	Bryan College	Dayton, TN	B
Bryn Mawr C	Bryn Mawr College	Bryn Mawr, PA	D
Bucknell U	Bucknell University	Lewisburg, PA	M
Buena Vista U	Buena Vista University	Storm Lake, IA	M
Bunker Hill CC	Bunker Hill Community College	Boston, MA	A
Butler County CC	Butler County Community College	El Dorado, KS	A
Butler U	Butler University	Indianapolis, IN	M
BYU	Brigham Young University	Provo, UT	D
BYU HI	Brigham Young University Hawaii Campus	Laie Oahu, HI	B
C Atlantic	College of the Atlantic	Bar Harbor, ME	M
C Bois-de-Boulogne	College de Bois-de-Boulogne	Montreal, QC	A
C Canyons	College of the Canyons	Santa Clarita, CA	A
C Charleston	College of Charleston	Charleston, SC	M
C Edouard Montpetit	College Edouard-Montpetit	Longueuil, QC	A
C Holy Cross	College of the Holy Cross	Worcester, MA	B
C Insurance	St. John's University Manhattan Campus	New York, NY	M
C Lake Co	College of Lake County	Grayslake, IL	A
C Merici	Collège Mérici	Quebec, QC	A

A=Associates   B=Bachelors   M=Masters   D=Doctorate

117

KEY TO PARTICIPATING INSTITUTIONS

Institution	Full Name of Institution	Location	Carnegie Class
C Mt St Joseph	College of Mount Saint Joseph	Cincinnati, OH	M
C Mt St Vincent	College of Mount Saint Vincent	Riverdale, NY	M
C New Caledonia	College of New Caledonia	Prince George, BC	A
C New Jersey	The College of New Jersey	Ewing, NJ	M
C Redwoods	College of the Redwoods	Eureka, CA	A
C St Benedict	College of Saint Benedict	Saint Joseph, MN	B
C St Jean Richelieu	College St-Jean-sur-Richelieu	St-Jean-sur-Richelieu, QC	A
C St Thomas More	The College of Saint Thomas More	Fort Worth, TX	M
C Visual Arts	College of Visual Arts	St. Paul, MN	B
C William & Mary	College of William and Mary	Williamsburg, VA	D
C WV	The College of West Virginia	Beckley, WV	M
CA C Arts & Crafts	California College Of The Arts	Oakland, CA	M
CA Inst Arts	California Institute of the Arts	Santa Clara, CA	M
CA St U - Sacramento	California State University-Sacramento	Sacramento, CA	M
CA ST U Bakersfield	California State University-Bakersfield	Bakersfield, CA	M
CA ST U Dominguez Hills	California State University-Dominguez Hills	Carson, CA	M
CA ST U Fresno	California State University-Fresno	Fresno, CA	M
CA ST U Fullerton	California State University-Fullerton	Fullerton, CA	M
CA ST U Hayward	California State University-Hayward	Hayward, CA	M
CA ST U LA	California State University-Los Angeles	Los Angeles, CA	M
CA ST U Long Beach	California State University-Long Beach	Long Beach, CA	M
CA ST U Northridge	California State University-Northridge	Northridge, CA	M
CA ST U San Marcos	California State University-San Marcos	San Marcos, CA	M
CA ST U Stanislaus	California State University, Stanislaus	Turlock, CA	M
CA West Sch Law	California Western School of Law	San Diego, CA	M
Cabrini C	Cabrini College	Radnor, PA	M
Calvin C	Calvin College	Grand Rapids, MI	D
Camden County C	Camden County College	Blackwood, NJ	A
Cameron U	Cameron University	Lawton, OK	M
Campion C	Campion College	Regina, SK	B
Canadian U C	Canadian University College	Lacombe, AB	B
Canisius C	Canisius College	Buffalo, NY	M
Cape Fear CC	Cape Fear Community College	Wilmington, NC	A
Capital CC	Capital Community College	Hartford, CT	A
Capital U	Capital University	Columbus, OH	D
Carl Sandburg C	Carl Sandburg College	Galesburg, IL	A
Carleton C	Carleton College	Northfield, MN	B
Carlow C	Carlow College	Pittsburgh, PA	M
Carnegie Mellon U	Carnegie Mellon University	Pittsburgh, PA	D
Carroll C-Helena	Carroll College	Helena, MT	B
Carroll Tech Inst	West Central Tech. College- Carroll Campus	Waco, GA	A

A=Associates   B=Bachelors   M=Masters   D=Doctorate

KEY TO PARTICIPATING INSTITUTIONS

Institution	Full Name of Institution	Location	Carnegie Class
Carteret CC	Carteret Community College	Morehead City, NC	A
Case Western Res U	Case Western Reserve University	Cleveland, OH	D
Catholic U Am	The Catholic University of America	Washington, DC	D
Cazenovia C	Cazenovia College	Cazenovia, NY	B
Cedar Crest C	Cedar Crest College	Allentown, PA	M
Cedar Valley	Cedar Valley College	Lancaster, TX	A
Cedarville U	Cedarville University	Cedarville, OH	M
CEGEP Beauce-Appalaches	CEGEP de Beauce-Appalaches	Saint-Georges, QC	A
CEGEP Trois-Rivieres	CEGEP de Trois-Rivieres	Trois-Rivières, QC	A
Centenary C	Centenary College	Hackettstown, NJ	M
Centenary C LA	Centenary College of Louisiana	Shreveport, LA	M
Centennial C	Centennial College	Scarborough, ON	B
Central Alabama CC	Central Alabama Community College	Alexander City, AL	A
Central C	Central College	Pella, IA	B
Central Carolina Tech C	Central Carolina Technical College	Sumter, SC	A
Central CT ST U	Central Connecticut State University	New Britain, CT	M
Central ME Tech C	Central Maine Technical College	Auburn, ME	A
Central MI U	Central Michigan University	Mount Pleasant, MI	D
Central MO ST U	Central Missouri State University	Warrensburg, MO	M
Central Piedmont CC	Central Piedmont Community College	Charlotte, NC	A
Central TX C	Central Texas College	Killeen, TX	A
Centralia C	Centralia College	Centralia, WA	A
Centre C	Centre College	Danville, KY	B
Chabot C	Chabot College	Hayward, CA	A
Chapman U	Chapman University	Orange, CA	D
Charleston Sthrn U	Charleston Southern University	Charleston, SC	M
Chattahoochee Tech	Chattahoochee Technical College	Marietta, GA	A
Chestnut Hill C	Chestnut Hill College	Philadelphia, PA	M
Chicago ST U	Chicago State University	Chicago, IL	M
Chippewa V Tech C	Chippewa Valley Technical College	Eau Claire, WI	A
Christendom C	Christendom College	Front Royal, VA	M
Christian Brothers U	Christian Brothers University	Memphis, TN	M
Christian Heritage C	Christian Heritage College	El Cajon, CA	B
Christian Theo Sem	Christian Theological Seminary	Indianapolis, IN	D
Clackamas CC	Clackamas Community College	Oregon City, OR	A
Clark C-WA	Clark College	Vancouver, WA	A
Clarke C-IA	Clarke College	Dubuque, IA	M
Clayton C&ST U	Clayton College & State University	Morrow, GA	B
Clear Creek Bible	Clear Creek Baptist Bible College	Pineville, KY	B
Clemson U	Clemson University	Clemson, SC	D
Cleveland Chiro C-CA	Cleveland Chiropractic College	Los Angeles, CA	D

A=Associates   B=Bachelors   M=Masters   D=Doctorate

KEY TO PARTICIPATING INSTITUTIONS

Institution	Full Name of Institution	Location	Carnegie Class
Cleveland Inst Art	Cleveland Institute of Art	Cleveland, OH	M
Cleveland ST U	Cleveland State University	Cleveland, OH	D
Clinton CC	Clinton Community College	Plattsburgh, NY	A
Cloud Co CC	Cloud County Community College	Concordia, KS	A
Cmty Hosp C Health	Jefferson College of Health Sciences	Roanoke, VA	B
Coastal GA CC	Coastal Georgia Community College	Brunswick, GA	A
Colby C	Colby College	Waterville, ME	B
Colby CC	Colby Community College	Colby, KS	A
Colby Sawyer C	Colby-Sawyer College	New London, NH	B
Colgate U	Colgate University	Hamilton, NY	M
Colorado C	Colorado College	Colorado Springs, CO	B
Colorado Christian U	Colorado Christian University	Lakewood, CO	M
Colorado NorthWstrn CC	Colorado Northwestern Community College	Rangely, CO	A
Columbia C	Columbia College	Chicago, IL	M
Columbia C MO	Columbia College	Columbia, MO	M
Columbia C SC	Columbia College	Columbia, SC	M
Columbia Intl U	Columbia International University	Columbia, SC	D
Columbia Junior C	Columbia Junior College	Columbia, SC	A
Columbia ST CC	Columbia State Community College	Columbia, TN	A
Columbia U	Columbia University in the City of New York	New York, NY	D
Columbia Union C	Columbia Union College	Takoma Park, MD	B
Columbus ST CC	Columbus State Community College	Columbus, OH	A
Columbus ST U	Columbus State University	Columbus, GA	M
Compton CC	Compton Community College	Compton, CA	A
Concordia C-NY	Concordia College	Bronxville, NY	B
Concordia Theo Sem	Concordia Theological Seminary	Fort Wayne, IN	D
Concordia U St Paul	Concordia University, St. Paul	Saint Paul, MN	M
Connecticut C	Connecticut College	New London, CT	M
Connors ST C	Connors State College	Warner, OK	A
Conservatory Music PR	Conservatory of Music of Puerto Rico	San Juan, PR	M
Cooper Union	Cooper Union	New York, NY	M
Cornell C	Cornell College	Mount Vernon, IA	B
Cornell U	Cornell University	Ithaca, NY	D
Corning CC	Corning Community College	Corning, NY	A
Cornish C Arts	Cornish College of the Arts	Seattle, WA	B
Cosumnes River C	Cosumnes River College	Sacramento, CA	A
Creighton U	Creighton University	Omaha, NE	M
Crichton C	Crichton College Library	Memphis, TN	B
Crowder C	Crowder College	Neosho, MO	A
Crown C-MN	Crown College	St. Bonifacius, MN	B
Cuesta C	Cuesta College	San Luis Obispo, CA	A

A=Associates   B=Bachelors   M=Masters   D=Doctorate

KEY TO PARTICIPATING INSTITUTIONS

Institution	Full Name of Institution	Location	Carnegie Class
Culver Stockton C	Culver-Stockton College	Canton, MO	B
Cumberland Co C	Cumberland County College	Vineland, NJ	A
CUNY BMB C	City University of New York Bernard M. Baruch College	New York, NY	M
CUNY Borough Manhattan CC	City University of New York Borough of Manhattan Community College	New York, NY	A
CUNY Bronx CC	City University of New York Bronx Community College	Bronx, NY	A
CUNY Brooklyn C	City University of New York Brooklyn College	Brooklyn, NY	M
CUNY C Stn Island	City University of New York College of Staten Island	Staten Island, NY	M
CUNY City C	City University of New York City College	New York, NY	M
CUNY Grad Ctr	City University of New York Graduate Center	New York, NY	D
CUNY HH Lehman C	City University of New York Herbert H. Lehman College	Bronx, NY	M
CUNY Hostos CC	City University of New York Hostos Community College	Bronx, NY	A
CUNY Hunter C	City University of New York Hunter College	New York, NY	M
CUNY John Jay C Crim Just	City University of New York John Jay College of Criminal Justice	New York, NY	M
CUNY LaGuardia CC	City University of New York,La Guardia Community College	Long Island City, NY	A
CUNY NYC Tech C	City University of New York New York City Technical College	Brooklyn, NY	B
CUNY Queensborough CC	City University of New York Queensborough Community College	Bayside, NY	A
CUNY York C	City University of New York York College	Jamaica, NY	B
Curtis Inst Music	Curtis Institute of Music	Philadelphia, PA	M
D.S. Lancaster CC	Dabney S. Lancaster Community College	Clifton Forge, VA	A
Daemen C	Daemen College	Amherst, NY	M
Dakota ST U	Dakota State University	Madison, SD	M
Dakota Wesleyan U	Dakota Wesleyan University	Mitchell, SD	B
Dalton ST C	Dalton State College	Dalton, GA	B
Daniel Webster C	Daniel Webster College	Nashua, NH	M
Darton C	Darton College	Albany, GA	A
Davis & Elkins C	Davis & Elkins College	Elkins, WV	B
Dawson CC	Dawson Community College	Glendive, MT	A
DE Valley C	Delaware Valley College	Doylestown, PA	M
Dean C	Dean College	Franklin, MA	B
Defiance C	The Defiance College	Defiance, OH	M
Del Mar C	Del Mar College	Corpus Christi, TX	A
Delaware Co CC	Delaware County Community College	Media, PA	A
Delta ST U	Delta State University	Cleveland, MS	D
Denison U	Denison University	Granville, OH	B
DePaul U	DePaul University	Chicago, IL	D
DeSales U	DeSales University	Center Valley, PA	M
Diablo Valley C	Diablo Valley College	Pleasant Hill, CA	A
Divine Word C	Divine Word College	Epworth, IA	B
DN Myers C	Davis N. Myers University	Cleveland, OH	M
Dodge City CC	Dodge City Community College	Dodge City, KS	A
Dominican C San Rafael	Dominican University of California	San Rafael, CA	M

A=Associates   B=Bachelors   M=Masters   D=Doctorate

KEY TO PARTICIPATING INSTITUTIONS

Institution	Full Name of Institution	Location	Carnegie Class
Dominican U	Dominican University	River Forest, IL	M
Douglas C	Douglas College	New Westminster, BC	B
Dowling C	Dowling College	Oakdale Long Island, NY	D
Drake U	Drake University	Des Moines, IA	M
Drexel MCPH	Drexel Universities	Philadelphia, PA	D
Drury C	Drury College	Springfield, MO	M
Duke U	Duke University	Durham, NC	D
Dyersburg ST CC	Dyersburg State Community College	Dyersburg, TN	A
E R Aero U	Embry-Riddle Aeronautical University	Daytona Beach, FL	M
Earlham C	Earlham College	Richmond, IN	M
East Carolina U	East Carolina University	Greenville, NC	D
East Central C	East Central College	Union, MO	A
East CT ST U	Eastern Connecticut State University	Willimantic, CT	M
East Georgia C	East Georgia College	Swainsboro, GA	A
East Los Angeles C	East Los Angeles College	Monterey Park, CA	A
East Tenn ST U	East Tennessee State University	Johnson City, TN	D
Eastern IL U	Eastern Illinois University	Charleston, IL	M
Eastern KY U	Eastern Kentucky University	Richmond, KY	M
Eastern Mennonite U	Eastern Mennonite University	Harrisonburg, VA	M
Eastern MI U	Eastern Michigan University	Ypsilanti, MI	D
Eastern WA U	Eastern Washington University	Cheney, WA	M
Eastrn NM U Main	Eastern New Mexico University Main Campus	Portales, NM	M
Eckerd C	Eckerd College	Saint Petersburg, FL	B
Ecole Polytech Mtl	Ecole polytechnique de Montreal	Montreal, QC	M
Eden Theo Sem	Webster University and Eden Theological Seminary	Webster Groves, MO	D
Edinboro U PA	Edinboro University of Pennsylvania	Edinboro, PA	M
El Paso CC	El Paso Community College	El Paso, TX	A
Elizabethtown C	Elizabethtown College	Elizabethtown, PA	M
Elmhurst C	Elmhurst College	Elmhurst, IL	M
Elon U	Elon University	Elon, NC	M
Emmanuel C MA	Emmanuel College	Boston, MA	M
Emmanuel Sch Rel	Emmanuel School of Religion	Johnson City, TN	D
Emperor's C Trad Oriental Med	Emperor's College of Traditional Oriental Medicine	Santa Monica, CA	D
Emporia ST U	Emporia State University	Emporia, KS	D
Erie CC North	Erie Community College North Campus	Williamsville, NY	A
Escuela Artes Plasticas-PR	Escuela de Artes Plasticas de Puerto Rico	San Juan, PR	B
Estrn Arizona C	Eastern Arizona College	Thatcher, AZ	A
Estrn Idaho Tech C	Eastern Idaho Technical College	Idaho Falls, ID	A
Estrn Maine Tech C	Eastern Maine Technical College	Bangor, ME	A
Eugene Bible C	Eugene Bible College	Eugene, OR	B
Eureka C	Eureka College	Eureka, IL	B

A=Associates   B=Bachelors   M=Masters   D=Doctorate

KEY TO PARTICIPATING INSTITUTIONS

Institution	Full Name of Institution	Location	Carnegie Class
Evergreen ST C	The Evergreen State College	Olympia, WA	M
F Hardeman U	Freed-Hardeman University	Henderson, TN	M
F&M C	Franklin & Marshall College	Lancaster, PA	B
Fairleigh Dickinson U	Fairleigh Dickerson University	Teaneck, NJ	D
Fairmont ST C	Fairmont State College	Fairmont, WV	B
Faith Bap Bible C & Theo Sem	Faith Baptist Bible College and Theological Seminary	Ankeny, IA	M
Fanshawe C	Fanshawe College	London, ON	B
Fashion Inst Tech	Fashion Institute of Technology	New York, NY	B
Fayetteville Tech CC	Fayetteville Technical Community College	Fayetteville, NC	A
Fergus Falls CC	Fergus Falls Community College	Fergus Falls, MN	A
Ferris ST U	Ferris State University	Big Rapids, MI	D
Ferrum C	Ferrum College	Ferrum, VA	B
Finlandia U	Finlandia University	Hancock, MI	B
Fisher C	Fisher College	Boston, MA	B
Fitchburg ST C	Fitchburg State College	Fitchburg, MA	M
FL A & M U	Florida Agricultural and Mechanical University	Tallahassee, FL	D
FL Atlantic U	Florida Atlantic University	Boca Raton, FL	D
FL Christian C	Florida Christian College	Kissimmee, FL	B
FL GCU	Florida Gulf Coast University	South Ft. Myers, FL	M
FL Intl U	Florida International University	North Miami, FL	D
Flagler C	Flagler College	St. Augustine, FL	B
Flor Dar Tech C	Florence - Darlington Technical College	Florence, SC	A
Florida C	Florida College	Temple Terrace, FL	B
Florida Inst Tech	Florida Institute of Technology	Melbourne, FL	D
Floyd C	Floyd College	Rome, GA	A
Fontbonne C	Fontbonne University	Saint Louis, MO	M
Fordham U	Fordham University Library	Bronx, NY	D
Fort Hays ST U	Fort Hays State University	Hays, KS	M
Fort Peck CC	Fort Peck Community College	Poplar, MT	A
Francis Marion U	Francis Marion University	Florence, SC	M
Franklin U	Franklin University	Columbus, OH	M
Free Will Baptist Bible C	Free Will Baptist Bible College	Nashville, TN	B
Frostburg ST U	Frostburg State University	Frostburg, MD	M
Fult Montgom CC	The Evans Library, Fulton-Montgomery Community College	Johnstown, NY	A
Furman U	Furman University	Greenville, SC	M
G Adolphus C	Gustavus Adolphus College	Saint Peter, MN	B
GA Southrn U	Georgia Southern University	Statesboro, GA	D
GA ST U	Georgia State University	Atlanta, GA	D
GA SWstrn ST U	Georgia Southwestern State University	Americus, GA	M
Gadsden ST CC	Gadsden State Community College	Gadsden, AL	A
Gainesville C	Gainesville College	Gainesville, GA	A

A=Associates   B=Bachelors   M=Masters   D=Doctorate

KEY TO PARTICIPATING INSTITUTIONS

Institution	Full Name of Institution	Location	Carnegie Class
Gannon U	Gannon University	Erie, PA	D
Gardner-Webb U	Gardner-Webb University	Boiling Springs, NC	M
Gavilan C	Gavilan College	Gilroy, CA	A
GC Wallace CC	George Corley Wallace State Community College - Selma	Selma, AL	A
George Fox U	George Fox University	Newberg, OR	D
George Mason U	George Mason University	Fairfax, VA	D
Georgetown C	Georgetown College	Georgetown, KY	M
Georgia C & ST U	Georgia College & State University	Milledgeville, GA	M
Georgia Inst Tech	Georgia Institute of Technology	Atlanta, GA	D
Gettysburg C	Gettysburg College	Gettysburg, PA	B
Glendale CC	Glendale Community College	Glendale, AZ	A
Glenville ST C	Glenville State College	Glenville, WV	B
Gogebic CC	Gogebic Community College	Ironwood, MI	A
Gonzaga U	Gonzaga University	Spokane, WA	D
Gordon C-GA	Gordon College	Barnesville, GA	A
Gordon-C TheoSem	Gordon-Conwell Theological Seminary	South Hamilton, MA	D
Goucher C	Goucher College	Baltimore, MD	M
Governors ST U	Governors State University	University Park, IL	M
Grambling ST U	Grambling State University	Grambling, LA	D
Grand Rapids CC	Grand Rapids Community College	Grand Rapids, MI	A
Grand Sem Montreal	Grand Seminaire de Montreal	Montreal, QC	M
Greenville C	Greenville College	Greenville, IL	M
Grinnell C	Grinnell College	Grinnell, IA	B
Guilford C	Guilford College	Greensboro, NC	B
Gwynedd Mercy C	Gwynedd-Mercy College	Gwynedd Valley, PA	M
H LaGrange C	Hannibal-La Grange College	Hannibal, MO	B
Hagerstown Bus C	Hagerstown Business College	Hagerstown, MD	A
Hanover C	Hanover College	Hanover, IN	B
Harding U Grad Schl Rel	Harding University Graduate School of Religion	Memphis, TN	D
Harding U Main	Harding University Main Campus	Searcy, AR	M
Harrisburg Area CC	Harrisburg Area Community College	Harrisburg, PA	A
Harvard U	Harvard University	Cambridge, MA	D
Haverford C	Haverford College	Haverford, PA	B
Hawaii Pacific U	Hawaii Pacific University	Honolulu, HI	A
Hawkeye CC	Hawkeye Community College	Waterloo, IA	A
Hebrew C	Hebrew College	Newton Center, MA	M
Hebrew U C Jewish Inst Rel-CA	Hebrew Union College-Jewish Institute of Religion (California Branch)	Los Angeles, CA	D
Hebrew U C Jewish Inst Rel-OH	Hebrew Union College - Jewish Institute of Religion Central Office	Cincinnati, OH	D
Heidelberg C	Heidelberg College	Tiffin, OH	M
Heritage C-WA	Heritage College	Toppenish, WA	M
Herkimer Co CC	Herkimer County Community College	Herkimer, NY	A

A=Associates   B=Bachelors   M=Masters   D=Doctorate

KEY TO PARTICIPATING INSTITUTIONS

Institution	Full Name of Institution	Location	Carnegie Class
Highland CC KS	Highland Community College	Highland, KS	A
Hillsborough CC	Hillsborough Community College	Tampa, FL	A
Hillsdale C	Mossey Library, Hillsdale College	Hillsdale, MI	B
Hillsdale Free Will Baptist C	Hillsdale Free Will Baptist College	Moore, OK	M
Hinds CC	Hinds Community College	Raymond, MS	A
Hiram C	Hiram College	Hiram, OH	B
Hiwassee C	Hiwassee College	Madisonville, TN	A
Hocking Tech C	Hocking Technical College	Nelsonville, OH	A
Hofstra U	Hofstra University	Hempstead, NY	D
Hollins U	Hollins University	Roanoke, VA	M
Holy Family C	Holy Family College	Philadelphia, PA	M
Holy Trinity Orth Sem	Holy Trinity Orthodox Seminary	Jordanville, NY	B
Hope C	Hope College	Holland, MI	B
Hope Int'l U	Hope International University	Fullerton, CA	M
Hopkinsville CC	Hopkinsville Community College	Hopkinsville, KY	A
Horry GTown Tech	Horry-Georgetown Technical College	Conway, SC	A
Houghton C	Houghton College	Houghton, NY	B
Houston Baptist U	Houston Baptist University	Houston, TX	M
Howard C	Howard College	Big Spring, TX	A
Howard CC	Howard Community College	Columbia, MD	A
Howard Payne U	Howard Payne University	Brownwood, TX	B
Humboldt ST U	Humboldt State University	Arcata, CA	M
Huntington C-ON	Huntington College	Sudbury, ON	M
Hutch CC&Voc Sch	Hutchinson Community College and Area Vocational School	Hutchinson, KS	A
Idaho ST U	Idaho State University Library	Pocatello, ID	D
IL C Optometry	Illinois College of Optometry	Chicago, IL	D
IL E CC Wabash Cntrl C	Illinois Eastern Community Colleges Wabash Valley College	Olney, IL	A
IL Estrn CC-Frontier	Illinois Eastern Community Colleges Frontier Community College	Olney, IL	A
IL Estrn CC-Lincoln Trail	Illinois Eastern Community Colleges (Lincoln Trail Campus)	Olney, IL	A
IL Inst Tech	Illinois Institute of Technology	Chicago, IL	D
IL Sch Prof Psych	Illinois School of Professional Psychology/Chicago	Chicago, IL	D
IL Valley CC	Illinois Valley Community College	Oglesby, IL	A
Iliff Sch Theo	The Iliff School of Theology	Denver, CO	D
Illinois ST U	Illinois State University	Normal, IL	D
IN Inst of Tech	Indiana Institute of Technology	Fort Wayne, IN	M
IN Purdue U Inpolis	Indiana University-Purdue University Indianapolis	Indianapolis, IN	D
IN U Kokomo	Indiana University Kokomo	Kokomo, IN	M
IN U PA	Indiana University of Pennsylvania	Indiana, PA	D
IN U S Bend	Indiana University South Bend	South Bend, IN	M
IN U-Bloomington	Indiana University at Bloomington	Bloomington, IN	D
IN U-Purdue U Ft Wayne	Indiana University-Purdue University Fort Wayne	Fort Wayne, IN	M

A=Associates   B=Bachelors   M=Masters   D=Doctorate

125

KEY TO PARTICIPATING INSTITUTIONS

Institution	Full Name of Institution	Location	Carnegie Class
IN Wesleyan U	Indiana Wesleyan University	Marion, IN	D
Independence CC	Independence Community College	Independence, KS	A
Indiana ST U	Indiana State University	Terre Haute, IN	D
Inst Com PR Jr C Arecibo	Instituto Comercial de Puerto Rico Junior College	Arecibo, PR	A
Inst Native Culture	Institute of American Indian and Alaska Native Culture and Arts Development	Santa Fe, NM	A
Iona C	Iona College	New Rochelle, NY	M
Iowa ST U	Iowa State University	Ames, IA	D
Isothermal CC	Isothermal Community College	Spindale, NC	A
J.F. Drake ST Tech C	J.F. Drake State Technical College	Huntsville, AL	A
Jacksonville C	Jacksonville College	Jacksonville, TX	A
Jacksonville ST U	Jacksonville State University	Jacksonville, AL	M
James Madison U	James Madison University	Harrisonburg, VA	D
Jamestown C	Jamestown College	Jamestown, ND	B
Jefferson CC-NY	Jefferson Community College	Watertown, NY	A
Jefferson C-MO	Jefferson College	Hillsboro, MO	A
Jewish Theol Sem	Jewish Theological Seminary of America	New York, NY	D
John Carroll U	John Carroll University Grasselli Library and Breen Learning Center	Cleveland, OH	M
Johnson Bible C	Johnson Bible College	Knoxville, TN	M
Johnston CC	Johnston Community College	Smithfield, NC	A
Jones County Jr C	Jones County Junior College	Ellisville, MS	A
JS Reynolds CC	J. Sargeant Reynolds Community College	Richmond, VA	A
Judson C	Judson College	Elgin, IL	B
Justice Inst BC	Justice Institute of British Columbia	New Westminster, BC	A
Kaplan C	Kaplan College	Davenport, IA	B
Kaskaskia C	Kaskaskia College	Centralia, IL	A
Keene State C	Keene State College	Keene, NH	M
Kent St U E Liverpool	Kent State University East Liverpool Campus	East Liverpool, OH	A
Kent ST U Salem	Kent State University Salem Campus	Salem, OH	B
Kent ST U Stark	Kent State University Stark Campus	Canton, OH	M
Kent St U Tuscarawas	Kent State University Tuscarawas Campus	New Philadelphia, OH	A
Kentucky Christian C	Kentucky Christian College	Grayson, KY	M
Kentucky ST U	Kentucky State University	Frankfort, KY	M
Kenyon C	Kenyon College	Gambier, OH	B
Kettering C Med	Kettering College of Medical Arts	Kettering, OH	B
Kettering U	Kettering University	Flint, MI	M
Kilgore C	Kilgore College	Kilgore, TX	A
King C TN	King College	Bristol, TN	B
King's C PA	King's College	Wilkes-Barre, PA	M
King's U C-AB	The King's University College	Edmonton, AB	B
Kirksville C Med	Kirksville College of Osteopathic Medicine	Kirksville, MO	D
Kirkwood CC	Kirkwood Community College	Cedar Rapids, IA	A

A=Associates   B=Bachelors   M=Masters   D=Doctorate

126

KEY TO PARTICIPATING INSTITUTIONS

Institution	Full Name of Institution	Location	Carnegie Class
Kirtland CC	Kirtland Community College	Roscommon, MI	A
Knox C	Knox College	Galesburg, IL	B
Kwantlen UC	Kwantlen University College	Langley, BC	B
Labette CC	Labette Community College	Parsons, KS	A
Laboure C	Laboure College	Boston, MA	A
LaGrange C	LaGrange College	La Grange, GA	M
Lake City CC	Lake City Community College	Lake City, FL	A
Lakeland CC-OH	Lakeland Community College	Kirtland, OH	A
Lakeland Sheboygan	Lakeland College	Sheboygan, WI	M
Lakeview C Nursing	Lakeview College of Nursing	Danville, IL	B
Lambuth U	Lambuth University	Jackson, TN	B
Lancaster Bible C	Lancaster Bible College	Lancaster, PA	M
Lancaster Theo Sem	Lancaster Theological Seminary	Lancaster, PA	D
Lander U	Lander University	Greenwood, SC	M
Lane CC-OR	Lane Community College	Eugene, OR	A
Langston U	Langston University	Langston, OK	D
Lansdale Sch of Bus	Lansdale School of Business	North Wales, PA	A
Laramie Co CC	Laramie County Community College	Cheyenne, WY	A
Lassen CC	Lassen Community College	Susanville, CA	A
Laurentian U JN	Laurentian University	Sudbury, ON	D
Lawrence U	Lawrence University	Appleton, WI	B
Le Moyne C	Noreen Reale Falcone Library, Le Moyne College	Syracuse, NY	M
Lebanon Valley C	Lebanon Valley College	Annville, PA	D
Lee U Theo Sem	Lee University/Ch. of God Theological Seminary	Cleveland, TN	M
Lehigh U	Lehigh University	Bethlehem, PA	D
Lemoyne-Owen C	Lemoyne-Owen College	Memphis, TN	B
Lenoir Rhyne C	Lenoir-Rhyne College	Hickory, NC	M
LeTourneau U	LeTourneau University	Longview, TX	M
Lewis&Clark C	Lewis and Clark College	Portland, OR	M
Lexington CC	Lexington Community College	Lexington, KY	A
Liberty U	Liberty University	Lynchburg, VA	D
Lincoln U-MO	Lincoln University	Jefferson City, MO	M
Lindsey Wilson C	Lindsey Wilson College	Columbia, KY	M
Linn ST Tech C	Linn State Technical College	Linn, MO	A
Lipscomb U	Lipscomb University	Nashville, TN	M
Lock Haven U PA	Lock Haven University of Pennsylvania	Lock Haven, PA	M
Long Island U	Long Island University	Brookville, NY	D
Longwood C	Longwood College	Farmville, VA	M
Lord Fairfax CC	Lord Fairfax Community College	Middletown, VA	A
Los Angeles Valley C	Los Angeles Valley College	Valley Glen, CA	A
Louisville Pres Theo	Louisville Presbyterian Theological Seminary	Louisville, KY	D

A=Associates   B=Bachelors   M=Masters   D=Doctorate

KEY TO PARTICIPATING INSTITUTIONS

Institution	Full Name of Institution	Location	Carnegie Class
Lourdes C	Lourdes College	Sylvania, OH	M
Loyola Marymount U	Loyola Marymount University	Los Angeles, CA	M
Loyola U New Orleans	Loyola University New Orleans	New Orleans, LA	M
Lubbock Christian U	Lubbock Christian University	Lubbock, TX	M
Lutheran Sch Theo Chicago	Lutheran School of Theology at Chicago	Chicago, IL	D
Luzerne County CC	Luzerne County Community College	Nanticoke, PA	A
Lyon C	Lyon College	Batesville, AR	B
Macon ST C	Macon State College	Macon, GA	B
Madison Area Tech C	Madison Area Technical College	Madison, WI	A
Malone C	Malone College	Canton, OH	M
Manatee CC	Manatee Community College	Bradenton, FL	A
Manchester C	Manchester College	North Manchester, IN	M
Manhattan C	Manhattan College	Bronx, NY	M
Manhattan Christ C	Manhattan Christian College	Manhattan, KS	B
Manhattanville C	Manhattanville College	Purchase, NY	M
Mansfield U PA	Mansfield University of Pennsylvania	Mansfield, PA	M
Maple Woods CC	Maple Woods Community College Library	Kansas City, MO	A
Marietta C	Marietta College	Marietta, OH	B
Marist C	Marist College Cannavino Library	Poughkeepsie, NY	M
Marlboro C	Marlboro College	Marlboro, VT	B
Marquette U	Marquette University	Milwaukee, WI	D
Marshall U	Marshall University	Huntington, WV	D
Martin Luther C	Martin Luther College	New Ulm, MN	B
Mary Baldwin C	Mary Baldwin College	Staunton, VA	M
Mary Washington C	Mary Washington College	Fredericksburg, VA	M
Marylhurst U	Marylhurst University	Marylhurst, OR	D
Marymount C CA	Marymount College	Rancho Palos Verdes, CA	A
Marymount Manhattan C	Marymount Manhattan College	New York, NY	B
Marymount U	Marymount University	Arlington, VA	M
Maryville C	Maryville College	Maryville, TN	B
Maryville U St Louis	Maryville University of Saint Louis	Saint Louis, MO	M
Mass C Liberal Arts	Massachusetts College of Liberal Arts	North Adams, MA	B
Massasoit CC	Massasoit Community College	Brockton, MA	A
Master's C & Sem	The Master's College and Seminary	Santa Clarita, CA	M
Mayo Med Schl	Mayo Medical School	Rochester, MN	D
Mayville ST U	Mayville State University	Mayville, ND	B
McCormick Theo Sem	McCormick Theological Seminary	Chicago, IL	D
McDowell Tech CC	McDowell Technical Community College	Marion, NC	A
McKendree C	McKendree College	Lebanon, IL	B
McMurry U	McMurry University	Abilene, TX	B
McPherson C	McPherson College	McPherson, KS	B

A=Associates   B=Bachelors   M=Masters   D=Doctorate

KEY TO PARTICIPATING INSTITUTIONS

Institution	Full Name of Institution	Location	Carnegie Class
Medical U SC	Medical University of South Carolina	Charleston, SC	D
Medicine Hat C	Medicine Hat College	Medicine Hat, AB	B
Mercy C	Mercy College	Dobbs Ferry, NY	M
Merrimack C	Merrimack College	North Andover, MA	M
Mesa CC	Mesa Community College	Mesa, AZ	A
Messiah C	Messiah College	Grantham, PA	B
Metropolitan CC	Metropolitan Community College	Omaha, NE	A
Miami U	Miami University Libraries	Oxford, OH	D
MidAmer Nazarene U	MidAmerica Nazarene University	Olathe, KS	M
Middle TN ST U	Middle Tennessee State University	Murfreesboro, TN	D
Middlebury C	Middlebury College	Middlebury, VT	D
Middlesex Co C-NJ	Middlesex County College	Edison, NJ	A
Midland C	Midland College	Midland, TX	A
Midwestern U	Midwestern University	Downers Grove, IL	D
Miles CC	Miles Community College	Miles City, MT	A
Mills C	Mills College	Oakland, CA	D
Millsaps C	Millsaps College	Jackson, MS	M
Milwaukee Inst Art Design	Milwaukee Institute of Art & Design	Milwaukee, WI	B
Minnesota ST U-Mankato	Minnesota State University, Mankato	Mankato, MN	M
MiraCosta C	MiraCosta College	Oceanside, CA	A
Mississippi C	Mississippi College	Clinton, MS	M
MIT	Massachusetts Institute of Technology	Cambridge, MA	D
MO Baptist C	Missouri Baptist College	Saint Louis, MO	B
MO Southrn ST C	Missouri Southern State College	Joplin, MO	B
MO Western ST C	Missouri Western State College	Saint Joseph, MO	B
Monmouth C	Monmouth College	Monmouth, IL	B
Monroe CC	Monroe Community College	Rochester, NY	A
Montserrat C Art	Montserrat College of Art	Beverly, MA	B
Moorhead ST U	Moorhead State University	Moorhead, MN	M
Moravian C	Moravian College	Bethlehem, PA	M
Morehead ST U	Morehead State University	Morehead, KY	M
Morningside C	Morningside College	Sioux City, IA	M
Mount Royal C	Mount Royal College	Calgary, AB	B
Mount Union C	Mount Union College	Alliance, OH	B
Mountain Empire CC	Mountain Empire Community College	Big Stone Gap, VA	A
MS County CC	Mississippi County Community College	Blytheville, AR	A
MS Delta CC	Mississippi Delta Community College	Moorhead, MS	A
MS ST U	Mississippi State University	Mississippi State, MS	D
MS Valley ST U	Mississippi Valley State University	Itta Bena, MS	M
Mt Hood CC	Mt. Hood Community College	Gresham, OR	A
Mt Holyoke C	Mount Holyoke College	South Hadley, MA	M

A=Associates   B=Bachelors   M=Masters   D=Doctorate

KEY TO PARTICIPATING INSTITUTIONS

Institution	Full Name of Institution	Location	Carnegie Class
Mt Marty C	Mount Marty College	Yankton, SD	M
MT ST U Northern	Montana State University - Northern	Havre, MT	M
MT ST U Billings	Montana State University - Billings	Billings, MT	M
MT ST U-Bozeman	Montana State University - Bozeman	Bozeman, MT	D
Mt St Vincent U	Mount St Vincent University	Halifax, NS	M
MT Tech U Montana	Montana Tech of The University of Montana	Butte, MT	M
Mt Vernon Nazarene C	Mount Vernon Nazarene University	Mount Vernon, OH	M
Muhlenberg C	Muhlenberg College	Allentown, PA	B
Multnomah Bible C & Sem	Multnomah Bible College and Biblical Seminary	Portland, OR	M
Murray ST U-KY	Murray State University	Murray, KY	M
Muskingum C	Muskingum College	New Concord, OH	M
N Alberta Inst	Northern Alberta Institute of Technology	Edmonton, AB	A
N GA C & ST U	Stewart Library/North Georgia College & State University	Dahlonega, GA	M
Naropa U	Naropa University	Boulder, CO	M
National Hispanic U	The National Hispanic University	San Jose, CA	A
National U	National University Library	San Diego, CA	M
National U Health Sci	National University of Health Sciences	Lombard, IL	D
Natl Defense U	National Defense University	Washington, DC	M
Naval Postgrad Sch	Naval Postgraduate School	Monterey, CA	D
Naval War C	Naval War College	Newport, RI	M
Nazareth C Rochester	Nazareth College of Rochester	Rochester, NY	M
NC A&T ST U	North Carolina Agricultural and Technical State University	Greensboro, NC	D
NC Sch Arts	North Carolina School of the Arts	Winston-Salem, NC	M
NC ST U	North Carolina State University Libraries	Raleigh, NC	D
NC Wesleyan C	North Carolina Wesleyan College	Rocky Mount, NC	B
ND ST C Science	North Dakota State College of Science	Wahpeton, ND	A
NE ST U	Northeastern State University	Tahlequah, OK	M
NE WI Tech C	Northeast Wisconsin Technical College	Green Bay, WI	A
NEastrn IL U	Northeastern Illinois University	Chicago, IL	M
NEastrn U	Northeastern University	Boston, MA	D
Neumann C	Neumann College	Aston, PA	M
New C U South FL	New College of Florida	Sarasota, FL	B
New Eng Cons Music	New England Conservatory of Music	Boston, MA	D
New School Arch Design	New School of Architecture and Design	San Diego, CA	M
New York U	New York University	New York, NY	D
Newberry C	Newberry College	Newberry, SC	B
NH CC-Berlin	New Hampshire Community Technical College	Berlin, NH	A
NH CC-Berlin	New Hampshire Community Technical College, Laconia	Laconia, NH	A
Nicholls ST U	Nicholls State University	thibodaux, LA	M
Nicolet Area Tech C	Nicolet Area Technical College	Rhinelander, WI	A
Nipissing U	Nipissing University	North Bay, ON	M

A=Associates   B=Bachelors   M=Masters   D=Doctorate

KEY TO PARTICIPATING INSTITUTIONS

Institution	Full Name of Institution	Location	Carnegie Class
NJ City U	New Jersey City University	Jersey City, NJ	M
NJ Inst Tech	New Jersey Institute of Technology	Newark, NJ	D
NM St U-Carlsbad	New Mexico State University at Carlsbad	Carlsbad, NM	A
Norfolk ST U	Norfolk State University	Norfolk, VA	D
Normandale CC	Normandale Community College	Bloomington, MN	A
North AR C	North Arkansas College	Harrison, AR	A
North Central U	North Central University	Minneapolis, MN	B
North Park U	North Park University	Chicago, IL	D
Northeast ST Tech CC	Northeast State Technical Community College	Blountville, TN	A
Northeastern JC	Northeastern Junior College	Sterling, CO	A
Northern AZ U	Northern Arizona University	Flagstaff, AZ	D
Northern IL U	Northern Illinois University	De Kalb, IL	D
Northern KY U	Northern Kentucky University	Highland Heights, KY	M
Northern Lights C	Northern Lights College	Dawson Cr, BC	B
Northern ST U	Northern State University	Aberdeen, SD	M
Northwest C	Northwest College	Powell, WY	A
Northwest C	Northwest College	Kirkland, WA	M
Northwestern C-IA	Northwestern College	Orange City, IA	B
Northwestern C-MN	Northwestern College	St. Paul, MN	B
NorthWstrn U	Northwestern University	Evanston, IL	D
Notre Dame C NH	Notre Dame College	Manchester, NH	M
Nthrn Marianas C	Northern Marianas College	Saipan, MP	A
NW C Chiropractic	Northwestern College of Chiropractic	Bloomington, MN	D
NW MO ST U	Northwest Missouri State University	Maryville, MO	M
Nwestern Business C	Edward G. Schumacher Memorial Library	Chicago, IL	A
Nwestern CT Tech CC	Northwestern Connecticut Community College	Winsted, CT	A
Nwestern ST U	Northwestern State University	Natchitoches, LA	M
NY Chiropractic C	New York Chiropractic College	Seneca Falls, NY	D
NY Inst Tech Main	New York Institute of Technology Main Campus - Old Westbury	Old Westbury, NY	M
NY Med C	New York Medical College	Valhalla, NY	D
NY Sch Int Design	New York School of Interior Design	New York, NY	M
Oakland U	Oakland University	Rochester, MI	D
Oberlin C	Oberlin College	Oberlin, OH	M
Occidental C	Occidental College	Los Angeles, CA	B
Oglethorpe U	Oglethorpe University	Atlanta, GA	M
OH Dominican C	Ohio Dominican University	Columbus, OH	B
OH ST U Ag Tech Inst	The Ohio State University Agricultural Technical Institute	Wooster, OH	A
OH U Lancaster	Ohio University Lancaster Campus	Lancaster, OH	M
OH Wesleyan U	Ohio Wesleyan University	Delaware, OH	B
Ohio C Pod Med	Ohio College of Podiatric Medicine	Cleveland, OH	D
Ohio U Main Campus	Ohio University Main Campus	Athens, OH	D

A=Associates   B=Bachelors   M=Masters   D=Doctorate

KEY TO PARTICIPATING INSTITUTIONS

Institution	Full Name of Institution	Location	Carnegie Class
Ohlone C	Ohlone College	Fremont, CA	A
OK Panhandle ST U	Oklahoma Panhandle State University	Goodwell, OK	B
OK ST U Okmulgee	Oklahoma State University - Okmulgee	Okmulgee, OK	A
Okaloosa-Walton CC	Okaloosa-Walton Community College	Niceville, FL	A
Old Dominion U	Perry Library,Old Dominion University	Norfolk, VA	D
Olivet Nazarene U	Olivet Nazarene University	Bourbonnais, IL	M
Olympic C	Olympic College	Bremerton, WA	A
OR Health Sci U	Oregon Health and Science University	Portland, OR	D
Oral Roberts U	Oral Roberts University	Tulsa, OK	D
Orange County CC	Orange County Community College	Middletown, NY	A
Otterbein C	Otterbein College	Westerville, OH	M
Owensboro	Owensboro Community College	Owensboro, KY	A
Owensboro Jr C Bus	Daymar college- Owensboro	Owensboro, KY	A
Oxnard C	Oxnard college library	Oxnard, CA	A
PA C Optometry	Pennsylvania College of Optometry	Elkins Park, PA	D
Pacific Grad Sch Psych	Pacific Graduate School of Psychology	Palo Alto, CA	D
Pacific Lutheran U	Pacific Lutheran University	Tacoma, WA	M
Pacific U	Pacific University	Forest Grove, OR	D
Pacific Union C	Pacific Union College	Angwin, CA	M
Palm Beach Atl C	Palm Beach Atlantic College	West Palm Beach, FL	M
Palmer C Chiropractic-CA	Palmer College of Chiropractic-West	San Jose, CA	D
Panola C	Panola College	Carthage, TX	A
Passaic County CC	Passaic County Community College	Paterson, NJ	A
Paul D. Camp CC	Paul D. Camp Community College	Suffolk, VA	A
Peace C	Peace College	Raleigh, NC	B
Pellissippi ST Tech CC	Pellissippi State Technical Community College	Knoxville, TN	A
Penn ST	Penn State University Park	University Park, PA	D
Pensacola Jr C	Pensacola Junior College	Pensacola, FL	A
Petit Jean C	University of Arkansas Community College at Morrilton	Morrilton, AR	A
Pfeiffer U	Pfeiffer University	Misenheimer, NC	M
Philadelphia U	Philadelphia University	Philadelphia, PA	M
Phillips Grad Inst	Phillips Graduate Institute	Encino, CA	D
Piedmont Baptist C	Piedmont Baptist College	Winston-Salem, NC	M
Piedmont Tech C	Piedmont Technical College	Greenwood, SC	A
Pine Manor C	Pine Manor College	Chesnut Hill, MA	B
Pittsburgh Tech Inst	Pittsburgh Technical Institute	Pittsburgh, PA	A
Pittsburgh Theo Sem	Pittsburgh Theological Seminary	Pittsburgh, PA	D
Plymouth ST C	Plymouth State College	Plymouth, NH	M
Point Park C	Point Park College	Pittsburgh, PA	M
Pont C Josephinum	Pontifical College Josephinum	Columbus, OH	M
Portland CC	Portland Community College	Portland, OR	A

A=Associates   B=Bachelors   M=Masters   D=Doctorate

KEY TO PARTICIPATING INSTITUTIONS

Institution	Full Name of Institution	Location	Carnegie Class
Potomac C	Potomac College	Washington, DC	B
Potomac St C-WVU	Potomac State College of West Virginia University	Keyser, WV	A
Prairie Bible C	Prairie Bible College	Three Hills, AB	B
Prairie ST C	Prairie State College	Chicago Heights, IL	A
Prairie View A&M U	Prairie View A & M University	Prairie View, TX	M
Presb C-Montreal	Presbyterian College of Montreal	Montreal, QC	M
Presbyterian C	Presbyterian College	Clinton, SC	B
Prescott C	Prescott College	Prescott, AZ	M
Prince George CC	Prince George's Community College	Largo, MD	A
Princeton TheoSem	Princeton Theological Seminary	Princeton, NJ	D
Principia C	Principia College	Elsah, IL	B
Pueblo CC	Pueblo Community College	Pueblo, CO	A
Pulaski Tech C	Pulaski Technical College	North Little Rock, AR	A
Purchase C SUNY	Purchase College, State University of New York	Purchase, NY	M
Purdue U Calumet	Purdue University Calumet	Hammond, IN	M
Purdue U Main	Purdue University Main Campus	West Lafayette, IN	D
Queens C	Queens University of Charlotte	Charlotte, NC	M
Queen's U	Queen's University	Kingston, ON	A
Quincy U	Quincy University	Quincy, IL	M
Quinebaug Vally Comm TC	Quinebaug Valley Community College	Danielson, CT	A
Quinsigamond CC	Quinsigamond Community College	Worcester, MA	A
R Morris C PA	Robert Morris University	Moon Township, PA	D
R.Wesleyan C	Roberts Wesleyan College	Rochester, NY	M
Radford U	Radford University	Radford, VA	M
Ramapo C NJ	Ramapo College of New Jersey	Mahwah, NJ	M
Randolph-Macon C	Randolph-Macon College	Ashland, VA	B
Randolph-Macon WC	Randolph-Macon Woman's College	Lynchburg, VA	B
Reading Area CC	Reading Area Community College	Reading, PA	A
Recnstrctnst Rabbinical C	Reconstructionist Rabbinical College	Wyncote, PA	M
Red Deer C	Red Deer College	Red Deer, AB	A
Redlands CC	Redlands Community College	El Reno, OK	A
Reformed Bible C	Reformed Bible College	Grand Rapids, MI	B
Reformed Theo Sem-MS	Reformed Theological Seminary	Jackson, MS	D
Regent	Regent University	Virginia Beach, VA	D
Regis C	Regis College	Toronto, ON	M
Rend Lake C	Rend Lake College	Ina, IL	A
Renton Tech C	Renton Technical College	Renton, WA	A
RI Sch Design	Rhode Island School of Design	Providence, RI	M
Rice U	Rice University	Houston, TX	D
Ricks C	BYU-Idaho	Rexburg, ID	B
Rider U	Rider University	Lawrenceville, NJ	M

A=Associates   B=Bachelors   M=Masters   D=Doctorate

KEY TO PARTICIPATING INSTITUTIONS

Institution	Full Name of Institution	Location	Carnegie Class
Ringling Sch Art & Design	Ringling School of Art and Design	Sarasota, FL	B
Ripon C	Ripon College	Ripon, WI	B
Rivier C	Rivier College	Nashua, NH	M
Robeson CC	Robeson Community College	Lumberton, NC	A
Rochester C	Rochester College	Rochester Hills, MI	B
Rochester Inst Tech	Rochester Institute of Technology	Rochester, NY	D
Rock Valley	Rock Valley College	Rockford, IL	A
Rockford C	Rockford College	Rockford, IL	M
Rockhurst U	Rockhurst University	Kansas City, MO	M
Rocky Mountain C	Rocky Mountain College	Billings, MT	B
Roger Williams U	Roger Williams University	Bristol, RI	M
Rogue CC	Rogue Community College	Grants Pass, OR	A
Rollins C	Rollins College	Winter Park, FL	M
Roosevelt U	Roosevelt University	Chicago, IL	D
Rosemont C	Rosemont College	Rosemont, PA	M
Rowan U	Rowan University	Glassboro, NJ	D
Rutgers ST U	Rutgers the State University of New Jersey Central Office	New Brunswick, NJ	D
S.F.Austin ST U	Stephen F. Austin State University	Nacogdoches, TX	D
Sacramento City C	Sacramento City College	Sacramento, CA	A
Sacred Heart Schl Theo	Sacred Heart School of Theology	Hales Corners, WI	M
Sacred Heart U	Sacred Heart University	Fairfield, CT	M
Saginaw Valley ST U	Saginaw Valley State University	University Center, MI	M
Saint Joseph C	Saint Joseph College	West Hartford, CT	M
Salem Teiko U	Salem International University	Salem, WV	M
Salisbury ST U	Salisbury University	Salisbury, MD	M
Salt Lake CC	Salt Lake Community College	Salt Lake City, UT	A
Salve Regina U	Salve Regina University	Newport, RI	D
Sam Houston ST U	Sam Houston State University	Huntsville, TX	D
Samford U	Samford University	Birmingham, AL	D
Samuel Merritt C	Samuel Merritt College	Oakland, CA	M
San Antonio C	San Antonio College	San Antonio, TX	A
San Jacinto C South	San Jacinto College South	Houston, TX	A
San Joaquin Delta C	San Joaquin Delta College	Stockton, CA	A
San Jose ST U	San Jose State University	San Jose, CA	M
Santa Barbara City C	Santa Barbara City College	Santa Barbara, CA	D
Santa Clara U	Santa Clara University	Santa Clara, CA	M
Santa Fe CC-NM	Santa Fe Community College	Santa Fe, NM	A
Santa Monica C	Santa Monica College	Santa Monica, CA	A
Sch Visual Arts	Visual Arts Library, School of Visual Arts	New York, NY	M
Schreiner C	Schreiner College	Kerrville, TX	M
Scripps C	Scripps College	Claremont, CA	B

A=Associates   B=Bachelors   M=Masters   D=Doctorate

KEY TO PARTICIPATING INSTITUTIONS

Institution	Full Name of Institution	Location	Carnegie Class
SD Sch Mines & Tech	South Dakota School of Mines and Technology	Rapid City, SD	D
SE C Assemblies God	Southeastern College of the Assemblies of God	Lakeland, FL	B
SE LA U	Southeastern Louisiana University	Hammond, LA	M
SE MO ST U	Southeast Missouri State University	Cape Girardeau, MO	M
SE Oklahoma St U	Southeastern Oklahoma State University	Durant, OK	M
Seattle Pacific U	Seattle Pacific University	Seattle, WA	D
Seattle U	Seattle University	Seattle, WA	D
Selkirk C	Selkirk College	Castlegar, BC	A
Seton Hill C	Seton Hill College	Greensburg, PA	M
Seward County CC	Seward County Community College	Liberal, KS	A
Shaw U	Shaw University	Raleigh, NC	M
Shawnee ST U	Shawnee State University	Portsmouth, OH	M
Shenandoah U	Shenandoah University	Winchester, VA	D
Shepherd C	Shepherd College	Shepherdstown, WV	B
Shippensburg U PA	Shippensburg University of Pennsylvania	Shippensburg, PA	M
Siena C	Siena College	Loudonville, NY	B
Silver Lake C	Silver Lake College	Manitowoc, WI	M
Simon Fraser U	Simon Fraser University	Burnaby, BC	D
Simpson C IA	Dunn Library -- Simpson College	Indianola, IA	B
Sisseton-Wahpeton CC	Sisseton-Wahpeton Community College	Sisseton, SD	M
Skidmore C	Skidmore College	Saratoga Springs, NY	M
South AR CC	South Arkansas Community College	El Dorado, AR	A
South Baylo U	South Baylo University	Anaheim, CA	M
South Florida CC	South Florida Community College	Avon Park, FL	A
South Puget Sound CC	South Puget Sound Community College	Olympia, WA	A
Southeast CC	Southeast Community College	Cumberland, KY	A
Southrn Adventist U	Southern Adventist University	Collegedale, TN	M
Southrn C Opt	Southern College of Optometry	Memphis, TN	D
Southrn IL U Carbondale	Southern Illinois University at Carbondale	Carbondale, IL	D
Southrn IL U Edward	Southern Illinois University at Edwardsville	Edwardsville, IL	M
Southrn Methodist U	Southern Methodist University	Dallas, TX	D
Southrn NH U	Southern New Hampshire University	Manchester, NH	D
Southrn OR U	Southern Oregon University	Ashland, OR	M
Southrn ST CC	Southern State Community College	Hillsboro, OH	A
Southrn U A&M Baton	Southern University and Agricultural and Mechanical College at Baton Rouge	Baton Rouge, LA	D
Southrn Utah U	Southern Utah University	Cedar City, UT	M
Southside VA CC	Southside Virginia Community College	Alberta, VA	A
Southwest U	Southwestern University	Georgetown, TX	B
Southwest VA CC	Southwest Virginia Community College	Richlands, VA	A
Spartan Aeronautics-Tech	Spartan School of Aeronautics and Technology	Tulsa, OK	B
Spartanburg Tech C	Spartanburg Technical College	Spartanburg, SC	A

A=Associates   B=Bachelors   M=Masters   D=Doctorate

135

KEY TO PARTICIPATING INSTITUTIONS

Institution	Full Name of Institution	Location	Carnegie Class
Spoon River C	Spoon River College	Canton, IL	A
Spring Hill C	Spring Hill College	Mobile, AL	M
St Andrews Presby C	St Andrews Presbyterian College	Laurinburg, NC	B
St Anthony C Nursing	St. Anthony College of Nursing	Rockford, IL	B
St Charles County CC	St. Charles County Community College	St. Peters, MO	A
St Clair C Arts Tech	St Clair College of Arts & Technology	Windsor, ON	B
St Cloud ST U	Saint Cloud State University	Saint Cloud, MN	M
St Francis C NY	St. Francis College	Brooklyn, NY	B
St Francis C PA	Saint Francis University	Loretto, PA	M
St John Fisher C	St. John Fisher College	Rochester, NY	M
St John Vianney C Sem	St. John Vianney College Seminary	Miami, FL	B
St John's C	St. John's College	Annapolis, MD	M
St John's U MN	Saint John's University	Collegeville, MN	M
St John's U NY	Saint John's University	Jamaica, NY	D
St Joseph's C NY	Saint Joseph's College, New York	Brooklyn, NY	M
St Joseph's U	Saint Joseph's University	Philadelphia, PA	M
St Louis U	Saint Louis University	Saint Louis, MO	D
St Mary's C CA	Saint Mary's College of California	Moraga, CA	D
St Mary's C IN	Saint Mary's College	Notre Dame, IN	B
St Mary's U TX	Blume Library, St. Mary's University	San Antonio, TX	D
St Mary's U Halifax	Saint Mary's University	Halifax, NS	D
St Mary's U MN	Saint Mary's University of Minnesota	Winona, MN	D
St Meinrad Theo	Saint Meinrad School of Theology	St. Meinrad, IN	M
St Michael's C	Saint Michael's College	Colchester, VT	M
St Norbert C	Saint Norbert College	De Pere, WI	M
St Patrick's Sem	Saint Patrick's Seminary	Menlo Park, CA	M
St Peter's Abbey & C	St Peter's Abbey & College	Muenster, SK	M
St Thomas U	St. Thomas University	Miami, FL	M
ST U W GA	State University of West Georgia	Carrollton, GA	D
St Vincent Sem	St. Vincent De Paul Regional Seminary	Boynton Beach, FL	M
St Vladimir TheoSem	Saint Vladimir's Orthodox Theological Seminary	Crestwood, NY	D
St. Bonaventure U	St. Bonaventure University	St. Bonaventure, NY	M
St. Edward's U	St. Edward's University	Austin, TX	M
St. Mary's C Maryland	St. Mary's College of Maryland	Saint Mary's City, MD	B
Sterling C-KS	Sterling College	Sterling, KS	M
Sterling C-VT	Sterling College	Craftsbury Common, VT	B
Stetson U	Stetson University	DeLand, FL	M
Stevens Inst Tech	Stevens Institute of Technology	Hoboken, NJ	D
Sthrn Arkansas U Tech	Southern Arkansas University Tech	Camden, AR	D
Sthrn CA C Opt	Southern California College of Optometry	Fullerton, CA	D
Sthrn Polytech ST U	Southern Polytechnic State University	Marietta, GA	M

A=Associates   B=Bachelors   M=Masters   D=Doctorate

KEY TO PARTICIPATING INSTITUTIONS

Institution	Full Name of Institution	Location	Carnegie Class
Sthrn U-Shreveport/Bossier	Southern University at Shreveport	Shreveport, LA	A
Stonehill C	Stonehill College	Easton, MA	M
SUNY A&T Cobleskill	State University of New York College of Agriculture and Technology at Coble	Cobleskill, NY	B
SUNY Binghamton	State University of New York at Binghamton	Binghamton, NY	D
SUNY Buffalo	State University of New York at Buffalo	Buffalo, NY	D
SUNY C Tech-Canton	State University of New York College of Technology at Canton	Canton, NY	B
SUNY C-Geneseo	State University of New York College at Geneseo	Geneseo, NY	B
SUNY Fredonia	State University of New York College at Fredonia	Fredonia, NY	M
SUNY Health Sci Ctr - Brooklyn	State University of New York Health Science Center at Brooklyn	Brooklyn, NY	D
SUNY Health Sci Ctr - Syracuse	State University of New York Health Science Center at Syracuse	Syracuse, NY	M
SUNY Hlth Sci Ctr Stony Brook	State University of New York Health Science Center at Stony Brook	Stony Brook, NY	D
SUNY IT Utica	State University of New York Institute of Technology at Utica-Rome	Utica, NY	M
SUNY Optometry	State University of New York College of Optometry	New York, NY	D
SUNY Oswego	State University of New York College at Oswego	Oswego, NY	M
Susquehanna U	Susquehanna University	Selinsgrove, PA	B
SW MO ST U	Southwest Missouri State University	Springfield, MO	M
SW TX U	Southwest Texas State University	San Marcos, TX	D
Sweet Briar C	Sweet Briar College	Sweet Briar, VA	M
SWstrn C	Southwestern College	Chula Vista, CA	A
SWstrn OK ST U	Southwestern Oklahoma State University	Weatherford, OK	D
SWstrn OR CC	Southwestern Oregon Community College	Coos Bay, OR	A
Syracuse U Main	Syracuse University main campus	Syracuse, NY	D
T Stevens C Tech	Thaddeus Stevens College of Technology	Lancaster, PA	A
Tacoma CC	Tacoma Community College	Tacoma, WA	A
Talladega C	Talladega College	Talladega, AL	B
Tallahassee CC	Tallahassee Community College	Tallahassee, FL	A
Taylor U	Taylor University	Upland, IN	M
Taylor U-Ft Wayne	Taylor University	Fort Wayne, IN	D
Teachers C Columbia	Teachers College, Columbia University	New York, NY	D
Tech C Lowcountry	Technical College of the Lowcountry	Beaufort, SC	A
Teikyo Post U	Teikyo Post University	Waterbury, CT	B
Temple C	Temple College	Temple, TX	A
Temple U	Temple University	Philadelphia, PA	D
Texas Sthrn U	Texas Southern University	Houston, TX	D
Thiel C	Thiel College	Greenville, PA	B
Three Rivers CTC	Three Rivers Community-Technical College	Norwich, CT	A
Thunderbird Schl Intl Mngmnt	Thunderbird, The American Graduate School of International Management	Glendale, AZ	M
Tiffin U	Tiffin University	Tiffin, OH	M
TN ST U	Tennessee State University	Nashville, TN	D
Touro C	Touro College	New York, NY	M
Trevecca Nazarene U	Trevecca Nazarene University	Nashville, TN	D

A=Associates   B=Bachelors   M=Masters   D=Doctorate

KEY TO PARTICIPATING INSTITUTIONS

Institution	Full Name of Institution	Location	Carnegie Class
Tri County CC	Tri-County Community College	Murphy, NC	A
Tri County Tech C	Tri-County Technical College	Pendleton, SC	A
Trinidad ST Jr C	Trinidad State Junior College	Trinidad, CO	A
Trinity Luth Sem	Trinity Lutheran Seminary	Columbus, OH	M
Trinity U	Trinity University	San Antonio, TX	M
Trocaire C	Trocaire College	Buffalo, NY	A
Troy ST U	Troy State University	Troy, AL	M
Truett McConnell C	Truett McConnell College	Cleveland, GA	B
Truman ST U	Truman State University	Kirksville, MO	M
Tunxis CC Tech	Tunxis Community College	Farmingtom, CT	A
TX A & M-Med	Texas A & M University-Medical Sciences	College Station, TX	D
TX A&M Comm	Texas A & M University - Commerce	Commerce, TX	D
TX Chiro C	Texas Chiropractic College	Pasadena, TX	D
TX Christian U	Texas Christian University	Fort Worth, TX	D
TX Lutheran U	Texas Lutheran University	Seguin, TX	B
TX ST Tech C Waco	Texas State Technical College - Waco	Waco, TX	A
TX Tech U, Health Sci Ctr	Texas Tech University Health Sciences Center	Lubbock, TX	D
TX Woman's U	Texas Woman's University	Denton, TX	D
U Adventista Antillas	Universidad Adventista de las Antillas	Mayaguez, PR	M
U AK Fairbanks	University of Alaska Fairbanks	Fairbanks, AK	D
U Akron Wayne C	University of Akron-Wayne College	Orrville, OH	A
U Akron-Main	The University of Akron, Main Campus	Akron, OH	D
U AL Birmingham	University of Alabama at Birmingham	Birmingham, AL	D
U AL Huntsville	University of Alabama in Huntsville	Huntsville, AL	D
U Alabama	The University of Alabama	Tuscaloosa, AL	D
U Alberta	University of Alberta	Edmonton, AB	D
U AR - Monticello	University of Arkansas at Monticello	Monticello, AR	M
U Arts	University of the Arts	Philadelphia, PA	M
U AS Little Rock	University of Arkansas at Little Rock	Little Rock, AR	D
U AS Main Campus	University of Arkansas Main Campus	Fayetteville, AR	D
U Baltimore	University of Baltimore	Baltimore, MD	D
U C Cape	University College of Cape	Sydney, NS	B
U CA - San Diego	University of California-San Diego	La Jolla, CA	D
U CA Davis	University of California-Davis	Davis, CA	D
U CA Riverside	University of California - Riverside	Riverside, CA	D
U CA Santa Barbara	University of California - Santa Barbara	Santa Barbara, CA	D
U CA Santa Cruz	University of California-Santa Cruz	Santa Cruz, CA	D
U Calgary	University of Calgary	Calgary, AB	D
U California - Berkeley	University of California - Berkeley	Berkeley, CA	D
U Central FL	University of Central Florida	Orlando, FL	D
U Charleston	University of Charleston	Charleston, WV	D

A=Associates   B=Bachelors   M=Masters   D=Doctorate

KEY TO PARTICIPATING INSTITUTIONS

Institution	Full Name of Institution	Location	Carnegie Class
U CO - Colorado Springs	University of Colorado at Colorado Springs	Colorado Springs, CO	D
U CO Boulder	University of Colorado at Boulder	Boulder, CO	D
U CO Denver	University of Colorado at Denver	Denver, CO	D
U CT	University of Connecticut	Storrs, CT	D
U CT Health Ctr	University of Connecticut Health Center	Farmington, CT	D
U Dallas	University of Dallas	Irving, TX	D
U Dayton	University of Dayton	Dayton, OH	D
U DC	University of the District of Columbia	Washington, DC	M
U Delaware	University of Delaware	Newark, DE	D
U Denver	University of Denver	Denver, CO	D
U Detroit Mercy	University of Detroit Mercy	Detroit, MI	D
U Dubuque	University of Dubuque	Dubuque, IA	D
U Findlay	The University of Findlay	Findlay, OH	M
U FL	University of Florida	Gainesville, FL	D
U GA	University of Georgia	Athens, GA	D
U Great Falls	University of Great Falls	Great Falls, MT	M
U Guam	University of Guam	Mangilao, GU	M
U Hawaii-Hilo	University of Hawaii at Hilo	Hilo, HI	D
U HI-Kapiolani CC	University of Hawaii Kapiolani Community College	Honolulu, HI	A
U HI-Kauai CC	University of Hawaii Kauai Community College	Lihue, HI	A
U HI-Leeward CC	University of Hawaii, Leeward Community College	Pearl City, HI	A
U HI-Manoa	University of Hawaii at Manoa	Honolulu, HI	D
U HI-Windward CC	University of Hawaii Windward Community College	Kaneohe, HI	A
U Houston	University of Houston - Clear Lake	Houston, TX	M
U Idaho	University of Idaho	Moscow, ID	D
U IL Chicago	University of Illinois at Chicago	Chicago, IL	D
U IL Springfield	University of Illinois at Springfield	Springfield, IL	D
U IL Urbana Champaign	University of Illinois at Urbana-Champaign	Urbana, IL	D
U Indianapolis	University of Indianapolis	Indianapolis, IN	D
U Iowa	University of Iowa	Iowa City, IA	D
U Judaism	University of Judaism	Los Angeles, CA	D
U Kentucky	University of Kentucky	Lexington, KY	D
U LA Lafayette	University of Louisiana at Lafayette	Lafayette, LA	D
U LA Monroe	University of Louisiana at Monroe	Monroe, LA	D
U Laval	Universite Laval	Sainte-Foy, QC	D
U LaVerne	University of LaVerne	La Verne, CA	D
U Lethbridge	University of Lethbridge	Lethbridge, AB	D
U M.Hardin-Baylor	University of Mary Hardin-Baylor	Belton, TX	M
U MA Boston	University of Massachusetts Boston	Boston, MA	D
U Maine	University of Maine	Orono, ME	D
U Mass Lowell	University of Massachusetts Lowell	Lowell, MA	D

A=Associates   B=Bachelors   M=Masters   D=Doctorate

KEY TO PARTICIPATING INSTITUTIONS

Institution	Full Name of Institution	Location	Carnegie Class
U MD C Park	University of Maryland College Park	College Park, MD	D
U ME Fort Kent	University of Maine at Fort Kent	Fort Kent, ME	B
U ME Presque Isle	University of Maine at Presque Isle	Presque Isle, ME	B
U Memphis	The University of Memphis	Memphis, TN	D
U MI AnnArbor	University Of Michigan-Ann Arbor	Ann Arbor, MI	D
U MI Dearborn	University of Michigan-Dearborn	Dearborn, MI	M
U Miami	University of Miami	Coral Gables, FL	D
U MN Duluth	University of Minnesota-Duluth	Duluth, MN	M
U MN Twin	University of Minnesota-Twin Cities	Minneapolis, MN	D
U MO Columbia	University of Missouri - Columbia	Columbia, MO	D
U MO KS City	University of Missouri-Kansas City	Kansas City, MO	D
U MO Rolla	University of Missouri - Rolla	Rolla, MO	D
U MO St Louis	University of Missouri-Saint Louis	Saint Louis, MO	D
U Mobile	University of Mobile	Mobile, AL	M
U Montana	The University of Montana	Missoula, MT	B
U Montreal	Universite de Montreal	Montreal, QC	D
U MS	University of Mississippi	University, MS	D
U N Iowa	University of Northern Iowa	Cedar Falls, IA	D
U ND Main	University of North Dakota Main Campus	Grand Forks, ND	D
U NE Kearney	University of Nebraska at Kearney	Kearney, NE	M
U NE Linocln	University of Nebraska - Lincoln	Lincoln, NE	D
U New Orleans	University of New Orleans	New Orleans, LA	D
U NH	University of New Hampshire	Durham, NH	D
U NM Gallup Branch	University of New Mexico Gallup Branch	Gallup, NM	A
U NM Main Campus	University of New Mexico Main Campus	Albuquerque, NM	D
U North FL	University of North Florida	Jacksonville, FL	D
U North TX	University of North Texas	Denton, TX	D
U Northern CO	University of Northern Colorado	Greeley, CO	D
U Notre Dame	University of Notre Dame	Notre Dame, IM	D
U NV Las Vegas	University of Nevada-Las Vegas	Las Vegas, NV	D
U Ottawa	Universite d'Ottawa	Ottawa, ON	D
U PA	University of Pennsylvania	Philadelphia, PA	D
U Pacific	University of the Pacific	Stockton, CA	D
U Pitt-Oakland	University of Pittsburgh- Oakland Campus	Pittsburgh, PA	M
U Portland	University of Portland	Portland, OR	M
U PQ Ecole tech	École de Technologie Supérieure	Montreal, QC	D
U Quebec	Universite du Quebec	Quebec, QC	D
U Quebec-Montreal	Université du Québec à Montréal	Montreal, QC	D
U Quebec-Rimouski	Universite du Quebec a Rimouski	Rimouski, QC	D
U Regina	University of Regina	Regina, SK	D
U RI	University of Rhode Island	Kingston, RI	D

A=Associates   B=Bachelors   M=Masters   D=Doctorate

KEY TO PARTICIPATING INSTITUTIONS

Institution	Full Name of Institution	Location	Carnegie Class
U Richmond	University of Richmond	Richmond, VA	M
U Rio Grande	University of Rio Grande	Rio Grande, OH	M
U S Dakota	University of South Dakota	Vermillion, SD	D
U San Fran	University of San Francisco	San Francisco, CA	D
U SC - Sumter	University of South Carolina - Sumter	Sumter, SC	B
U SC Columbia	University of South Carolina-Columbia	Columbia, SC	D
U SC Spartanburg	University of South Carolina Spartanburg	Spartanburg, SC	M
U Sci & Arts OK	University of Science and Arts of Oklahoma	Chickasha, OK	B
U Sciences Phila	University of the Sciences in Philadelphia	Philadelphia, PA	D
U South AL	University of South Alabama	Mobile, AL	D
U South FL	University of South Florida	Tampa, FL	D
U St Thomas	University of Saint Thomas	Houston, TX	D
U Sthn CA	University of Southern California	Los Angeles, CA	D
U Sthn IN	University of Southern Indiana	Evansville, IN	M
U Sthrn Maine	University of Southern Maine	Portland, ME	D
U Sthrn Mississippi	University of Southern Mississippi	Hattiesburg, MS	D
U Tampa	University of Tampa	Tampa, FL	M
U Theo Sem Presb	Union Theological Seminary and Presbyterian School of Christian Education	Richmond, VA	D
U TN Chatt	University of Tennessee at Chattanooga	Chattanooga, TN	D
U TN Martin	University of Tennessee at Martin	Martin, TN	D
U TN-Knoxville	University of Tennessee, Knoxville	Knoxville, TN	D
U Toledo	University of Toledo	Toledo, OH	D
U Toronto	University of Toronto	Toronto, ON	D
U TX Arlington	University of Texas at Arlington	Arlington, TX	D
U TX Austin	University of Texas at Austin	Austin, TX	D
U TX Dallas	University of Texas at Dallas	Richardson, TX	D
U TX El Paso	University of Texas at El Paso	El Paso, TX	D
U TX Hlth Sci Ctr-Houston	University of Texas Health Science Center at Houston	Houston, TX	D
U TX Pan Amer	University of Texas - Pan American	Edinburg, TX	D
U TX Tyler	University of Texas at Tyler	Tyler, TX	M
U VA	University of Virginia	Charlottesville, VA	D
U Victoria	University of Victoria	Victoria, BC	D
U Waterloo	University of Waterloo	Waterloo, ON	D
U West AL	The University of West Alabama	Livingston, AL	M
U West FL	University of West Florida	Pensacola, FL	D
U WI E Claire	University of Wisconsin-Eau Claire	Eau Claire, WI	M
U WI La Crosse	University of Wisconsin-La Crosse	La Crosse, WI	M
U WI Madison	University of Wisconsin - Madison	Madison, WI	D
U WI Milwaukee	University of Wisconsin - Milwaukee	Milwaukee, WI	D
U WI Platteville	University of Wisconsin-Platteville	Platteville, WI	M
U Windsor	University of Windsor	Windsor, ON	D

A=Associates   B=Bachelors   M=Masters   D=Doctorate

KEY TO PARTICIPATING INSTITUTIONS

Institution	Full Name of Institution	Location	Carnegie Class
U Winnipeg	University of Winnipeg	Winnipeg, MB	M
U Wisconsin-River Falls	University of Wisconsin-River Falls	River Falls, WI	M
U Wstrn Ontario	University of Western Ontario	London, ON	D
U Wyoming	University of Wyoming	Laramie, WY	D
UNBC	University of Northern British Columbia	Prince George, BC	M
UNC Asheville	University of North Carolina at Asheville	Asheville, NC	B
UNC Chapel Hill	University of North Carolina at Chapel Hill	Chapel Hill, NC	D
UNC Charlotte	University of North Carolina at Charlotte	Charlotte, NC	D
UNC Pembroke	University of North Carolina at Pembroke	Pembroke, NC	M
UNC Wilmington	University of North Carolina at Wilmington	Wilmington, NC	D
Union C-NE	Union College	Lincoln, NE	M
Union C-NY	Union College	Schenectady, NY	M
United Theo Sem-Twin Cities	United Theological Seminary of the Twin Cities	New Brighton, MN	D
Unity C	Unity College	Unity, ME	B
UNT HSC Ft Worth	University of North Texas Health Science Center at Fort Worth	Fort Worth, TX	D
Ursuline C	Ursuline College	Cleveland, OH	M
US C Guard Acad	United States Coast Guard Academy	New London, CT	B
US Merchant Marine Acad	United States Merchant Marine Academy	Kings Point, NY	B
USC - Aiken	University of South Carolina - Aiken	Aiken, SC	B
UT Valley ST C	Utah Valley State College	Orem, UT	B
Utah ST	Utah State University	Logan, UT	D
VA Union U	Virginia Union University	Richmond, VA	D
VA Wesleyan C	Virginia Wesleyan College	Norfolk, VA	B
VA Western CC	Virginia Western Community College	Roanoke, VA	A
Valdosta ST U	Valdosta State University	Valdosta, GA	D
Valley City ST U	Valley City State University	Valley City, ND	B
Valparaiso U	Valparaiso University	Valparaiso, IN	M
Vanderbilt U	Vanderbilt University	Nashville, TN	D
VanderCook C Music	VanderCook College of Music	Chicago, IL	M
Vassar C	Vassar College	Poughkeepsie, NY	M
VCU	Virginia Commonwealth University	Richmond, VA	D
Victoria U	Victoria University	Toronto, ON	D
Villa Julie C	Villa Julie College	Stevenson, MD	M
Villanova U	Villanova University	Villanova, PA	D
W.Carey College	William Carey College	Hattiesburg, MS	M
W.Rainey Harper C	William Rainey Harper College	Palatine, IL	A
Wake Forest U	Wake Forest University	Winston-Salem, NC	D
Walla Walla C	Waldorf College	Forest City, IA	B
Walla Walla C	Walla Walla College	College Place, WA	M
Walsh U	Walsh University	North Canton, OH	A
Walters ST CC	Walters State Community College	Morristown, TN	A

A=Associates   B=Bachelors   M=Masters   D=Doctorate

KEY TO PARTICIPATING INSTITUTIONS

Institution	Full Name of Institution	Location	Carnegie Class
Warner Sthrn C	Warner Southern College	Lake Wales, FL	B
Warren Wilson C	Warren Wilson College	Asheville, NC	B
Wartburg Theo Sem	Wartburg Theological Seminary	Dubuque, IA	M
Washburn U Topeka	Washburn University of Topeka	Topeka, KS	M
Washington C	Washington College	Chestertown, MD	M
Washington Theo Union	Washington Theological Union	Washington, DC	M
Washington U	Washington University in St. Louis	Saint Louis, MO	D
Waycross C	Waycross College	Waycross, GA	A
Weatherford C	Weatherford College	Weatherford, TX	A
Wellesley C	Wellesley College	Wellesley, MA	B
Wells C	Wells College	Aurora, NY	B
Wesley C	Wesley College	Dover, DE	M
Wesley Theo Sem	Wesley Theological Seminary	Washington, DC	D
West Chester U PA	West Chester University of Pennsylvania	West Chester, PA	M
West TX A & M U	West Texas A&M University	Canyon, TX	M
West VA U	West Virginia University	Morgantown, WV	D
West VA Wesleyan C	West Virginia Wesleyan College	Buckhannon, WV	M
Westark C	University of Arkansas - Fort Smith	Fort Smith, AR	B
Western IA Tech CC	Western Iowa Tech Community College	Sioux City, IA	A
Western MD C	McDaniel College	Westminster, MD	M
Western MI U	Western Michigan University	Kalamazoo, MI	D
Western OR U	Western Oregon University - Wayne and Lynn Hamersly Library	Monmouth, OR	M
Western Sem	Western Seminary	Portland, OR	D
Western ST C	Western State College	Gunnison, CO	B
Western WA U	Western Washington University	Bellingham, WA	M
Westminster C-MO	Westminster College	Fulton, MO	B
Westminster C-UT	Westminster College	Salt Lake City, UT	M
Westminster Theo Sem-CA	Westminster Theological Seminary in California	Escondido, CA	M
Westmont C	Westmont College	Santa Barbara, CA	B
Wharton Co Jr C	Wharton County Junior College	Wharton, TX	A
Whatcom CC	Whatcom Community College	Bellingham, WA	A
Wheaton C	Wheaton College	Wheaton, IL	D
Wheeling Jesuit U	Wheeling Jesuit University	Wheeling, WV	M
Wheelock C	Wheelock College	Boston, MA	M
Whitman C	Whitman College	Walla Walla, WA	B
Whitworth C	Whitworth College	Spokane, WA	M
WI Lutheran C	Wisconsin Lutheran College	Milwaukee, WI	B
Wichita ST U	Wichita State University	Wichita, KS	D
Widener U	Widener University	Chester, PA	D
Wiley C	Wiley College	Marshall, TX	B
Wilfrid Laurier U	Wilfrid Laurier University	Waterloo, ON	D

A=Associates   B=Bachelors   M=Masters   D=Doctorate

KEY TO PARTICIPATING INSTITUTIONS

Institution	Full Name of Institution	Location	Carnegie Class
Wilkes U	Willamette University	Salem, OR	M
William Woods U	William Woods University	Fulton, MO	M
Williams C	Williams College	Williamstown, MA	M
Wilmington C DE	Wilmington College	New Castle, DE	D
Wilson C	Wilson College	Chambersburg, PA	B
Winston-Salem ST U	Winston-Salem State University	Winston-Salem, NC	M
Winthrop U	Winthrop University	Rock Hill, SC	M
Wittenberg U	Wittenberg University	Springfield, OH	B
Wofford C	Wofford College	Spartanburg, SC	B
Woodbury U	Woodbury University	Burbank, CA	M
Worchester PTech Inst	Worcester Polytechnic Institute	Worcester, MA	D
Wright ST U-Lake	Wright State University Lake Campus	Celina, OH	D
Wright ST U-Main	Wright State University Main Campus	Dayton, OH	D
Wstrn CT ST U	Western Connecticut State University	Danbury, CT	D
Wstrn New England C	Western New England College	Springfield, MA	M
WV U Inst Tech	West Virgina Universtiy Institute of Technology	Montgomery, WV	M
Wytheville CC	Wytheville Community College	Wytheville, VA	A
Xavier U	Xavier University	Cincinnati, OH	D
Xavier U LA	Xavier University of Louisiana	New Orleans, LA	D
Yakima Valley CC	Yakima Valley Community College	Yakima, WA	A
Yale U	Yale University	New Haven, CT	D
Yavapai C	Yavapai College	Prescott, AZ	A
Yeshiva U	Yeshiva University	New York, NY	D
York C	York College	York, NE	B

A=Associates   B=Bachelors   M=Masters   D=Doctorate

ACRL STATISTICS 2004-05
WORKSHEET

This worksheet is designed to help you plan your submission for the 2004-05 *ARL Statistics*. The figures on this worksheet should be similar to those in the "Summary" page of your web form, except in cases where data are unavailable. If an exact figure is unavailable, use "NA/UA". If the appropriate answer is zero or none, use "0."

Reporting Institution _____ Date Returned to ARL _____

Report Prepared by (name) _____

Title _____

Email address_____ Phone number _____

Contact person (if different) _____

Title _____

Email address_____ Phone number _____

PAGE ONE – VOLUMES

    1. Volumes held June 30, 2005

        1a. Volumes held June 30, 2004   (1.a) _____

        1b. Volumes added during the year

                (i) Volumes added – Gross   (1.b.i) _____

                (ii) Volumes withdrawn during year   (1.b.ii) _____

        (Net Volumes Added: 1.b.i – 1.b.ii)   (1.b) _____

        (Volumes held June 30, 2005: 1.a + 1.b)   (1) _____

    2. Number of monographic volumes purchased   (2) _____

    3. Basis of volume count is: (3) _____ Physical

                                    _____ Bibliographical

OTHER COLLECTIONS

SERIALS

    4. Total number of current serials received, including periodicals

        4a. Number of current serials <u>purchased</u>   (4a) _____

4b. Number of current serials <u>received but not purchased</u>   (4b) _____
(Exchanges, gifts, deposits, etc. See instructions.)

(Total serials received: 4.a + 4.b)   (4) _____

5. Government documents are included in count of Current Serials? (5) _____ Yes _____ No

OTHER LIBRARY MATERIALS

6. Microform units   (6) _____

7. Government documents not counted elsewhere   (7) _____

8. Computer files   (8) _____

9. Manuscripts and archives (linear ft.)   (9) _____

AUDIOVISUAL MATERIALS

10. Cartographic   (10) _____

11. Graphic   (11) _____

12. Audio   (12) _____

13. Film and Video   (13) _____

EXPENDITURES

14. Are the below figures reported in Canadian dollars?   (14) _____Yes _____No

15. Total Library Materials Expenditures

15a. Monographs   (15a) _____

15b. Current serials, including periodicals   (15b) _____

15c. Other Library Materials   (15c) _____

15d. Miscellaneous   (15d) _____

(Total library materials: 15.a + 15.b + 15.c + 15.d)   (15) _____

16. Contract binding   (16) _____

17. Total Salaries and Wages

17a. Professional staff   (17a) _____

17b. Support staff   (17b) _____

17c. Student assistants   (17c) _____

(Total salaries and wages: 17.a + 17.b + 17.c)   (17) _____

18. Fringe benefits are included in expenditures for salaries and wages?   (18) _____ Yes

_____ No

19. Other operating expenditures   (19) _____

20. Total library expenditures (*15 + 16 + 17 + 19)*   (20) _____

ELECTRONIC MATERIALS EXPENDITURES

21. Computer files *(One-time/monographic purchases.)*   (21) _____

22. Electronic serials   (22) _____

23. Bibliograhpic Utilities, Networks, and Consortia

23a. From internal library sources   (23a) _____

23b. From external sources   (23b) _____

24. Computer hardware and software   (24) _____

25. Document Delivery/Interlibrary Loan   (25) _____

PERSONNEL AND PUBLIC SERVICES

PERSONNEL (Round figures to nearest whole number.)

26. Total Staff FTE

26a. Professional staff   (26a) _____

26b. Support staff   (26b) _____

26c. Student assistants   (26c) _____

(Total staff FTE: 26.a + 26.b + 26.c)   (26) _____

STAFFED SERVICE POINTS AND HOURS

27. Number of staffed library service points   (27) _____

28. Number of weekly public service hours   (28) _____

INSTRUCTION

29. Number of library presentations to groups   (29) _____

29a. Figure based on sampling? (29a) _____Yes _____No

30. Number of total participants in group presentations reported in line 29

(30) _____

30a. Figure based on sampling? (30a) _____Yes _____No

REFERENCE

31. Number of reference transactions (31) _____

31a. Figure based on sampling? (31a) _____Yes _____No

PUBLIC SERVICES AND LOCAL CHARACTERISTICS

CIRCULATION

32. Number of initial circulations (excluding reserves) (32) _____

33. Total circulations (initial and renewals, excluding reserves) (33) _____

INTERLIBRARY LOANS

34. Total number of filled requests provided to other libraries (34) _____

35. Total number of filled requests received from other libraries or providers

(35) _____

Ph.D. DEGREES AND FACULTY

36. Number of Ph.D.s awarded in FY2004-05 (36) _____

37. Number of fields in which Ph.D.s can be awarded (37) _____

38. Number of full-time instructional faculty in FY2004-05 (38) _____

ENROLLMENT – FALL 2004
(Line numbers refer to IPEDS survey form.)

39. Full-time students, undergraduate and graduate (39) _____
(Add line 8, columns 15 & 16, and line 14, columns 15 & 16.)

40. Part-time students, undergraduate and graduate (40) _____
(Add line 22, columns 15 & 16, and line 28, columns 15 & 16.)

41. Full-time graduate students *(Line 14, columns 15 & 16.)* (41) _____

42. Part-time graduate students *(Line 28, columns 15 & 16.)* (42) _____

FOOTNOTES

ACRL STATISTICS QUESTIONNAIRE, 2004-05
INSTRUCTIONS FOR COMPLETING THE QUESTIONNAIRE

General Instructions

Definitions of statistical categories can be found in NISO Z39.7-2004, *Information Services and Use: Metrics & statistics for libraries and information providers--Data Dictionary* (http://www.niso.org/emetrics/current/index.html). ARL has been modifying the interpretation of the standard definitions to address questions posed by by the library staff at various member institutions that complete the survey and with feedback from the ARL Statistics and Assessment Committee (http://www.arl.org/stats/program/meeting.html).

Please do not use decimals. All figures should be rounded to the nearest whole number.

Please respond to every question. If an exact figure cannot be provided, use NA/UA to indicate that the figure is either unavailable or not applicable. If the appropriate answer is zero or none, use **0**. Although the form allows for data to be entered from both main and branch campuses, an effort should be made to report figures for the main campus only. (The U.S. National Center for Education Statistics, Integrated Postsecondary Education Data System (IPEDS) defines a **branch institution** as "a campus or site of an educational institution that is not temporary, is located in a community beyond a reasonable commuting distance from its parent institution, and offers organized programs of study, not just courses.") If figures for libraries located at branch campuses are reported, please specify which branch libraries are included and which ones are excluded in the notes below. A **branch library** is defined as an auxiliary library service outlet with quarters separate from the central library of an institution, which has a basic collection of books and other materials, a regular staffing level, and an established schedule. A branch library is administered either by the central library or (as in the case of some law and medical libraries) through the administrative structure of other units within the university. Departmental study/reading rooms are not included. The questionnaire assumes a fiscal year ending **June 30, 2005**. If your fiscal year is different, please indicate this in the notes below by adjusting the reporting period.

Footnotes. Explanatory footnotes will be included with the published statistics. Provide any notes you may have in the footnotes area at the end of the survey. Reporting libraries are urged to record there any information that would clarify the figures submitted in that line, e.g., the inclusion and exclusion of branch campus libraries. Please make an effort to word your footnotes in a manner consistent with notes appearing in the published report, so that the ARL Office can interpret your footnotes correctly.

Specific Instructions

Question 1. Volumes in Library. Use the ANSI/NISO Z39.7-2004 definition for **volume** as follows:

> *a single physical unit of any printed, typewritten, handwritten, mimeographed, or processed work, distinguished from other units by a separate binding, encasement, portfolio, or other clear distinction, which has been cataloged, classified, and made ready for use, and which is typically the unit used to charge circulation transactions. Either a serial volume is bound, or it comprises the serial issues that would be bound together if the library bound all serials.*

Include duplicates and bound volumes of periodicals. For purposes of this questionnaire, unclassified bound serials arranged in alphabetical order are considered classified. Exclude microforms, maps, nonprint materials, and uncataloged items. If any of these items cannot be excluded, please provide an explanatory footnote Include government document volumes that are accessible through the library's catalogs regardless of whether they are separately shelved. "Classified" includes documents arranged by Superintendent of Documents, CODOC, or similar numbers. "Cataloged" includes documents for which records are provided by the library or downloaded from other sources into the library's card or online catalogs. Documents should, to the extent possible, be counted as they would if they were in bound volumes (e.g., 12 issues of an annual serial would be one or two volumes). Title and piece counts should not be considered the same as volume counts. If a volume count has not been kept, it may be estimated through sampling a representative group of title records and determining the corresponding number of volumes, then extrapolating to the rest of the collection. As an alternative, an estimate may be made using the following formulae:

52 documents pieces per foot

10 "traditional" volumes per foot

5.2 documents pieces per volume

Include e-book units, as long as these e-books have been purchased and are owned by your library. If you have access to netLibrary titles as a result of participating in various consortia, **do not** report these e-books as your library's property unless the e-books actually belong to your library. If the books were purchased by a consortium, they may belong to the consortium itself and not to the participating libraries. Report only the number of e-books that belong to your library and are cataloged, classified and made ready for use. Provide a footnote explaining how many e-books you are reporting, preferably by specifying the products and the number of titles in a note. For information on how to count items housed in remote storage, see the Interim Guidelines for Counting Materials Housed in Library Storage Centers, at http://www.arl.org/stats/arlstat/storage.html. If either formulas or sampling are used for deriving your count, please indicate in a footnote.

Question 1b. Volumes Added. Include only volumes cataloged, classified, and made ready for use. Include government documents if they have been included in the count of volumes on line 1a. Do not include as part of Volumes Added Gross any government documents or other collections (such as large gift collections or e-book packages) that were added to the collection as the result of a one time download or addition to the OPAC. Include these items in Volumes Held of the previous year (Line 1a) and provide a footnote explaining the revision of Line 1a. Include e-book units, as long as these e-books have been purchased and are owned by your library. If you have access to netLibrary titles as a result of participating in various consortia, **do not** report these e-books as your library's property unless the e-books actually belong to your library. If the books were purchased by a consortium, they may belong to the consortium itself and not to the participating libraries. Report only the number of e-books that belong to your library and are cataloged, classified and made ready for use. Provide a footnote explaining how many e-books you are reporting, preferably by specifying the products and the number of titles in a note.

Question 2. Monographic Volumes Purchased. Report number of volumes purchased; do not include volumes received or cataloged. Include all volumes for which an expenditure was made during 2004-05, including volumes paid for in advance but not received during the fiscal year. Include monographs in series and continuations. Include e-books that fit the netLibrary model, i.e., electronic manifestations of physical entities and/or units; provide a footnote explaining how many ebooks you are reporting, preferably by specifying the products and the number of titles. If only number of titles purchased can be reported, please report the data and provide an explanatory footnote.

Question 3: Basis of Volume Count. A physical count is a piece count; a bibliographic count is a catalog record count.

Questions 4-5. Serials. Report the total number of subscriptions, not titles. Include duplicate subscriptions and, to the extent possible, all government document serials even if housed in a separate documents collection. Verify the inclusion or exclusion of document serials in Question 5. Exclude unnumbered monographic and publishers' series. Electronic serials acquired as part of an aggregated package (e.g., Project MUSE, BioOne, ScienceDirect) should be counted by title. A **serial** is

a publication in any medium issued in successive parts bearing numerical or chronological designations and intended to be continued indefinitely. This definition includes periodicals, newspapers, and annuals (reports, yearbooks, etc.); the journals, memoirs, proceedings, transactions, etc. of societies; and numbered monographic series.

In the case of consortial agreements, count under Q4a only those subscriptions to titles for which the library pays directly from its budgeted expenditures reported under Q15b (expenditures for serials). Count under Q4a only those titles and subscriptions for which your library pays. Report other subscriptions that your library receives and does not pay for directly under Q4b (serials received and not purchased). If a purchased subscription includes electronic access to the title, count that subscription twice: once for the print version and once for the electronic version. If serials have been purchased through a consortium whose budget is centrally funded and independent from the library's budget, these serials should be reported under Q4b. **Do not include** the full-text serials from such indexing/abstracting products as Wilson Social Sciences Abstracts Full Text, Lexis-Nexis, ABI/INFORM, and other indexes with access to the full text of articles. These full-text titles are counted in in the ARL Supplementary Statistics.

Question 4b. Serials: Not Purchased. Record those serials whose subscriptions were received without purchase for whatever reason. If separate counts of nonpurchased and purchased serials are not available, report only the total number of current serials received on line 4, and report U/A for lines 4a and 4b.

Question 6. Microforms. Report the total number of physical units: reels of microfilm, microcards, and microprint and microfiche sheets. Include all government documents in microform; provide a footnote if documents are excluded.

Question 7. Government documents. Report the total number of physical units (pieces) of government documents in paper format that have not been counted elsewhere. Include local, state, national, and international documents; include documents purchased from a commercial source if shelved with separate documents collections and not counted above. Include serials and monographs. To estimate pieces from a measurement of linear feet, use the formula
   1 foot = 52 pieces
and indicate in a footnote that the count is based on this estimate. Exclude microforms and nonprint formats such as maps or CD-ROMs. Adjust line 1a, i.e., last year's Volumes Held, and provide a footnote if you are adding records to the OPAC for government documents previously held but not counted as part of Volumes Held (line 1a).

Question 8. Computer files. Include the number of pieces of computer-readable disks, tapes, CD-ROMs, and similar machine-readable files comprising data or programs that are **locally held as part of the library's collections** available to library clients. Examples are U.S. Census data tapes, sample research software, locally-mounted databases, and reference tools on CD-ROM, tape or disk. Exclude bibliographic records used to manage the collection (i.e., the library's own catalog in machine-readable form), library system software, and microcomputer software used only by the library staff.

Question 9. Manuscripts and archives. Include both manuscripts and archives measured in linear feet.

Question 10. Cartographic materials. Include the numbers of pieces of two- and three-dimensional maps and globes. Include satellite and aerial photographs and images.

Question 11. Graphic materials. Include the number of pieces of prints, pictures, photographs, postcards, slides, transparencies, film strips, and the like.

Question 12. Audio materials. Include the number of pieces of audiocassettes, phonodiscs, audio compact discs, reel-to-reel tapes, and other sound recordings.

Question 13. Film and video materials. Include the number of pieces of motion pictures, videocassettes, video laser discs, and similar visual materials.

Questions 14-20. Expenditures. Report all expenditures of funds that come to the library from the regular institutional budget, and from sources such as research grants, special projects, gifts and endowments, and fees for service. (For question 17, include non-library funds; see instruction Q17.) Do not report encumbrances of funds that have not yet been expended. **Canadian libraries should report expenditures in Canadian dollars.** (For your information, if interested in determining figures in U.S. dollars, divide Canadian dollar amounts by 1.24971, the average monthly noon exchange rate published in the Bank of Canada *Review* for the period July 2004-June 2005.) **Please round figures to the nearest dollar.**

Question 15a. Monographs. Report expenditures for volumes counted on line 2.

Question 15b. Current Serials. Report expenditures for serials counted on line 4a. Exclude unnumbered monographic and publishers' series, and encumbrances.

Question 15c. Other library materials. Include expenditures for all materials not reported in Questions 15a and 15b, e.g., backfiles of serials, charts and maps, audiovisual materials, manuscripts, etc. If expenditures for these materials are included in lines 15a and/or 15b and cannot be disaggregated, please report U/A and provide a footnote. Do not include encumbrances.

Question 15d. Miscellaneous expenditures. Include any other **materials funds expenditures** not included in questions 15a-c, e.g., expenditures for bibliographic utilities, literature searching, security devices, memberships for the purposes of publications, etc. Please list categories, with amounts, in a footnote. **Note:** If your library does not use materials funds for non-materials expenditures—i.e., such expenditures are included in "Other Operating Expenditures"— **report 0, not U/A,** on line 15d.

Question 16. Contract Binding. Include only contract expenditures for binding done outside the library. If all binding is done in-house, state this fact and give in-house expenditures in a footnote; do not include personnel expenditures. (This figure should also be reported in the 2004-05 ARL Preservation Survey, question 7b.)

Questions 17. Salaries and wages. Exclude fringe benefits. If professional and support staff salaries cannot be separated, enter **U/A,** on lines 17a and 17b and enter total staff on line 17.

Question 17c. Salaries and wages: Student Assistants. Report 100% of student wages regardless of budgetary source of funds. Include federal and local funds for work study students.

Question 19. Other operating expenditures. Exclude expenditures for buildings, maintenance, and fringe benefits.

Questions 21-25. Electronic materials expenditures. These items are intended to indicate what portion of your institution's total library expenditures are dedicated to electronic resources and services. Please use the Footnotes to indicate any electronic materials expenditures you believe not to be covered by these questions. **Many expenditures recorded in these questions should have been included in Question 20, total library expenditures.**

Question 21. Computer files. Report expenditures that are not current serials (i.e. are non-subscription, one-time, or monographic in nature) for software and machine-readable materials considered part of the collections. Examples include periodical backfiles, literature collections, one-time costs for JSTOR membership, etc. Expenditures reported here may be derived from any of the following categories: Monographs (Q15a), Other Library Materials (Q15c), Miscellaneous (Q15d), or Other Operating Expenditures (Q19).

Question 22. Electronic Serials. Report subscription expenditures (or those which are expected to be ongoing commitments) for serial publications whose primary format is electronic and for online searches of remote databases such as OCLC FirstSearch, DIALOG, Lexis-Nexis, etc. Examples include paid subscriptions for electronic journals and indexes/abstracts available via the Internet, CD-ROM serials, and annual access fees for resources purchased on a "one-time" basis, such as literature collections, JSTOR membership, etc. Not all items whose expenditures are counted here will be included in Total Current Serials (Question 4) or Current Serial Expenditures (Question 15b).

Q23. Bibliographic Utilities, Networks, and Consortia. Because it is increasingly common for ARL Libraries to enter into consortial arrangements to purchase access to electronic resources, both "Library" and "External" expenditure blanks and instructions are provided. Please use afootnote to describe expenditures that you believe are not covered by the question, or situations that do not seem to fit the instructions.

Q23a. From internal library sources. Report expenditures paid by the Library for services provided by national, regional, and local bibliographic utilities, networks, and consortia, such as OCLC and RLG, unless for user database access and subscriptions, which should be reported in Questions 21 or 22. Include only expenditures that are part of Other Operating Expenditures (Q19).

Q23b. From external sources. If your library receives access to computer files, electronic serials or search services through one or more centrally-funded system or consortial arrangements for which it does not pay fully and/or directly (for example, funding is provided by the state on behalf of all members), enter the amount paid by external bodies on its behalf. If the specific dollar amount is not known, but the total student FTE for the consortium and amount spent for the academic members are known, divide the overall amount spent by your institution's share of the total student FTE.

Q24. Computer hardware and software. Report expenditures from the library budget for computer hardware and software used to support library operations, whether purchased or leased, mainframe or microcomputer, and whether for staff or public use. Include expenditures for: maintenance; equipment used to run information service products when those expenditures can be separated from the price of the product; telecommunications infrastructure costs, such as wiring, hubs, routers, etc. Include only expenditures that are part of Other Operating Expenditures (Q19).

Q25. Document Delivery/Interlibrary Loan. Report expenditures for document delivery and interlibrary loan services (both borrowing and lending). Include fees paid for photocopies, costs of telefacsimile transmission, royalties and access fees paid to provide document delivery or interlibrary loan. Include fees paid to bibliographic utilities if the portion paid for interlibrary loan can be separately counted. Include only expenditures that are part of Miscellaneous Materials Expenditures (Q15d) or Other Operating Expenditures (Q19), and only for those ILL/DD programs with data recorded in Questions 34-35.

Questions 26. Personnel. Report the number of staff in filled positions, or positions that are only temporarily vacant. ARL defines temporarily vacant positions as positions that were vacated during the fiscal year for which ARL data were submitted, for which there is a firm intent to refill, and for which there are expenditures for salaries reported on line 17. Include cost recovery positions and staff hired for special projects and grants, but provide an explanatory footnote indicating the number of such staff. If such staff cannot be included, provide a footnote. To compute full-time equivalents of part-time employees and student assistants, take the total number of hours per week (or year) worked by part-time employees in each category and divide it by the number of hours considered by the reporting library to be a full-time work week (or year). **Round figures to the nearest whole numbers.**

Question 26a. Professional Staff. Since the criteria for determining professional status vary among libraries, there is no attempt to define the term "professional." Each library should report those staff members it considers professional, including, when appropriate, staff who are not librarians in the strict sense of the term, for example computer experts, systems analysts, or budget officers.

Question 26c. Student Assistants. Report the total FTE (see instruction Q26) of student assistants employed on an hourly basis whose wages are paid from funds under library control or from a budget other than the library's, including federal work-study programs. Exclude maintenance and custodial staff.

Question 27. Number of staffed library service points. Count the number of staffed public service points in the main library and in all branch libraries reported in this inventory, including reference desks, information desks, circulation, current periodicals, reserve rooms, reprographic services (if staffed as a public facility), etc. Report the number of designated locations, not the number of staff.

Question 28. Number of weekly public service hours. Report an unduplicated count of the total public service hours per typical full-service week (i.e., no holidays or other special accommodations) across both main library and branches using the following method (corresponds to IPEDS): If a library is open from 9:00 a.m. to 5:00 p.m. Monday through Friday, it should report 40 hours per week. If several of its branches are also open during these hours, the figure remains 40 hours per week. Should Branch A also be open one evening from 7:00 p.m. to 9:00 p.m., the total hours during which users can find service somewhere within the system becomes 42 hours per week. If Branch B is open the same hours on the same evening, the count is still 42, but if Branch B is open two hours on another evening, or remains open two hours later, the total is then 44 hours per week. **Exclude 24-hour unstaffed reserve or similar reading rooms.** The maximum total is 168 (i.e., a staffed reading room open 7 days per week, 24 hours per day).

Questions 29-30. Instruction. Sampling based on a typical week may be used to extrapolate TO A FULL YEAR for Questions 29 and 30. Please indicate if responses are based on sampling.

Question 29. Presentations to Groups. Report the total number of sessions during the year of presentations made as part of formal bibliographic instruction programs and through other planned class presentations, orientation sessions, and tours. If the library sponsors multi-session or credit courses that meet several times over the course of a semester, each session should be counted. Presentations to groups may be for either bibliographic instruction, cultural, recreational, or educational purposes. Presentations both on and off the premises should be included as long as they are sponsored by the library. Do not include meetings sponsored by other groups using library meeting rooms. Do not include training for library staff; the purpose of this question is to capture information about the services the library provides for its clientele. Please indicate if the figure is based on sampling.

Question 30. Participants in Group Presentations. Report the total number of participants in the presentations reported on line 29. For multi-session classes with a constant enrollment, count each person only once. Personal, one-to-one instruction in the use of sources should be counted as reference transactions on line 31. Please indicate if the figure is based on sampling. Use a footnote to describe any special situations.

Question 31. Reference Transactions. Report the total number of reference transactions. A **reference transaction** is

> *an information contact that involves the knowledge, use, recommendations, interpretation, or instruction in the use of one or more information sources by a member of the library staff. The term includes information and referral service. Information sources include (a) printed and nonprinted material; (b) machine-readable databases (including computer-assisted instruction); (c) the library's own catalogs and other holdings records; (d) other libraries and institutions through communication or referral; and (e) persons both inside and outside the library. When a staff member uses information gained from previous use of information sources to answer a question, the transaction is reported as a reference transaction even if the source is not consulted again.*

If a contact includes both reference and directional services, it should be reported as one reference transaction. Duration should not be an element in determining whether a transaction is a reference transaction. Sampling based on a typical week may be used to extrapolate TO A FULL YEAR for Question 31. Please indicate if the figure is based on sampling. EXCLUDE SIMPLE DIRECTIONAL QUESTIONS. A directional transaction is an information contact that facilitates the logistical use of the library and that does not involve the knowledge, use, recommendations, interpretation, or instruction in the use of any information sources other than those that describe the library, such as schedules, floor plans, and handbooks.

Questions 32-33. Circulation. For Question 32, count the number of initial circulations during the fiscal year from the general collection for use usually (although not always) outside the library. Do not count renewals. Include circulations to and from remote storage facilities for library users (i.e., do not include transactions reflecting transfers or stages of technical processing). Count the total number of items lent, not the number of borrowers. For Question 33, report total circulation for the fiscal year including initial transactions reported on line 32 and renewal transactions. Exclude reserve circulations; these are no longer reported.

Questions 34-35. Interlibrary Loans. Report the number of requests for material (both returnables and non-returnables) provided to other libraries on line 34 and the number of filled requests received from other libraries or providers on line 35. On both lines, include originals, photocopies, and materials sent by telefacsimile or other forms of electronic transmission. Include patron-initiated transactions. Exclude requests for materials locally owned and available on the shelves or electronically. Do not include transactions between libraries covered by this questionnaire.

Questions 36. Ph.D. Degrees. Report the number awarded during the 2004-05 fiscal year. Please note that only the number of Ph.D. degrees are to be counted. Statistics on all other advanced degrees (e.g., D.Ed., D.P.A., M.D., J.D.) should not be reported in this survey. If you are unable to provide a figure for Ph.D.s only, please add a footnote.

Question 37. Ph.D. Fields. For the purposes of this report, Ph.D. fields are defined as the specific discipline specialties enumerated in the U.S. Department of Education's Integrated Postsecondary Education Data System (IPEDS) "Completions" Survey. Although the IPEDS form requests figures for all doctoral degrees, only fields in which Ph.D.s are awarded should be reported on the ARL questionnaire. Any exceptions should be footnoted.

Question 38. Instructional Faculty. Instructional faculty are defined by the U.S. Dept. of Education as
members of the instruction/research staff who are employed full-time as defined by the institution, including faculty with released time for research and faculty on sabbatical leave.
Full-time counts generally exclude faculty who are employed to teach fewer than two semesters, three quarters, two trimesters, or two four-month sessions; replacements for faculty on sabbatical leave or leave without pay; faculty for preclinical and clinical medicine; faculty who are donating their services; faculty who are members of military organizations and paid on a different pay scale from civilian employees; academic officers, whose primary duties are administrative; and graduate students who assist in the instruction of courses. Please be sure the number reported, and the basis for counting, are consistent with those for 2003-04 (unless in previous years faculty were counted who should have been excluded according to the above definition). Please footnote any discrepancies.

Questions 39-42. Enrollment. U.S. libraries should use the Fall 2004 enrollment figures reported to the Department of Education on the Integrated Postsecondary Education Data System survey. Please check these figures against the enrollment figures reported to ARL last year to ensure consistency and accuracy. **Note:** In the past, the number of part-time students reported was FTE; the number now reported to IPEDS is a head count of part-time students. Canadian libraries should note that the category "graduate students" as reported here includes all post-baccalaureate students.

FOOTNOTES
Please consult the printed copy of the *ACRL Statistics 2004* for a copy of last year's footnotes. A pdf version is available at: http://www.arl.org/stats/arlstat/. Explanatory footnotes will be included with the published statistics. Reporting libraries are urged to record in the footnote section any information that would clarify the figures submitted, e.g., the inclusion and exclusion of branch campus libraries (see the "General Instructions" for definition of branch campus libraries). Please make an effort to word your footnotes in a manner consistent with notes appearing in the published report, so that your footnotes can be interpreted correctly.

ACRL SUPPLEMENTARY STATISTICS 2004-05
WORKSHEET

Reporting Institution _____

Report Prepared by (name) _____

Title_____

Email address_____ Phone number_____

Contact person (if different) _____

Title_____

Email address_____ Phone number_____

Definitions of the statistical categories used in this questionnaire can be found in the COUNTER Code of Practice, April 2005 (http://www.projectcounter.org/code_practice.html) and in *Information Services and Use: Metrics & statistics for libraries and information providers--Data Dictionary*, NISO Z39.7-2004 (http://www.niso.org/emetrics/current/index.html).

Please read all instructions carefully before you answer the questionnaire. Make sure your responses are as complete and accurate as possible. Give estimates when you must, but please do not make wild guesses. Use footnotes to expand upon or clarify your responses. All questions assume a ***fiscal year ending June 30, 2005***. If your library's fiscal year is different, please use footnotes to explain.

If your library does not perform a given function or had no activity for this function or if the appropriate answer is zero or none, use **0**. If an exact figure is unavailable, check NA/UA.

Please do not use decimals. All figures should be rounded to the nearest whole number.

Number of Networked Electronic Resources
1. Number of electronic journals purchased. (1) _____

> Number of electronic journal subscriptions that the library provides to users and for which the library pays some fee for access either through an individual institutional licensing contract with the provider of journals or through other arrangements (e.g., library-funded consortia, centrally-funded consortia or through state or national purchasing plans). Include electronic journals offered by established scholarly journal publishing houses (e.g., Elsevier's ScienceDirect); scholarly societies (e.g., American Chemical Society journals and American Institute of Physics Online); services that aggregate journal content (e.g., Expanded Academic ASAP or Lexis/Nexis); and, from those publishers using an external delivery platform (BioOne, EbscoOnline, Highwire, and OCLC ECO). The number of electronic journals purchased reported here could include journals for which you may have reported expenditures in the *ARL Statistics*.

2. Number of electronic "full-text" journals purchased. (2) _____

> This is a subset of #1, *Number of electronic journals purchased*. "Full-text" journals, such as those from Elsevier's Science Direct or Kluwer Online Journals, should contain the journals' complete contents. Include electronic full-text journals from the sources described above. Exclude services that

aggregate or provide only partial coverage of journal content (e.g., Expanded Academic ASAP or Lexis/Nexis).

3. Number of electronic journals not purchased. (3) _____

Number of unique electronic journals for which the library pays no fee and for which the library has taken responsibility for providing access either through cataloging in its OPAC or other forms of local organization (web site, databases, etc.). Include journals that are free through centrally-funded consortia. Include government documents.

4. Number of electronic reference sources. (4) _____

This includes licensed citation indexes and abstracts; full-text reference sources (e.g. encyclopedias, almanacs, biographical and statistical sources, and other quick fact-finding sources); full-text journal and periodical article collection services (e.g., EBSCOhost, ProQuest, Academic Universe, and INFOTRAC OneFile); dissertation and conference proceedings databases; and, those databases that institutions mount locally. Include databases that contain journals reported in #1. Please describe in the Footnotes, if e-books are included in this count.

5. Number of electronic books. (5) _____

Number of electronic full-text monographs that the library offers to its users and for which the library pays some fee for access either through an individual institutional licensing contract with the provider of journals or through other arrangements (e.g., library-funded consortia, centrally-funded consortia or through state or national purchasing plans). This includes electronic books purchased through vendors, such as netLibrary and Books24x7, and electronic books that come as part of aggregate services. Include individual volumes of e-book sets that are counted as individual reference sources reported in #4. Exclude locally digitized electronic books, electronic theses and dissertations, locally created digital archival collections, and other special collections. Do not include machine-readable books distributed on CD-ROM, or accompanied by print books.

Expenditures for Networked Electronic Resources

6. Are the below figures reported in Canadian dollars? (6) _____Yes _____No

7. Expenditures for current electronic journals purchased. (7) _____

Include membership fees (such as JSTOR) as well as annual access and service fees paid directly or through consortia arrangements. Include initial purchase cost only for items purchased this fiscal year. Expenditures reported here are for journals reported in #1.

8. Expenditures for electronic "full-text" journals. (8) _____

Include membership fees (such as JSTOR) as well as annual access and service fees paid directly or through consortia arrangements. Include initial purchase cost only for items purchased this fiscal year. Expenditures here are for journals reported in #2.

9. Expenditures for electronic reference sources. (9) _____

Include annual access and service fees paid directly or through consortia arrangements. Include initial purchase cost only for items purchased this fiscal year. Expenditures here are for the reference sources reported in #4.

10. Expenditures for electronic books.   (10) _____

Include annual access and service fees paid directly or through consortia arrangements. Include initial
purchase cost only for items purchased this fiscal year. Expenditures here are for the electronic books
report in #5.

Use of Networked Electronic Resources and Services

11. Number of virtual reference transactions.   (11) _____

Virtual reference transactions are conducted via email, a library's website, or other network
communications mechanisms designed to support electronic reference. A virtual reference transaction
must include a question *either* received electronically (e.g., via e-mail, WWW form, etc.) *or* responded
to electronically. A transactions that is both received and responded to electronically is counted as *one*
transaction. Exclude phone and fax traffic unless either the question or answer transaction occurs via
the manner described above. Include counts accrued from participation in any local and national
projects, such as DigiRef and the Library of Congress's CDRS (Collaborative Digital Reference
Service). A reference transaction is an information contact, which involves the knowledge, use,
recommendations, interpretation, or instruction in the use of one or more information sources by any
member of the library staff (e.g., circulation, technical or reference services).

12. Does your library offer federated searching across networked electronic resources?

                                                  (12) _____Yes _____No

Networked electronic resources may include any information resource, such as databases, journals, ebooks,
reference materials, and non-textual resources that are provided to the library's users through
licensing and contractual agreements. Include electronic resources that institutions mount locally.

13. Number of sessions (logins) to databases or services.   (13) _____

13a. Number of resources for which you are reporting.   (13.a) _____

A session or login is one cycle of user activities that typically starts when a user connects to an
electronic resource and ends with explicit termination of activities (by leaving through logout or exit)
or implicit termination (time out due to user inactivity). Report here those figures that you derive from
Database Report 1 and Database Report 3 in the COUNTER Code of Practice. In a footnote, please
include the types of resources reported in 13a.

14. Number of searches (queries) in databases or services. (14) _____

14a. Number of resources for which you are reporting.   (14.a) _____

A search is intended to represent a unique intellectual inquiry. Typically, a search is recorded each
time a search request is sent/submitted to the server. Report here those figures that you derive from
Database Report 1 and Database Report 3 in the COUNTER Code of Practice. In a footnote, please
include the types of resources reported in 14a.

15. Number of successful full-text article requests.   (15) _____

15a. Number of resources for which you are reporting.   (15.a) _____

Items reported should include only full-text articles as defined in the COUNTER Code of Practice. Report here those figures that you derive from Journal Report 1 in the COUNTER Code of Practice. In a footnote, please include the types of resources reported in 15a.

16. Number of virtual visits.

16a. Number of virtual visits to library's website.   (16.a) _____

16b. Number of virtual visits to library's catalog.   (16.b) _____

16c. Excludes virtual visits from inside the library?   (16.c) ____Yes ____No

Virtual visits include a user's request of the library web site or catalog from outside the library building excluding the number of pages or gratuitous elements (images, style sheets) viewed. Exclude, if possible, virtual visits from within the library, from robot or spider crawls and from page reloads. A visit is usually determined by a user's IP address, which can be misleading due to Internet Service Providers (ISPs) and Firewalls or Proxy Servers. Thus, this measure is actually an estimate of the visits.

Library Digitization Activities

17. Number and Size of Library Digital Collections.

17a. Number of Collections.   (17.a) _____

17b. Size (in megabytes).   (17.b) _____

17c. Items.   (17.c) _____

Library digital collections can include born digital materials or those created in or converted from different formats (e.g., paper, microfilm, tapes, etc.) by the library and made available to users electronically. This includes locally held digital materials that are not purchased or acquired through other arrangements (e.g., vendor, individual or consortia licensing agreements). Born digital collections can include materials self-archived in an institutional repository. Created or converted digital collections can include electronic theses and dissertations (ETDs); special collections materials; maps; sound recordings; and, films. For each type of collection (e.g., text, image, multimedia), include the size (in megabytes) and, if possible, the number of items (e.g. unique files) in each collection. Exclude back up copies or mirror sites since items should be counted only once. Exclude e-reserves and ETDs provided by ProQuest or other vendors. In the footnote, provide a paragraph describing the general nature of library digital collections and, if possible, provide the URL where collections are listed.

18. Use of Library Digital Collections.

18a. Number of times items accessed.   (18.a) _____

18b. Number of queries conducted.   (18.b) _____

Number of times library digital collection items (unique files) were accessed and the number of searches (queries) conducted (if there is such a capability) during the reporting period. Please explain in a footnote how library digital collections are accessed, and if possible, list the URLs of those collections.

19. Direct cost of digital collections construction and management.

19a. Direct cost of personnel (19.a) _____

19b. Direct cost of equipment, software or contracted services. (19.b) _____

Annual direct costs (personnel, equipment, software, contracted services and similar items) spent to create digital materials (texts, images, and multimedia) or to convert existing materials into digital form for the purpose of making them electronically available to users. Include expenditures related to digitization, OCR, editorial, creation of markup texts, and preparation of metadata for access to digitized materials, data storage, and copyright clearance. Exclude expenditures for information resources purchased or acquired from outside the institution through individual or consortia licensing agreements. In the footnote, please describe any additional funding (university, state, private grants, etc.) provided specifically for the library's digitization activities.

20. Volumes Held Collectively (20) _____

The defining criterion is that the library has devoted financial resources for the purchase of these items and is taking responsibility for their availability through participation in a cooperative that supports shared ownership. The library demonstrates commitment to the shared storage facility by supporting the consortium financially through a legally binding arrangement. Include here volumes originally held and now withdrawn from the local collection because they are held in a "shared" remote storage facility starting with volumes that have been transferred during fiscal year 2004-05. Exclude volumes held collectively because they are held by other organizations such as the Center of Research Libraries (CRL) that are supported by membership dues and determination on whether to maintain membership may vary from year to year.

Footnotes:

Printed in the United States
59130LVS00003B/1-172